THE NEW BALLYMALOE BREAD BOOK

Darina Allen

GILL BOOKS

Gill Books
Hume Avenue
Park West
Dublin 12
www.gillbooks.ie

Gill Books is an imprint of M.H. Gill and Co.

9780717195855

Edited by Kristin Jensen
Indexed by Adam Pozner
Design origination by www.grahamthew.com
Designed by Luke Doyle
Printed and bound by L.E.G.O. SpA, Italy
This book is typeset in Freight Text Pro.

The paper used in this book comes from the wood pulp of sustainably managed forests.

A CIP catalogue record for this book is available from the British Library.

5 4 3 2 1

MIX
Paper | Supporting
responsible forestry
FSC
www.fsc.org   FSC® C023419

CONTENTS

INTRODUCTION

The Ballymaloe Bread Book was published in 2001 and is still in print over 20 years later. Since then we have added many new recipes to our repertoire, including several favourites contributed by teachers and students throughout the years.

In 2016 the Ballymaloe Bread Shed, a tiny artisan bakery and classroom where magic happens every day, was established in a trailer beside the cookery school. Our natural sourdough bread recipe in the sourdough chapter, made from just four ingredients (flour, water, salt and natural starter), is fermented for a minimum of 48 hours or up to 72 or 96 hours over the weekend. Also included, of course, is the soda bread taught to me by my mother and the original Ballymaloe brown yeast bread, so beloved of guests at Ballymaloe House. The original loaf was based on a recipe by Doris Grant, which, from what I understand, was shared with my mother-in-law Myrtle Allen in the 1950s by Lucy Pearce of Shanagarry Pottery. I urge everyone who has been fortunate enough to learn the simple art of bread-making to spread the joy by passing on the skill to others.

This revised edition was triggered by several considerations. Remember the frenzy of sourdough bread-making during the pandemic, when many home bakers became intrigued by the challenge, frustration and occasional delight of making bread with a living starter? Many also discovered that a natural sourdough is easier to digest and infinitely better for your health than breads made by the super-fast Chorleywood method, with a multitude of artificial additives and enzymes. Those with a gluten intolerance (but not coeliacs) seem to be able to enjoy natural sourdough bread without ill effects.

Another incident also spurred me into action. When the 'Beast from the East' in 2018 resulted in violent snowstorms, the country almost came to a standstill. Within days, there were shortages of fresh food and bread. There was chaos in the supermarket aisles as elegantly dressed ladies wrenched sliced pans from each other in panic. Can you imagine?! Ironically, packs of flour, buttermilk and bicarbonate of soda were stacked up on nearby shelves, but many of us have lost the skill of making a simple loaf of soda bread, which can be made in mere minutes. Many of our grandparents cooked 'a cake of bread' in a pot oven over an open fire, so there's no excuse for us.

Something had to be done, so I picked up my pen and three years later, this revised edition, The New Ballymaloe Bread Book, is the result.

I fervently hope it will take the mystery out of bread-making for everyone and upskill those who feel that making a loaf of bread is beyond them. It's definitely not rocket science, but it *is* a science. I promise you that if you follow each tried-and-tested recipe, you will absolutely be able to bake irresistible bread at home. Anyone – and I mean *anyone* – can make a simple loaf of soda bread: just mix, pour (or if you don't have a bread tin, shape it into a floury round and transfer to a baking tray) and pop it in the oven. You wouldn't have found your car keys and be back from the shops by the time it's baked! When you share the joy of how to bake a loaf of bread, you give a gift for life. So if I could teach only one thing, it would be how to make a loaf of soda bread.

Once you get started, there are 180 master recipes in this book, from soda breads, yeast breads, sourdough breads and flatbreads to breads from all over the world, breads for celebrations and sweet treats for special occasions.

I've been making bread all of my adult life and most of my childhood, but I still get a thrill every time I take a loaf of crusty bread out of the oven. How wonderful is that? I hope that in this New Ballymaloe Bread Book, I've passed that excitement on to you.

Darina Allen, April 2023

BASIC EQUIPMENT AND TOOLS

You don't need lots of fancy gadgets or specialist equipment to make a good loaf, but for specialist breads, here are a few essentials.

Baker's
Couche

Not absolutely essential, but these are brilliant for baguettes. Couche is heavy unbleached or natural canvas or linen flax cloth that's easy to pleat. It's used to support artisan baguettes while proving before being gently flipped onto a baking tray and into the oven. The dough doesn't stick to the couche because of its rougher texture. Brush and dry the couche after use. Available from bakers' suppliers or specialist kitchen shops. Heavy glass cloths can be substituted, but the dough will stick to the cotton tea towels.

Baker's Knife

Known as a lame, this is used to slash the top of the dough before baking. A super-sharp knife or even a Stanley knife will also do the job.

Baking Tray(s)

For proving and baking. You can use a super-hot flat or upturned tray for baking pizza on.

Bannetons or Wicker Proving Baskets	For proving sourdough loaves, you can use a clean glass cloth inside the banneton or proving basket to avoid sticking. Bannetons now come in a choice of materials, such as timber, bamboo or plastic. Or you can improvise with an inexpensive breadbasket lined with a clean floured tea towel.

Bread Board	I love old-fashioned bread boards. They are great for serving all kinds of things on, not just bread.
Bread Tins	Choose best-quality tins (not non-stick). We find these sizes useful: + Loaf tin 13cm × 20cm (450g) approx. + Loaf tin 24cm × 13.5cm approx. + Small loaf tins 14.6cm × 7.6cm approx.
Casserole/Dutch Oven	A heavy, usually cast iron, cooking pot with a tight-fitting lid and handle isn't essential, but it's handy for so many things in the kitchen, including baking bread. We use the Lodge pre-seasoned 3-litre pot. Both the pot and lid have a handle at the side for ease of lifting.
Digital Thermometer	Not totally essential, but it eliminates some of the guesswork – the temperature of the dough has a significant effect on how slowly or quickly it ferments. You can also use it to check when bread is fully baked – the internal temperature will be above 95°C (200°F) and the loaf will sound hollow when you tap the base.
Measuring Jug	Look for one with a good spout for pouring that measures millilitres and fluid ounces if possible.

Mixing Bowl(s)	At least one large stainless steel bowl, one big enough to mix a couple of kilos of dough comfortably.
Oven Thermometer	Ovens vary in temperature and many have a 'hot spot', so it's useful to check the accuracy of the temperature with an oven thermometer before baking.
Pastry Brush	I like to have a couple of sizes to egg wash the surface of brioche, croissants, etc. evenly. Keep one dry for brushing dry flour off the worktop.
Plastic and Metal Scrapers	Plastic scrapers are a game changer and are many bakers' favourite tool, used to mix, turn out, stretch, scoop up and cut the dough. Available from specialist kitchen shops.
Rolling Pin	Choose either a solid timber pin or one with ball bearings, whichever feels most comfortable to you.
Serrated Bread Knife	Buy a good-quality serrated bread knife to slice your crusty loaves.
Sharp Scissors	To slash or snip the top of the loaf before baking.
Timer	Not essential, but it's heart-breaking when you overcook or burn your precious loaves.
Water Mister	A spotlessly clean plant sprayer from your local garden centre is perfect. Spray the inside of your preheated domestic oven before and after the loaves are put in to bake. This creates humidity, mimicking a professional baker's oven. It slows down the crust formation and allows the bread to rise fully before the crust traps the gas inside.

Weighing Scales	An accurate digital scale is an essential bit of kitchen kit. Baking is an exact science, so if you want to get consistent results, it's important to weigh accurately. Bakers even weigh their water and eggs.
	The volume and weight measurements of water are like for like: 1ml water = 1 gram.
	A standard egg weighs 55–60g, whereas free-range organic eggs will vary in size depending on the breed of the hen, their feed and the time of year.
Wire Rack	To allow the air to circulate when bread, scones, pastries, etc. are cooling.

HOW TO MEASURE

In a domestic situation we tend to use ordinary spoons for measuring, the sort of spoons that most people have in the cutlery drawer in the kitchen: a teaspoon, dessertspoon and tablespoon.

Unless it says otherwise, we measure in rounded spoonfuls. A *rounded* spoonful has exactly the same amount on top as underneath. A *heaped* teaspoon has as much of the ingredient as the spoon will hold. A *level* teaspoon is just that and is the equivalent of a half-rounded measuring teaspoon.

If you are using standard measuring spoons or American measuring spoons, always use level measurements. Our rounded measurements are the exact equivalent of a level measuring spoon.

However, please note that our tablespoon is the equivalent of 4 teaspoons, whereas a standard measuring spoon holds just 3 teaspoons.

For accuracy it is preferable to weigh everything on a digital scale. This is particularly important when scaling up from a small recipe:

```
1 teaspoon = 5g/5ml
1 dessertspoon = 10g/10ml
1 tablespoon = 15g/15ml
```

HOW TO LINE A TIN

Do you really need to line the tin? If not, brush the sides and base evenly with a good oil – the bread will be crustier. I like to use a light olive oil rather than sunflower or peanut oil. Alternatively, use parchment paper and follow the diagrams below.

FOR A RECTANGULAR OR SQUARE TIN

Place the tin on the parchment and cut towards the corners

Fold along the dotted line and fold into the tin

FOR A ROUND TIN

Trace around the tin and cut out the circle

Cut a piece of parchment long enough to fit the circumference of the tin. Make cuts along one edge.

Place the long piece in the tin, followed by the circle

HOW TO SEASON A TIN

When you buy new cake or loaf tins that are not non-stick, greasing them will not be enough to stop them from sticking. You'll need to do what's referred to as 'seasoning' the tins. You do this by brushing them with oil or clarified butter and putting them in the oven preheated to 180°C/350°F/gas mark 4 for 10–15 minutes at a time. Let them cool down and repeat this three or four times. Just to be on the safe side, put a bit of greased parchment paper on the base of the tin the first few times you use it to ensure it doesn't stick. I far prefer this method to using non-stick tins, which generally lose their coating over time and can even be dangerous because the chemical coatings can leach into your food.

YEAST
....

Yeast is a single-cell micro-organism that acts as a leavening agent to cause dough to rise. Unlike bicarbonate of soda, baking powder and cream of tartar, yeast is a living organism so you need to be nice to it, otherwise it won't rise your bread. In order to grow, it also requires warmth, moisture and nourishment. The yeast feeds on sugar and produces bubbles of carbon dioxide (CO_2), which expand in the heat of the oven and cause the bread to rise.

Like many of us, yeast likes to be warm, but not too warm. Cold doesn't kill yeast but heat over 50°C (122°F) will, so have all the ingredients at blood heat (35°C/90°F is the optimum temperature) and your equipment should be warm too. In cold weather, it helps to warm the flour a little in a low oven (150°C/300°F/gas mark 2) for 5–10 minutes.

The less yeast you use, the longer the dough will take to rise but the better the flavour.

Baker's Yeast	Baker's yeast (*Saccharomyces cerevisiae*) comes in three forms (fresh, dried and instant) and can be used for baking, wine-making and brewing. It's readily available from bakeries or supermarkets.
Fresh Yeast	Fresh yeast is also referred to as commercial or baker's yeast or compressed yeast. It needs to be used within two or three weeks and should be kept refrigerated in a tightly sealed container.
	Fresh yeast is pale in colour and crumbly. As it ages it becomes darker in colour, more putty-like in texture and less effective.
	Fresh yeast freezes well. Divide it into small convenient blocks (e.g. 25g pieces), wrap well, date and label and use within three months.

Dried Yeast	Dried yeast comes in granules, sometimes in 7g packets or in tubs. It's dormant and needs to be rehydrated before use. It has a long shelf life: 1½–2 years. If you can't source fresh yeast, use half the quantity of dried yeast, e.g. 12g dried instead of 25g fresh yeast.
Instant Yeast	Also known as rapid rise or easy blend, instant yeast also has a long shelf life: about two years unopened or three to four months once opened. Add it directly to the flour. The yeast feeds on sugars in the flour and produces little bubbles of CO_2 that expand in the heat of the oven to rise the bread. Use 1 × 7g sachet for 450g flour.
How to Sponge (Activate) Yeast	Crumble the yeast into a bowl, then add the sugar and warm water. Mix and put the bowl in a warm place to allow the yeast to start to work. After 4–5 minutes, it should be creamy and slightly frothy on top. At this point, it's ready to add to the flour.

FLOURS

One of the most exciting developments on the baking scene in recent years has been a revival of interest in heritage grains, with a growing number of farmers trialling different varieties. Here at Ballymaloe Cookery School we have been growing a small acreage of heritage milling wheat, which we have dried and milled for us by Robert Mosse at the Little Mill in Co. Kilkenny. The flavour of the bread made from freshly milled wheat is discernibly different. After milling, flour needs to be aged for at least two weeks before use.

Heritage grains are grains that were grown before the introduction of intensive scientific plant breeding for high-yielding hybridised grains during the Green Revolution in the mid-1900s. Ancient grains date back almost 10,000 years. They are thought to be more nutrient dense and richer in flavour than the modern, overprocessed wheat. Enthusiastic artisan bakers are greatly enjoying experimenting with different heritage wheat, such as emmer, khorasan/kamut, einkorn, Red Fife, Rouge de Bordeaux, White Sonora, Blue Beard durum, Olands … the list goes on.

Flours vary in gluten content. It's important to choose the appropriate flour for the bread (organic if possible).

+ For soda bread, use plain (all-purpose) white flour, wholemeal flour or a mixture. You want a soft flour that's low in gluten: between 9.5% and 11.5%.

+ For yeast bread, use strong white flour or baker's flour, which is higher in gluten (protein) – between 12% and 14% – than plain (all-purpose) flour. Kneading develops the gluten and makes the dough elastic, which traps in more air to produce a lighter loaf.

Buckwheat Flour	Despite its name, buckwheat is not a wheat. It doesn't contain any gluten, so it's typically used for flatbreads and pancakes but its slightly sour flavour works well in some breads when mixed with white and rye flour.
Cornmeal	Sometimes called maize meal or polenta, cornmeal is ground from corn. The texture can be coarse, medium or fine and can be milled from yellow or white kernels of corn. It can be used instead of flour to dust baguettes, ciabatta or a loaf of sourdough.
Plain Flour	Also known as white flour or all-purpose flour, this flour is low in gluten (8–11%, depending on the brand). Milled from soft varieties of wheat, it contains about 75% of the wheat grain with the bran and wheat germ removed. It's perfect for soda breads, scones, pastry, cakes, biscuits, pancakes and sauces. US all-purpose flour usually contains 11–12% gluten so it can also be used for yeast bread, hence the name. In theory plain flour does not contain a raising agent but check the brand, as some do.
Spelt	Spelt is an ancient grain, a species of wheat that was cultivated by earlier civilisations such as Mesopotamia in the Middle East around 9,000 years ago. Spelt (*Triticum spelta*) is an old relative of wheat and is one of the first cultivated cereals in written history. Studies show that spelt contains more zinc, phosphorus and thiamine (vitamin B1) than wheat. Spelt has another interesting property: its grains are tightly attached to the outer shell. The grains must be removed from the husks with a special

device before milling. The tight outer shell protects the grains from mechanical damage and perhaps even from environmental impurities. We use organic spelt from Emma Clutterbuck, Oak Forest Mills in County Kilkenny and Dunany Flour in County Louth.

Stone-Ground Flour

This flour is produced in the time-honoured way of grinding the grain between two millstones, resulting in a coarser texture with flakes of bran and wheat germ, better flavour and a higher nutrient content. Traditional stone grinding also keeps the temperatures lower and the proteins more stable. Commercial mass-produced flour is roller milled. Sadly we have lost many of our small mills in Ireland but perhaps there will be a revival now that the interest in heritage grains continues to gather momentum.

Strong White Flour

Also referred to as bread flour or baker's flour, strong white flour has a higher gluten content (12–14%) than plain white or brown wholemeal flour and is suitable for bread-making.

Wholemeal Flour

Also known as whole wheat flour or wheaten flour, ideally this is a brown flour milled from the wheat grain with all the elements intact. It can be stone-ground or roller milled, but commercial brands are more often blends of white flour with bran and white germ added back. It comes in different grades of coarseness.

How to Check for Weevils in Flour

Many years ago, when I was in hotel school, our lecturer told us we would need to know how to tell whether there were weevils in flour. We were appalled and doubted that we would ever be in a situation where we would need this information. But in reality it's very useful, particularly for people who don't bake very often and may find a bag of flour at the back of a kitchen cupboard.

Fill a dessertspoon or tablespoon with flour and smooth the surface with a knife. Leave the spoon sitting for a few minutes, then check. Weevils cannot be seen by the naked eye, so if the surface is even slightly broken, that means there are weevils in the flour. Cooking weevil-infested flour will kill the weevils but will result in a heavy-textured loaf. Wholemeal flour infested with weevils is even more obvious – when you look into the packet or bin, the flour will look dusty and brown on top.

Weevils can infest any grains, including nuts, seeds, rice, oats and breakfast cereals. Bags of rice with really dusty bottoms are another clue, as are strings like cobwebs. If you store flour in a bin, wash out and dry the bin meticulously between batches to avoid weevils passing from one batch of flour to another.

HOW TO KNEAD BREAD AND WHY WE DO IT

Unlike brown yeast bread, white yeast bread does involve kneading, double rising and knocking back. It takes time, but not your time, as much of it is in the rising and baking. It's tempting to use a food mixer to knead bread, but we always encourage people to knead by hand to begin with. It can seem like a chore, but in fact it can be enormously therapeutic and relaxing when you enter into the spirit and just enjoy the process. With each loaf you make, you will continue to perfect your technique and will become more observant of the changes in the dough depending on the flour, atmosphere and even your humour.

If you do want to use a food mixer, however, use the dough hook and knead for 5–6 minutes rather than 10 minutes if hand kneading.

Why Knead?	The process of kneading develops the elasticity of the dough. When the yeast feeds on the sugar and creates little bubbles of carbon dioxide, the strong, stretchy web will facilitate the rising process. It can be done by hand or in a machine using a dough hook.
What Is Gluten?	Gluten is the protein in the flour. When it is wet it becomes elastic, so flour with a higher gluten content will expand considerably more as it rises and is therefore desirable for white yeast bread.

There are several different styles of hand kneading, all equally effective, so choose the one that you feel most comfortable with. It doesn't matter which style or combination you settle for, but it's important to remember that you need to work and stretch the dough in order to develop the gluten structure, so don't just play with it. Kneading needs energy and has the added bonus of providing you with a physical workout, which surely can only be desirable!

To start, scrape the dough out of the mixing bowl onto a dry or lightly floured worktop. Begin to stretch and fold. It usually takes about 10 minutes to get the dough to the correct consistency, but the length of time will depend on your technique. Here are my three suggestions.

Hand Kneading: Method 1

Stand upright with one foot slightly ahead of the other in front of the worktop. Tidy the dough into a manageable round. Now, with your right hand, stretch the top right-hand side of the dough and then fold it back towards you. With your left hand, turn the dough anticlockwise and continue stretching and folding as you knead a different part of the dough, all the time, over and over. Reverse if left-handed.

Stretch the top
right-hand side
of the dough

Fold it back
towards you

Turn anticlockwise
and continue

Hand Kneading: Method 2

Stretch the top of the dough away from you

Stretch the top of the dough away from you while holding onto the end closest to you. Then roll the top edge of the dough inwards towards you and press away again with the heel of your hand. Roll it towards you again, give it another stretch and a final roll, which should bring all the dough as far as the bottom edge. Now you'll have what looks like a Swiss roll in front of you, so turn it 90° and start the kneading process again from the narrow end. Continue until the dough is fully kneaded.

Press away again

Roll towards you

Roll towards you again

Turn it 90° and start again

Hand Kneading: Method 3

This third method is effective but very noisy. It's the best method by far for getting rid of frustration, but only attempt it if you are on your own! Knead the dough until it becomes a coherent mass, then form it into a longish piece. Grip it by the bottom end with your right hand. Lift up the dough, flick your wrist forward and bang the dough onto the worktop, flicking your wrist to the right in the same movement, then pick up the other end of the dough and repeat the action over and over again – you'll soon feel better and the dough will benefit from the workout too!

Gripping the bottom end of the dough, lift it, flick your wrist forward

... and bang the dough onto the worktop

How Do I Know the Dough Is Kneaded Enough?

You will be aware of the dough changing texture as you knead. At first, if you lift up the dough and pull it apart, it will break into two distinct pieces. But as you continue to knead, you will be able to stretch it into a longer and longer piece without it breaking. It will also become much firmer and will spring back without sticking when you press it with your fingertip.

When it's kneaded enough, it will stretch into a long roll without breaking. You'll be able to see the long strand of gluten you've developed with your hard work.

Is It Possible to Over-Knead?

You can over-knead your bread, but it's unlikely to happen when you are hand kneading. A dough can be over-kneaded in a machine. The tell-tale signs are when the texture of the dough changes from silky and elastic to a coarse, sticky dough that is slightly curdled in appearance.

Where Can I Rise My Bread?

Bread will rise almost anywhere (within reason), but 27°C (80.6°F) is considered the optimum temperature. Cold doesn't kill yeast, so if your kitchen is a bit colder the bread may take a little longer to rise but it will still be fine. Keep it out of draughts but you don't need to put it in an airing cupboard or on top of a radiator – and no matter how much of a hurry you're in, don't be tempted to put it into a warming cupboard or a low oven. Remember, heat over 50°C (122°F) kills yeast – and breads that rise slowly have a much better flavour and are more nutritious and digestible than those that rise quickly. Dough can also rise slowly in a covered bowl overnight in the fridge.

What Is Happening When the Dough Is Rising?

When dough rises there is a lot of enzyme action going on, but basically the yeast is feeding on the natural sugar in the flour and creating bubbles of carbon dioxide gas. The yeast builds up flavour from the acids and other by-products of fermentation – even a short period of rising greatly enhances the flavour of your bread.

How to Knock Back
Dough

After the first rising, the dough needs to be 'knocked back' to eliminate large air pockets and to redistribute the yeast back in contact with the dough so that when it rises a second time, the texture will be more even.

To knock back dough, turn it out onto a lightly floured surface and knead or fold for a minute or two, until all the air has been knocked out of it. It seems counterintuitive, but the resulting loaf will have a more even texture.

Knead or fold until
all the air has been
knocked out of it

What Is Oven
Spring?

When a fully risen loaf of bread is put into a preheated oven, it will expand further (up to 30% of its original size) in the first 8–10 minutes of baking.

To prove the bread, put the tin in a warm place in your kitchen, out of a draught. Cover the tin with a clean tea towel to prevent a skin from forming. After 10–15 minutes, just as the bread comes to the top of the tin, remove the tea towel and pop the bread into the oven for 20 minutes. The bread will rise a little further in the oven – this is called oven spring. However, if the bread rises over the top of the tin before it goes into the oven, it may continue to rise as it bakes and may flow over the edges.

HOW TO CUT BREAD

Because of the prevalence of sliced pan, not every household has a bread knife so you may need to invest in one. A really good serrated bread knife is a joy to use.

Surprising as it may sound, there's a lot of skill to slicing bread. My mother-in-law, Myrtle Allen, did this enchanting drawing and pasted it on the wall in the Ballymaloe House kitchen to guide over-enthusiastic waitresses who squished the bread while attempting to slice it.

Please cut bread in straight, even slices — not too thick or too thin. Don't under-cut loaf.

wrong   right

Sandwiches must be buttered out to the edges of each slice.

Ballymaloe House, Shanagarry, Co. Cork, Ireland,
Telephone +353 (0)21 4652531, Fax +353 (0)21 4652021, Email: res@ballymaloe.ie   www.ballymaloe.ie

BREADS TO MAKE THROUGHOUT THE YEAR

+ St Patrick's Day: Shamrock scones
+ Easter: Hot cross buns, hot cross scones, Easter tea ring
+ Halloween: Barmbrack
+ Christmas: Christmas mincemeat scones with brandy butter, Christmas tree bread, Mary Jo's stollen

BREADS TO MAKE WITH KIDS

+ Soda bread
+ Teenie weenies
+ Kibbled wheat scones
+ Orange or chocolate swirls
+ Plaits
+ Pizza
+ Wiggly worms
+ Parma sticks
+ Lavash
+ Carta musica funny faces
+ Chocolate breadsticks
+ Snails
+ Balloons

IRISH ARTISAN MILLERS

+ **Ballyminane Mills (John Murphy)**
  Stone-ground wholemeal flour

  Enniscorthy, Wexford
  @Ballyminanemill

+ **Ballymore Organics (James Kelly)**
  Stone-ground flours (wholemeal, rye, plain flour and semolina)
  and porridge oats

  Ballymore Eustace, Kildare
  ballymoreorganics.ie

+ **Irish Organic Mill (Mark Gillanders and Michael Rafferty)**
  Stone-ground organic pasta, pastry and pizza flour, organic
  plain flour, organic wholemeal flour and organic semolina

  Ballybay Food Hub, Carrickmacross Road, Ballybay, Monaghan
  irishorganicmill.ie

+ **Dunany Mills (Workman family)**
  Organic oatmeal and flours (wholemeal, spelt and rye)

  Dunany, Drogheda, Louth
  dunanyflour.com

+ **Macroom Mills (Donal Creedon)**
  Oatmeal and wholemeal flour

  Macroom, Cork

+ **Oak Forest Mills (Emma Clutterbuck)**
  Irish-grown stone-ground flours (wholemeal spelt and white spelt flour)

  Piltown, Kilkenny
  oakforestmills.ie

+ **The Little Mill (Bill and Rob Mosse)**
  Seventh-generation millers – Irish-grown wholemeal, spelt and rye flours

  Bennetsbridge, Kilkenny
  thelittlemill.ie

+ **The Merry Mill (Kevin Scully)**
  Organic porridge oats

  Vicarstown, Laois
  themerrymill.ie

USEFUL WEBSITES

+ **Real Bread Ireland**
  realbreadireland.org

+ **The Real Bread Campaign (UK)**
  sustainweb.org/realbread

+ **The Grain Lab (UK)**
  ukgrainlab.com

A NOTE ON INGREDIENTS
AND OVEN TEMPERATURES

Butter

We use salted butter unless stated otherwise in a recipe. We are fortunate in Ireland to have beautiful butter. We use Kerrygold for virtually all our baking. It contains 1.8% salt, so if you are using unsalted butter you will need to add a pinch of salt to the recipe to enhance the flavour, otherwise the end result will be bland.

Eggs

The quality of eggs really matters. Here at Ballymaloe Cookery School we have a flock of organic hens that roam freely on grass. The flavour and texture of their eggs are discernibly different to the eggs with pale yolks produced by hens from overcrowded battery cages. It's really worth considering having a few hens of your own or sourcing fresh eggs from a local free-range or, better still, organic producer – you will be amazed by the difference it makes.

All eggs are a medium size unless stated otherwise in a recipe.

Salt

Salt is essential for life and important in bread-making for flavour, colour and the texture of the crust. As a general rule of thumb, use 20g salt to 1kg flour. Use pure salt, preferably natural sea salt. Processed salt will have been stripped of much of its mineral content. Dairy salt or vacuum salt is widely available, sold in simple plastic bags in supermarkets. It's less expensive than table salt. Seek out Oriel Sea Salt from County Louth (orielseasalt.com).

Yeast

Choose non-genetically modified (GM) yeast. If you can't source fresh yeast, use half the quantity of dried yeast to fresh yeast, e.g. 12g dried instead of 25g fresh yeast.

Oven Temperatures

All oven temperatures in this book are for a conventional oven unless stated otherwise. If you are using a fan-assisted oven, reduce the temperature in the recipe by 10°C–20°C depending on the brand of cooker (check the instruction booklet).

SODA BREAD

Soda bread is indigenous to Ireland and our climate. It reflects the soft, gentle nature of the people and the weather. It was first made in the early 19th century when bicarbonate of soda, also known as bread soda or baking soda, gradually became widely available. The varieties of wheat that were grown in Ireland at that time were low in gluten – not suitable for yeast bread but perfect for soda bread. The combination of our soft flour with readily available sour milk and bicarbonate of soda meant it became a staple in every Irish family. It was originally cooked in an iron pot oven (called a bastible) or on a griddle over an open fire and served with country butter. It was commonly referred to as a cake of bread, brown cake or white cake. Wholemeal bread is known as wheaten bread in Northern Ireland.

In some parts of Ireland, soda bread is called soda cake. It has continued to be made up to the present day in many Irish homes, where sour milk has been replaced by cultured buttermilk that can be bought in most shops around the country. However, in an emergency you can also make your own cheat's buttermilk by adding an acid such as lemon juice or vinegar to fresh milk (see page 25).

We often say that the skill of making soda bread well is more of an art than a science. It's all in your hands and the way you handle the flour and the dough.

There are many variations on the basic recipe for soda bread. As you will see, you can be adventurous and creative with the flavourings, though I'm not sure our ancestors would recognise the rosemary and sun-dried tomato soda bread let alone our stripy cat, a chocolate version of the traditional spotted dog. One could call it an Irish version of the French pain au chocolat!

There are a few crucial points when making soda bread to ensure a light loaf:

+ Bread should always be baked in a fully preheated oven, but ovens vary enormously so it may be necessary to adjust the temperature accordingly. It could be a good idea to buy an accurate oven thermometer to check your oven's temperature occasionally (see page 4).
+ Use a large enough bowl, at least 25.5cm wide. A plastic washing-up bowl or a large stainless steel bowl is ideal.

- Measure the ingredients accurately (see page 5).
- The quantity of buttermilk needed can vary depending on how thick it is. If using low-fat buttermilk, add 2–3 tablespoons of cream to enrich the buttermilk.
- Sieve the bicarbonate of soda or rub it between the palms of your hands in the time-honoured way to eliminate any lumps.
- The trick with all soda breads is not to overmix the dough – mix the dough as quickly and as gently as possible, keeping it really light and airy. Using one hand with the fingers stiff and outstretched, mix in a full circle from the centre to the outside of the bowl, gradually drawing in the flour from the sides. Add a little more buttermilk if necessary. The dough should be softish, not too wet and sticky. When it all comes together – a matter of seconds – turn it out onto a well-floured worked surface.
- With floured hands, roll the dough gently on the work surface and flip it over. DO NOT KNEAD!
- Place your dough on the baking tray before cutting the cross on top (the traditional blessing).
- Transfer to a hot oven immediately.

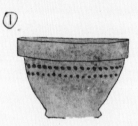

Mix the dry ingredients in a large (25cm) bowl

Make a well in the centre and add almost all the milk

Hold your hand like a claw and mix from the centre out in a circle

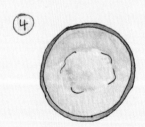

In moments, you'll have a loose dough. Add more milk if necessary.

Toss gently on a floured worktop

Place on a tray and cut a cross in the top to let the fairies out!

BICARBONATE OF SODA, BAKING POWDER AND CREAM OF TARTAR

Bicarbonate of soda and baking powder have been in common use only since the mid-19th century. They are well-suited to thin doughs such as drop scone batter that lack sufficient gluten to contain the carbon dioxide generated by yeast. These chemical raising agents are also used with low-gluten flours that cannot be leavened with yeast. They must be measured with care and can discolour doughs containing chocolate.

Bread soda, baking soda and bicarbonate of soda are all names for sodium bicarbonate. When combined with acidic ingredients such as buttermilk, lemon juice or vinegar, bicarbonate of soda generates carbon dioxide bubbles, thus raising the dough. The right balance of leavening agent and acid in a dough is important. For every ½ teaspoon bicarbonate of soda, use 225ml sour milk, buttermilk or yogurt or 1 tablespoon lemon juice or vinegar. Bicarbonate of soda can also be activated by combining it with cream of tartar (an acid in powder form) in a ratio of 4:5, then adding milk or water.

Baking powder is a ready-prepared combination of soda and acid (usually cream of tartar) designed to give consistent results. It generates carbon dioxide on contact with water. Double-acting baking powder contains two acids: one activated when liquid is added at room temperature, the other activated in the heat of the oven. As a rule, 1½ teaspoons baking powder are needed to leaven 125g flour.

The white, odourless powder known as cream of tartar is a product of grape fermentation. It is said to have been first isolated from the bottom of wine barrels by the Persian alchemist Jabir ibn Hayyan around 800 AD. Today, we know that tartaric acid, the acid component of cream of tartar, is found in the greatest concentration in grapes but is also present in bananas and tamarind. To make cream of tartar, the grape sediment, called beeswing, is scraped from wine barrels, purified and ground. Use cream of tartar to boost acidic flavour. It is most often incorporated into beaten egg whites for stability or into sugar syrup to help prevent crystallisation.

A NOTE ON BUTTERMILK

Buttermilk varies in thickness depending on the richness of the milk. Our Ballymaloe organic farm buttermilk is thick and gloopy – you will need slightly less cultured buttermilk. If your buttermilk is low fat, add 2–3 tablespoons cream to the buttermilk.

Cheat's Buttermilk

If you can't buy commercial buttermilk easily or want full-fat buttermilk, here is a simple method for producing your own. Commercial buttermilk is usually made with low-fat milk. This version, made with full-cream milk, will give you rich, thick buttermilk. To make low-fat buttermilk, use low-fat milk and 1 tablespoon white vinegar.

Traditionally, sour milk was used instead of buttermilk. Raw milk sours naturally and makes delicious soda breads, whereas the pasteurised, homogenised milk that is available in shops goes rotten before it sours. Traditionally buttermilk was milk left over from butter-making. Every house would have had a sour milk jug to which the milk left over from meals was added to. This was kept covered in a cold place – maybe a larder or pantry. The milk coagulated overnight and made wonderful soda bread.

MAKES 225ML
....

- 225ml full-cream milk
- 1 tablespoon freshly squeezed lemon juice

Put the milk in a deep bowl with the lemon juice and leave to stand at room temperature for about 15 minutes. The milk will start to curdle. Stir well before using and store in the fridge in a covered container. The 'buttermilk' will keep for a couple of days.

White Soda Bread

Soda breads are the traditional breads of our country. Making a loaf of soda bread is a simple life skill that everyone should know. A loaf or a tray of scones will be made in minutes and out of the oven before you find your car keys to drive to the shop!

Soda bread takes only a few minutes to make and 30–40 minutes to bake. It is certainly another of our 'great convertibles'. We have a lot of fun experimenting with different variations, from teeny weenies to crusty loaves and deep-pan pizza. The possibilities are endless for the hitherto humble soda bread.

MAKES 1 ROUND LOAF

- 450g plain flour
- 1 level teaspoon bicarbonate of soda
- 1 level teaspoon salt
- 350-400ml sour milk or buttermilk (the quantity needed depends on the thickness of the milk)

Preheat the oven to 230°C/450°F/gas mark 8. Soda bread is best cooked in a conventional oven rather than a fan or convection oven.

Sieve the dry ingredients into a large bowl. Make a well in the centre and pour most of the milk in at once. Using one hand with the fingers stiff and outstretched, mix in a full circular movement from the centre to the outside of the bowl, gradually drawing in the flour from the sides. Add a little more milk if necessary – shop-bought buttermilk is thinner than farm-fresh, so you will need less rather than more. The dough should be softish, not too wet and sticky. The trick with all soda breads is not to overmix the dough – mix the dough as quickly and as gently as possible, keeping it really light and airy. When it all comes together – a matter of seconds – turn it out onto a well-floured worked surface.

Wash and dry your hands, then dust them with flour. Tidy up the dough and flip it over gently. Pat into a round approx. 4cm deep. Gather some of the excess flour from the worktop and sprinkle it on the centre of a baking tray, then transfer the loaf to the tray. With a sharp knife, cut a deep cross on top and prick the four corners with the tip of your knife to let the fairies out, otherwise they will jinx your bread!

Bake in the preheated oven for 15 minutes, then reduce the temperature to 200°C/400°F/gas mark 6 and bake for 30 minutes more, until cooked. If you are in doubt, tap the bottom of the bread – if it's fully cooked, it will sound hollow. Allow to cool on a wire rack.

A Little White Soda Bread Loaf	Make the loaf as in the master recipe but add 425ml buttermilk and scoop it into an oiled 13cm × 20cm (450g) loaf tin. Sprinkle with oatmeal and sesame seeds or kibbled wheat seeds if you enjoy them. This is more convenient for slicing or using as sandwiches.
White Soda Scones	Make the dough as above but flatten the dough into a round or square approx. 2.5cm deep and stamp or cut into scones. Bake in the oven for about 20 minutes at 230°C/450°F/gas mark 8 or use to cover the top of a casserole or stew.
Teeny Weenies	Stamp out the dough into teeny weeny scones using a 4cm cutter. Bake at 230°C/450°F/gas mark 8 for 8–10 minutes, until cooked through.
Caraway Seed Soda Bread	Add 2 tablespoons caraway seeds and 1 tablespoon caster sugar to the dry ingredients.
Rosemary and Raisin Soda Bread	Add 75g raisins and 2 tablespoons chopped fresh rosemary to the dry ingredients.

Curry and Sultana Soda Bread	Add 1–2 teaspoons curry powder and 75g sultanas to the dry ingredients.
Seeded Tear-and-Share Soda Scones	Make the dough as above. Brush a 23cm round tin with olive or sunflower oil. Pat the dough into a round approx. 4cm deep and score into eight wedges. Put into the tin and brush the top of the scones with a selection of sesame, poppy, pumpkin and sunflower seeds. Bake as above. When cooked, remove from the tin and cool on a wire rack. The bread can then be torn apart and shared.
White Soda Bread with Herbs	Add 2 tablespoons chopped fresh herbs, such as rosemary, sage, thyme, chives, parsley, lemon balm or even freshly chopped seaweed or dried seaweed, to the dry ingredients. Shape into a loaf or scones and bake as for soda bread.
White Soda Bread with Spring Onions, Garlic Chives or Wild Garlic	Add 3–4 tablespoons chopped spring onions, garlic chives or wild garlic to the basic recipe.
Dillisk Soda Bread	Add 15–25g chopped fresh dillisk or 1–2 tablespoons dried dillisk to the dry ingredients.
Treacle Soda Bread	Whisk 2 tablespoons treacle into the buttermilk. Date syrup or pomegranate molasses are also fun to try and are delicious.
Bacon or Chorizo Soda Bread	Cut 75–110g streaky bacon or chorizo into lardons 5mm thick. Fry the bacon in a hot dry pan until almost crisp. To include the bacon and its fat in the measuring, put it in the measuring jug and pour in the buttermilk to bring it up to the 400ml mark. If using chorizo, be careful to just warm it through until the fat starts to run, as it's really easy to burn chorizo.

Multi-seed Soda Bread	Add 1 tablespoon sunflower seeds, 1 tablespoon sesame seeds, 1 tablespoon pumpkin seeds and 1 tablespoon kibbled wheat to the dry ingredients. Reserve a little of this mixture to scatter over the top.
Rosemary and Sun-blush Tomato Soda Bread	Add 1–2 tablespoons chopped fresh rosemary and 2 tablespoons roughly chopped sun-blush tomatoes to the flour and continue as in the basic recipe. Shape into a loaf of bread or scones.
Cheddar Cheese Soda Wedges	Brush a 23cm round tin with olive or sunflower oil. Pat the dough into a round approx. 4cm deep, then score into 6–8 wedges and brush the surface of the dough with egg wash. Scatter with 50g grated Cheddar cheese. Bake in the oven at 200°C/400°F/gas mark 6 for 35–40 minutes.
Cheddar Cheese Soda Scones or Herb and Cheese Scones	Make the white soda bread or white soda bread with herbs dough but stamp or cut into scones. Brush the top of each scone with egg wash, then dip into 110g grated mature Cheddar cheese or a cheese of your choice and bake as for soda scones.
Cheddar Cheese and Thyme Leaf Soda Scones	Substitute thyme leaves for the mixed herbs in the white soda bread with herbs variation on the previous page.
Cheddar Cheese and Wild Garlic Soda Scones	Add 1–2 tablespoons finely chopped wild garlic to the dry ingredients in the Cheddar cheese soda scones variation above.
Rosemary and Olive Soda Scones	Add 1½ tablespoons chopped fresh rosemary and 2 tablespoons roughly chopped stoned black olives to the dry ingredients.
Olive Soda Scones	Make a white soda bread dough with or without herbs. Flatten into a 2.5cm square and cut into square scones. Brush generously with olive oil, then put a whole olive and a small sprig of rosemary on top of each scone. Sprinkle with flaky sea salt and bake as above. Looks and tastes delicious.

Soda Farls

In Ulster, the term *farls* can refer to soda bread or potato bread cooked on a griddle. Farls are traditionally served with an Ulster fry. Preheat a griddle or heavy frying pan over a medium to low heat. On a floured surface, flatten the dough into a round approx. 2cm thick. Cut into four pieces. Cook on the pan for 6–10 minutes, depending on the thickness. Be careful not to let the farls burn. Serve immediately. Traditionally, this is the quickest way to make soda bread – delicious for a barbecue or picnic.

Soda Bread Swirls

These can be savoury or sweet – try chocolate and hazelnut spread, homemade jam, peanut butter and jam, orange butter ... Just omit the cheese and fresh herbs!

MAKES 12

....

- 1 batch of white soda
  bread dough (page 26)
- 175g finely grated
  Parmesan, Pecorino or
  mature Cheddar cheese
  (reserve some for
  dipping)
- 2 tablespoons finely
  chopped fresh parsley
- extra virgin olive
  oil, for greasing the
  tin
- 1 egg, beaten

....

TOPPING (CHOOSE ONE):
- 4-6 tablespoons basil,
  wild garlic, kale
  or watercress pesto
  (pages 312-13)
- 4-6 tablespoons
  tapenade (page 316)
  and 2-3 tablespoons
  finely chopped fresh
  rosemary
- 4-6 tablespoons
  anchoïade (page 316)
- 50g 'nduja mixed with
  2 tablespoons extra
  virgin olive oil

Preheat the oven to 230°C/450°F/gas mark 8.

Make the white soda bread dough in the usual way, adding the cheese and parsley to the dry ingredients. On a floured board, roll the dough into a rectangle to fit a well-oiled baking tray or a rectangular tin (approx. 31cm × 23cm × 5cm).

Slather the surface with the chosen topping. Brush the edge of one of the long ends with a little beaten egg, then roll it up tightly from the long side. Press to seal, then squeeze a little to elongate further. Cut the dough in half, then into quarters, then cut each quarter into three to make 12 swirls.

Brush one cut side of each swirl with egg wash, then dip into some grated cheese and arrange side by side on the baking tray, allowing a little space to expand. Alternatively, arrange in the well-oiled rectangular tin, cheese side up.

Bake in the preheated oven for 10–15 minutes, until fully cooked. The swirls in the tin will take longer to cook, possibly 20 minutes.

Cool on a wire rack, but these are best eaten warm or at room temperature.

Soda Bread Deep Pan Pizza

The idea to use soda bread as a base for a pizza was born out of desperation one day when I needed to whip up a dish of something filling and delicious in no time at all for a few hungry lads. It can be as simple as a topping of grated mature Cheddar cheese and spring onions or well-seasoned cherry tomatoes, a few basil leaves and a drizzle of extra virgin olive oil. This recipe is taken from my book *One Pot Feeds All*, published by Kyle Books.

SERVES 6-8

- 450g plain flour
- 1 level teaspoon bicarbonate of soda
- 1 level teaspoon fine sea salt
- 375-400ml buttermilk

TOPPINGS:
- extra virgin olive oil, for brushing
- ½-1 tablespoon chopped fresh rosemary
- 50g pepperoni or chorizo, cut into 5mm pieces
- 350g tomato fondue (page 306) or chopped fresh or tinned tomatoes mixed with seasoning/spices
- 8 bocconcini, halved
- 15g Parmesan cheese, grated
- lots of snipped fresh flat-leaf parsley

Preheat the oven to 230°C/450°F/gas mark 8.

Sieve the flour, bicarbonate of soda and salt into a large bowl. Make a well in the centre. Pour in 375ml of the buttermilk and, using one hand, mix in the flour from the sides of the bowl. Mix to a softish dough, not too wet or sticky, adding more buttermilk if necessary. When it all comes together, turn the dough out onto a floured board, tidy it up, knead lightly for a few seconds and flip it over.

Brush a roasting tin (approx. 31cm × 23cm × 5cm) with olive oil. Roll the dough lightly into a rectangle to fit the tin and sprinkle with the rosemary. Scatter the diced pepperoni or chorizo evenly over the surface, then spread a layer of tomato fondue on top (we add the pepperoni or chorizo first and cover it with the tomato fondue so that it doesn't burn). Arrange some halved bocconcini on top of the tomato fondue, then sprinkle with the grated Parmesan.

Transfer the tray to the fully preheated oven on a low rack and bake for 15 minutes. Reduce the heat to 200°C/400°F/gas mark 6 and bake for a further 20–25 minutes, until the dough is cooked and it's golden and bubbly on top.

Sprinkle with fresh parsley and serve with a good green salad.

'Nduja and Bocconcini

Omit the rosemary. Replace the chorizo with 100g 'nduja mixed with 2 tablespoons extra virgin olive oil to make it easier to spread. Sprinkle with fresh marjoram to serve.

Pesto and Parmesan	Omit the rosemary and chorizo. Replace the tomato fondue with 3 tablespoons loosened basil or wild garlic pesto. Top with 110–150g grated mozzarella or 110–150g soft goat's cheese and 15g grated Parmesan.
Tapenade and Soft Goat's Cheese	Omit the rosemary and chorizo. Replace the tomato fondue with 3 tablespoons tapenade (page 315) and replace the mozzarella with 110–150g soft goat's cheese.
Spiced Aubergine	Omit the rosemary and chorizo. Replace it with 6–8 tablespoons of spiced aubergine (page 311).
Cheddar Cheese and Spring Onion	Omit the chorizo. Replace the rosemary with 4 tablespoons thinly sliced spring onions and replace the Parmesan with 100g grated mature Cheddar cheese.
Peperonata	Spread a layer of peperonata (page 305) and a generous sprinkling of grated Parmesan over the dough. Add a few pitted whole olives and fresh basil leaves before serving.

Shanagarry Brown Soda Bread

This is a more modern version of soda bread. It couldn't be simpler – just mix and pour into a well-greased tin. This bread keeps very well for several days and is also great toasted.

....

- 400g stone-ground wholemeal flour
- 75g plain flour, preferably unbleached
- 1 level teaspoon bicarbonate of soda, finely sieved
- 1 teaspoon salt
- 1 egg
- 425ml buttermilk or sour milk (approx.)
- 1 tablespoon sunflower oil, plus extra for greasing
- 1 teaspoon honey or treacle
- sunflower or sesame seeds (optional)

Preheat the oven to 200°C/400°F/gas mark 6. Grease a 13cm × 20cm (450g) loaf tin or three small loaf tins (14.6cm × 7.6cm).

Put all the dry ingredients, including the sieved bicarb, in a large bowl and mix well. Whisk the egg, buttermilk, oil and honey or treacle together. Make a well in the centre of the dry ingredients and pour in all the liquid. Mix well and add more buttermilk if necessary. The mixture should be soft and slightly sloppy.

Pour into the oiled tin or tins. Using a butter knife, draw a slit down the middle. Sprinkle some sunflower or sesame seeds on the top (if using).

Bake in the preheated oven for approx. 60 minutes for a large loaf or 45–50 minutes for the small loaf tins, until the bread is nice and crusty and sounds hollow when tapped on the bottom. Cool on a wire rack.

Irish Stout and Walnut Soda Bread

Everyone loves this 'new age' soda bread and it keeps well. Try using a local stout from the many new Irish craft breweries. Thank you to Maggie Draddy for sharing her favourite recipe.

MAKES 1 LOAF OR
3 SMALL LOAVES

....

- 160g plain flour
- 10g bicarbonate of soda
- 315g wholemeal flour
- 60g porridge oats
- 60g walnuts, roughly chopped
- 40g caster sugar
- 10g salt
- 375ml milk
- 110g honey or golden syrup
- 110g treacle
- 40g butter, melted
- 100ml stout, such as Murphy's, Beamish, Guinness or your favourite craft stout

Preheat the oven to 150°C/300°F/gas mark 2. Line a 13cm × 20cm (450g) loaf tin or three small loaf tins (14.6cm × 7.6cm) with parchment paper.

Sieve the plain flour and bicarb into a large bowl. Add the wholemeal flour, oats, walnuts, sugar and salt. Mix together and make a well in the centre.

In a separate bowl, whisk the milk, honey or golden syrup, treacle, melted butter and stout together thoroughly. Combine the wet and dry ingredients and mix to a sloppy dough.

Scrape the dough into the lined tin or divide it between the three small tins. Bake in the preheated oven for 45 minutes, then increase the oven temperature to 180°C/350°F/gas mark 4 and bake for another 15 minutes. Remove from the tin and bake for a further 10 minutes to crisp the base. It should sound hollow when the base is tapped. Cool on a wire rack and serve buttered.

Kibbled Wheat and Oatmeal Soda Bread Scones

To enjoy for breakfast with marmalade, with soup at lunchtime or in your lunchbox – pop a few into the freezer.

MAKES 9

....

- 285g brown wholemeal flour
- 225g plain flour
- 25g oatmeal
- 25g kibbled wheat
- 1 rounded teaspoon bicarbonate of soda, finely sieved
- 1 rounded teaspoon salt
- 25g butter, chilled and diced
- 1 egg
- 425-450ml buttermilk (approx.)

....

TOPPING:
- 25g kibbled wheat
- 25g rolled oats

Preheat the oven to 230°C/450°F/gas mark 8.

Mix together the flours, oatmeal, kibbled wheat, finely sieved bicarb and salt in a large, wide bowl. Rub in the butter, then make a well in the centre.

Whisk the egg. Keeping a little back for the top, pour the rest of the egg into a measuring jug. Bring the liquid up to the 425ml mark with the buttermilk.

Pour most of the liquid into the well in the flour. Using one hand with the fingers open and stiff, mix in a full circle, drawing in the flour from the sides of the bowl, adding more milk and egg mixture if necessary. The dough should be softish but not too wet and sticky. Mix as quickly and gently as possible, keeping it light and airy. When the dough comes together, turn it out onto a well-floured work surface. Wash and dry your hands.

Roll the dough lightly, just enough to shape it into a square approx. 18cm × 18cm. Flatten it slightly to about 3cm high. Cut the dough into nine square scones. Brush the top of the scones with the remaining beaten egg, adding a little extra buttermilk if needed. Mix the topping of kibbled wheat and oatmeal together on a flat plate, then dip each scone into this mixture.

Transfer the scones to a very lightly floured baking sheet. Bake in the preheated oven for about 15 minutes. When cooked, they should sound hollow when tapped underneath. Cool on a wire rack.

Crunchy Tops Tear-and-Share Soda Bread Scones

These crunchy-topped scones join in a tin to make an irresistible tear-and-share loaf or they can be baked individually.

MAKES 7

....

- butter or olive oil, for greasing
- 450g plain flour, preferably unbleached
- 1 level teaspoon bicarbonate of soda
- 1 level teaspoon dairy salt
- 350-400ml buttermilk, depending on how thick it is

....

TOPPING:
- egg wash (page 325)
- sunflower seeds, sesame seeds, kibbled wheat, caraway seeds, poppy seeds, oat flakes, pumpkin seeds, amaranth seeds, puffed rice and/or grated mature Cheddar cheese

Preheat the oven to 230°C/450°F/gas mark 8. Grease a round tin measuring 23cm across × 4cm high with butter or olive oil.

Sieve the dry ingredients into a large bowl. Mix together and make a well in the centre. Pour in all the buttermilk at once. Using one hand, mix in the flour from the sides of the bowl, adding more buttermilk if necessary. The dough should be softish, not too wet and sticky. When it all comes together, turn it out onto a floured board.

Wash and dry your hands. Flip the dough over and pat it into a round approx. 4cm high. Stamp out seven scones with a 7.5cm scone cutter. Brush the top of each scone with egg wash or buttermilk, then dip in the seeds of your choice. Arrange the scones side by side in the well-greased tin, allowing a little space for expansion.

Bake in the preheated oven for 15 minutes, then reduce the temperature to 200°C/400°F/gas mark 6 and bake for a further 15 minutes. Remove from the tin and put back in the oven for a further 5–8 minutes, until fully cooked. If you are in doubt, tap the bottom of the scones. When they're cooked, they will sound hollow. Cool on a wire rack.

Teeny Weenies

Roll the dough to 3–4cm thick, then stamp into 2.5cm rounds and dip into the crunchy topping of your choice. Bake in the preheated oven at 230°C/450°F/gas mark 8 for 8–10 minutes.

Spotted Dog

In some parts of the country, spotted dog is called railway cake – 'a currant for every station', as the saying goes. In my case, though, it would be 'a sultana for every station'. I prefer them for their more luscious flavour.

This bread has always been a favourite with our children, freshly made on Sunday mornings for our picnics on the cliffs at Ballyandreen or relished with lashings of butter, jam and steaming mugs of drinking chocolate after a winter walk on Shanagarry strand.

Preheat the oven to 220°C/430°F/gas mark 7.

Sieve the flour and bicarb into a large mixing bowl, then add the fruit, sugar and salt. Mix the ingredients well by lifting them up above the bowl and letting them fall loosely back into the bowl through your fingers. This adds more air and therefore more lightness to the finished bread.

Now make a well in the centre of the flour. Break the egg into the bottom of the measuring jug, whisking to break it up, then add the buttermilk up to the 400ml level so that the egg makes up part of the total liquid measurement. Pour most of this milk and egg mixture into the flour.

With your fingers open and stiff, mix in a full circular movement, drawing in the flour from the sides of the bowl. Add more milk and egg mixture if necessary. The dough should be nice and soft, but not too wet and sticky. With spotted dog, as with all soda breads, mix as quickly and gently as possible to keep the dough light and airy but avoid over-mixing. When it comes together – a matter of seconds – turn it out onto a well-floured work surface. Wash and dry your hands.

With floured hands, roll the dough lightly for a few seconds, just enough to tidy it up. Pat the dough into a round and press gently with your fingers to about 6cm high.

Transfer the dough onto a baking tray dusted lightly with flour. Mark the top with a deep cross and prick each of the dough triangles with your knife to let the pesky fairies out.

Bake in the preheated oven for 5 minutes, then reduce the temperature to 180°C/350°F/gas mark 4 and bake for

a further 35 minutes, until the bottom sounds hollow when tapped.

Cut into thick slices and spread lavishly with Irish butter and jam. Spotted dog is also really good eaten with slices of Cheddar cheese.

Boozy Spotted Dog	Prick the sultanas and soak in 125ml warm whiskey for 15–30 minutes. Add to the ingredients and proceed as above.
Spotted Puppies	In the window of Eli's in New York City on St Patrick's weekend in 2005, I spied lots of little spotted puppies – they were selling like proverbial hot cakes. Make the spotted dog as above. Divide the dough into six pieces, then shape each piece into a little round loaf. Cut a cross on top and bake in the preheated oven for approx. 20 minutes. Cool on a wire rack.
Stripy Cat	When Paul and Jeannie Rankin taught at the school some years ago, their two eldest children were in the kitchen with me while I was making spotted dog. They asked if I ever added chocolate instead of sultanas. I'm always happy to try anything once, so in went some chocolate chips. Once it was out of the oven and by all accounts a success, I asked the girls what I should call it. 'Stripy cat, of course,' they declared in unison. So stripy cat was born. Substitute 75–110g dark chocolate, roughly chopped, for the fruit and proceed as in the spotted dog recipe. This is definitely best eaten warm, so serve this delicious, sweet bread freshly baked, cut into thick slices and generously smeared with butter.
Emigrant's Soda	Caraway seeds and sultanas were added to soda bread in Ireland long ago, but the tradition went by the wayside. Not so in America, where soda bread often has caraway seeds and sultanas in it. Usually when I go to the US I take Irish recipes there, but I was delighted to bring this one back to Ireland! Simply add 2 teaspoons caraway seeds to the spotted dog recipe and proceed as above.

Mary Walsh's Currant Bread

Mary Walsh lived in the little village of Cullohill in County Laois, where I lived as a child. She was famous for her currant bread, which falls somewhere between a cake and a very rich soda bread. She usually made it on Sunday mornings and as children we used to fight about who would collect the milk from their farm so we could have a slice of 'cake' fresh from the oven. One of the secrets of why it tastes so good is that she used sultanas, not currants, despite the name!

MAKES 1 LOAF

- 450g plain flour
- 25g caster sugar
- 1 level teaspoon bicarbonate of soda, finely sieved
- 1 level teaspoon salt
- 50g butter, diced, plus extra for greasing
- 150g good-quality sultanas or 90g sultanas and 60g currants
- 25g candied peel (page 298), chopped
- zest of 1 sweet orange
- 1 egg, whisked
- 350ml buttermilk (approx.)
- 2-3 tablespoons cream
- 2-3 tablespoons Demerara sugar

Preheat the oven to 220°C/430°F/gas mark 7. Grease a 23cm cake tin.

Put the flour, sugar, finely sieved bicarb and salt in a large bowl. Rub in the butter, then add the sultanas, mixed peel and orange zest. (Mary suggests plumping up the dried fruit for a minute or two in the oven or in a saucepan with some fresh orange juice.)

Whisk the beaten egg with the buttermilk and cream. Make a well in the centre of the dry ingredients, then add enough of the liquid to make a soft dough. Turn out onto a floured board, shape gently into a round and put in the greased tin.

Mark the top with a cross (the traditional blessing) and prick the four corners to let the fairies out! Brush the top with a little of the remaining liquid, then sprinkle with some crunchy brown sugar. Put on the middle or lower shelf in the preheated oven and immediately reduce the temperature to 180°C/350°F/gas mark 4. Cook for 35–40 minutes, covering the bread with parchment paper if the top of the bread begins to brown too much. To test for doneness, tap the base of the loaf – when it's cooked, it will sound hollow.

Cool on a wire rack. Cut into thick slices and eat while still warm slathered with Irish butter.

Currant Squares

Instead of cooking the currant cake in a tin, divide the round into four triangles. Transfer to a baking sheet and cook as above for 30–35 minutes. These are always called currant squares even though they are triangles!

Brown Seedy Soda Bread

This contemporary Irish soda bread is baked in a tin or tins. Just weigh, mix and pour into the tin and bake. The addition of seeds gives this bread a delicious extra crunch.

MAKES 1 LOAF OR
3 SMALL LOAVES

- oil, for greasing
- 225g plain flour
- 225g brown wholemeal flour
- 50g granary flour
- 50g kibbled wheat
- 2-3 teaspoons sesame seeds
- 1 rounded teaspoon dark soft brown sugar
- 1 rounded teaspoon salt
- 1 level teaspoon bicarbonate of soda, finely sieved
- 15g butter
- 1 small egg
- 450ml buttermilk (approx.)

TOPPING:
- ½ teaspoon kibbled wheat
- ½ teaspoon sesame seeds

Preheat the oven to 200°C/400°F/gas mark 6. Grease one 13cm × 20cm (450g) loaf tin or three small loaf tins (14.6cm × 7.6cm) well with oil.

In a large, wide bowl, mix the flours, kibbled wheat, sesame seeds, brown sugar, salt and bicarbonate of soda together, then rub in the butter. Make a well in the centre of the dry ingredients.

Break the egg into a measuring jug and add the buttermilk to the 475ml line, with the egg forming part of your total liquid measurement. Whisk to combine, then pour most of this mixture into the dry ingredients.

Using one hand, with the fingers open and stiff, mix in a full circle, drawing in the flour from the sides of the bowl, adding more of the buttermilk and egg mixture if necessary. Avoid over-mixing to keep the dough light and airy – the mixture should be soft and almost pourable. Transfer to the well-oiled tin(s), then sprinkle the top with the extra kibbled wheat and sesame seeds.

Bake in the fully preheated oven for 50–60 minutes for one loaf or 40–50 minutes for small loaves. Remove from the tin(s) 10–15 minutes before the end of the cooking time and return to the oven continue to bake. Tap the base of bread to check if it's cooked – it should sound hollow. Cool on a wire rack.

Traditional Wheaten Bread

Nowadays the buttermilk sold in Irish shops is usually low-fat. If you have access to beautiful rich, thick buttermilk, there is no need to add butter or extra cream. If a lighter bread is preferred, the proportion of white to brown flour can be adjusted to taste – we use 300g plain flour and 150g brown wholemeal flour. An egg adds to the flavour and richness.

MAKES 1 LOAF

....

- 225g brown wholemeal flour (preferably stone-ground)
- 225g plain flour
- 1 level teaspoon bicarbonate of soda, finely sieved
- 1 teaspoon salt
- 12-25g butter or 2 tablespoons sour or fresh cream (see the intro)
- 400-425ml sour milk or buttermilk
- 1 egg, beaten (optional)

Preheat the oven to 230°C/450°F/gas mark 8.

Mix all the dry ingredients together in a large, wide bowl, then rub in the butter (if using, or if using cream, add it to the buttermilk). Make a well in the centre and pour in all the sour milk or buttermilk and the beaten egg (if using). Using one hand, stir in a full circular movement from the centre to the outside of the bowl until all the flour has been incorporated. The dough should be soft but not too wet and sticky. When it all comes together – a matter of seconds – turn it out onto a well-floured board (use wholemeal flour).

Wash and dry your hands. Roll the dough around gently with floury hands for a second, just enough to tidy it up. Flip it over and flatten slightly into a round approx. 5cm thick. Sprinkle a little of the spare wholemeal flour from the worktop onto a baking tray, then put the round loaf on top of the flour. Mark the surface with a deep cross (the traditional blessing) and prick in each corner to let the fairies out of the bread!

Bake in the preheated oven for 10 minutes, then reduce the temperature to 200°C/400°F/gas mark 6 and bake for a further 30 minutes. Turn the bread upside down on the baking tray and continue to bake for 5-10 minutes more. The bread will sound hollow when tapped on both sides. Cool on a wire rack. Wrap in a clean tea towel while hot if you prefer a softer crust.

Kibbled Wheat Scones

Make the dough as above but form it into a round and flatten to 4cm thick approx. Stamp out into round scones with a glass or cookie cutter or cut into squares with a knife. Brush the top of each scone with buttermilk, then dip into kibbled wheat. Bake at 230°C/450°F/gas mark 8 for about 30 minutes, then reduce the temperature to 200°C/400°F/gas mark 6 and bake for another 5–10 minutes, depending on their size. When cooked, they should sound hollow when tapped.

Bastible Bread

A bastible is an iron pot, usually with three little legs underneath and a slightly domed lid. It was used as a pot oven to cook over an open fire. Everything from breads and tarts to stews and even a goose was cooked in the bastible. Breads and tarts cooked in a bastible always had more tender crusts because the steam was trapped inside the pot, softening the crust. You can recreate a similar tender crust by cooking the soda bread in a covered casserole in the oven.

Put a large casserole in the oven to preheat. Line the base of the casserole with a round of parchment paper. Make the dough as in the recipe for white soda bread (page 26) or the brown soda bread above. Pat the dough into a round approx. 4cm thick and just large enough to fit the casserole. Cut a deep cross on top and prick the centre of the four sections to let the fairies out, then transfer the dough to the hot casserole and cover with the lid. Bake in the preheated oven for 40–50 minutes, until fully cooked. Remove from the casserole and cool on a wire rack. The crust will be soft and tender and the bread will be almost spongy in texture.

Soda 'Squares'

Cut the dough into four quadrants and bake separately in the oven or cook for 6–10 minutes on each side on a griddle or frying pan, depending on thickness.

Brown Cake

Years ago, a loaf of soda bread was commonly referred to as a brown or a white cake, or a cake of bread, possibly because the texture is more 'cakey' than yeast bread. Double the quantities and bake in a bastible or 28cm diameter casserole.

Mrs McGilly-cuddy's Yellowmeal Bread

This bread tastes just as delicious today as it did over a hundred years ago and it deserves to be much better known. I've made it over and over again since Mrs McGillycuddy from Caragh Lake in County Kerry first showed me how to make it. I've also heard it referred to as 'yalla male' bread. This tradition dates back to Famine times, when cornmeal was imported into Ireland to help alleviate starvation. Other recipes from West Cork use equal quantities of yellowmeal and flour, which produces a slightly yellower bread with a grittier texture.

SERVES 4-8

- 275g plain flour
- 175g cornmeal (sometimes referred to as yellowmeal or Indian meal)
- 1 level teaspoon bicarbonate of soda
- 1 level teaspoon salt
- 350-375ml sour milk or buttermilk

Preheat the oven to 230°C/450°F/gas mark 8.

Sieve the dry ingredients into a large bowl. Make a well in the centre and pour most of the buttermilk in at once.

Using one hand, mix in the flour from the sides of the bowl in a full circular movement, adding more milk if necessary. The dough should be softish, not too wet and sticky. When it all comes together, turn it out onto a floured board. Wash and dry your hands and dust them with flour, then tidy it up. Flip over and pat the dough into a round approx. 4cm deep. Cut a cross on top and prick in the four corners to let the fairies out!

Transfer the round to a baking tray and bake in the preheated oven for 15 minutes, then turn down the temperature to 200°C/400°F/gas mark 6 and bake for 30 minutes more, until cooked. If you are in doubt about this, tap the bottom of the bread – when it's cooked, it will sound hollow. Cool on a wire rack.

Fadge or Potato Bread

In Ulster, people are passionate about fadge or potato bread. It can be cooked on a griddle, in a frying pan or in the oven. A little leftover mashed potato can be, and often was, added to soda bread.

SERVES 8

- 900g unpeeled 'old' potatoes, e.g. Golden Wonders or Kerr's Pinks
- 1 egg, beaten
- 25-50g butter, diced
- 40g plain flour
- fine sea salt and freshly ground black pepper
- creamy milk
- bacon fat, clarified butter (page 307) or olive oil, if frying

Bake or boil the potatoes in their jackets until soft, then pull off the skins and mash right away. Add the beaten egg, butter and flour. Season with lots of salt and freshly ground black pepper, adding a few drops of creamy milk if the mixture is too stiff. Taste and correct the seasoning.

Tip out onto a floured surface and shape into an 18cm round that's 2.5cm thick, then cut into eight wedges. Dip in seasoned flour.

Heat some bacon fat, melted clarified butter or olive oil in a cast iron or griddle pan on a gentle heat. Add the wedges to the pan and cook for 4–5 minutes, until the fadge is crusty and golden on one side. Flip it over and cook the other side for 4–5 minutes more, until crusty and golden. Alternatively, arrange the wedges on a baking tray and bake in an oven preheated to 180°C/350°F/gas mark 4 for 15–20 minutes.

Serve with an Ulster fry or just on its own on hot plates with a blob of butter melting on top.

Potato Bread Pizza

You can do lots of riffs on potato bread. Add chopped chives, wild garlic, thyme leaves, seaweed – or use it as the base of a pizza.

Preheat the oven to 220°C/430°F/gas mark 7. Brush a loose-bottomed 23cm tin generously with extra virgin olive oil. Roll the dough into a circle and press into the base of the tin, then bake in the preheated oven for 15 minutes. Remove from the oven and scatter with diced chorizo or crisp streaky bacon. Cover with a generous layer of tomato fondue (page 306), then sprinkle with chopped spring onions and top with grated cheese. Return to the oven for a further 10–15 minutes, until the base is fully cooked and the cheese has melted.

YEAST BREAD

When yeast was identified and then commercialised in the mid-1900s, it changed everything. Before that, in the words of Andrew Whitley, who started the Real Bread Campaign in the UK in 2008, 'Our forebears relied on the yeasts naturally present in the flour to make their bread rise. This took a long time, during which the bacteria that was also there could work their modest miracles – of flavour, nourishment and digestibility.'

When commercial baker's yeast became widely available, it enabled bakers to 'manufacture' bread in a fraction of the time. What is now known as the Chorleywood process (the method used to make most industrial bread) was developed in 1961 by Bill Collins, George Elton and Norman Chamberlain of the British Baking Industries Research Association. This fast process reduced the labour input and thus the manufacturing costs. Soft, fluffy bread could be made in less than half the time that it took to make bread the traditional way, but beneficial bacteria had less opportunity to develop. In addition, two to three times the quantity of yeast is used compared to traditional bread. This dramatic increase is being cited as a possible cause of the growth of yeast intolerance.

The Green Revolution resulted in high-yielding varieties of wheat. These were not designed to enhance the nutrient content but were specifically developed to work with the artificial fertilizers and pesticides used in intensive farming systems. However, it is now acknowledged that these new varieties of wheat have fewer vitamins and minerals than traditional varieties and more of the protein that causes leaky gut syndrome.

There are other concerns too. Until recently, hydrogenated fats, implicated in heart disease, were used in the industrial bread-making process. These are being replaced by vegetable oils, which are now thought to cause similar health problems.

Many people can no longer eat bread without discomfort. According to Coeliac UK, in 2022, at least one in every hundred people were diagnosed as coeliac and cannot eat gluten in wheat, rye, barley or oats, while one in every five are gluten intolerant. At Ballymaloe Cookery School, we have observed over many years that students who have a gluten intolerance (not coeliacs) seem to be able to digest and enjoy our natural sourdough, which is fermented for a minimum of 48 hours.

It's time to get baking and enjoy a delicious slice of crusty, nourishing bread again.

Ballymaloe Brown Yeast Bread

This wholemeal loaf has been made at Ballymaloe House since the 1950s and is a variation on the Grant loaf created accidentally by Doris Grant, who was keen to produce an easy-to-make, nourishing loaf. The main ingredients – wholemeal flour, treacle and yeast – are highly nutritious.

This bread is a brilliant introduction to yeast bread-making. There's no need for a machine – it's made entirely by hand; there's no kneading involved; there's only one rising; and it's easy to scale up the recipe to make 4–16 loaves.

Ballymaloe brown yeast bread takes approx. 1½ hours to make from start to finish. It takes time, but not your time – mixing is a matter of minutes and the remainder of the time is spent rising.

When making Ballymaloe brown yeast bread, remember that yeast is a living organism. In order to grow, it requires warmth, moisture and nourishment. The yeast feeds on the sugar and produces bubbles of carbon dioxide, which cause the bread to rise. Heat over 50°C (122°F) will kill yeast, so have all the ingredients and equipment at blood heat (37°C/99°F). In cold weather, it helps to warm the flour a little in a warm oven.

White or brown sugar, honey, golden syrup, treacle or molasses may be used. Each will give a slightly different flavour to the bread. At Ballymaloe, we use treacle.

The dough rises more rapidly with 30g yeast than with 25g yeast. Dried yeast may be used instead of baker's yeast. Follow the same method but use only **half the weight** given for fresh yeast. Allow longer to rise. Fast-acting yeast may also be used – follow the instructions on the packet. Add directly to the flour – 10–15g is adequate for 450g flour.

We use a stone-ground wholemeal, but you could use 400g stone-ground wholemeal flour **plus** 50g strong white flour **OR** 450g stone-ground wholemeal flour. Different flours produce breads of different textures and flavour. The amount of natural moisture in the flour varies according to atmospheric conditions, so the quantity of water will need to be altered accordingly. The dough should be just too wet to knead – in fact, it does not require kneading.

MAKES 1 LOAF OR 3 SMALL
LOAVES
....

- 450g stone-ground
  wholemeal flour (or
  see the intro)
- 9g salt
- 1 teaspoon black
  treacle or molasses
- 425ml tepid water
- 20-30g fresh yeast
  (or see the intro)
- light olive or
  sunflower oil,
  for greasing
- sesame seeds
  (optional)

Before you begin, all your ingredients should ideally be at room temperature.

Mix the flour and salt in a wide bowl.

In a small bowl or Pyrex jug, mix the treacle or molasses with 150ml of the tepid water, crumble in the yeast and stir once or twice. Put the bowl in a warm place for a few minutes to allow the yeast to start to work. Check to see if the yeast is working – after about 5 minutes, it will have a creamy, slightly frothy appearance on top.

When ready, stir and pour it into the flour with all the remaining water to make a loose, wet dough. The mixture should be too wet to knead. Allow to sit in the bowl for 4–5 minutes (the time varies depending on the room temperature).

Meanwhile, brush the base and sides of one regular 13cm × 20cm (450g) loaf tin or three small tins (14.6cm × 7.6cm) with a good light olive or sunflower oil.

Scoop the mixture into the greased tin(s). Sprinkle the top of the loaves with sesame seeds if you like. Put the tin in a warm place in your kitchen, out of a draught. Cover the tin with a clean tea towel to prevent a skin from forming.

Preheat the oven to 230°C/450°F/gas mark 8.

After 10–15 minutes, just as the bread comes to the top of the tin, remove the tea towel and pop the bread into the oven for 20 minutes. The bread will rise a little further in the oven – this is called oven spring. However, if the bread rises over the top of the tin before it goes into the oven, it will continue to rise as it bakes and will flow over the edges.

After 20 minutes, turn the oven temperature down to 200°C/400°F/gas mark 6 and bake for another 40–50 minutes, until it looks nicely browned and the bottom sounds hollow when tapped. We usually remove the loaf from the tin about 10 minutes before the end of the cooking time and put it back in the oven to crisp all round, but if you like a softer crust, there's no need to do this. Cool on a wire rack.

Fermented
Ballymaloe Brown
Yeast Bread

Make the bread as above but put only three-quarters of the dough in the oiled loaf tin. Put the remainder in a jar, cover it with a clean cloth, secure the cloth with a rubber band and leave it out at room temperature overnight (or refrigerate for several days). Add this starter to the next loaf to add extra flavour and complexity. The resulting loaf will have an even more complex flavour, slightly like a pumpernickel bread. It's delicious with charcuterie or smoked fish.

Russian Village Bread

We enjoyed several bread courses at the Village Bakery in Cumbria with Andrew Whitley, co-founder of the Real Bread Campaign. Andrew makes many Russian breads, including one with coriander seeds on the top and bottom. On our return we experimented with our brown yeast bread, and although it is not as complex as Andrew's sourdough version, it is still delicious.

Follow the master recipe but substitute the flour with 400g wholemeal flour, 50g rye flour and 50g strong white flour. Brush the tin with sunflower oil, then sprinkle a layer of lightly crushed whole coriander seeds over the base of the tin. After you put the bread in the tin, sprinkle another layer of crushed coriander seeds over the top of the bread. Bake as above and cool on a wire rack.

Ballymaloe Spelt Loaf

Spelt is an ancient variety of wheat that originated in the Persian Gulf 5,000 years ago. It has a fragile gluten structure, which makes it easier to digest than wheat.

There are three separate references to spelt flour in the New Testament. It was grown throughout Europe for centuries, but high-cost production meant that spelt production had virtually ceased in Britain by the Second World War. In recent years there has been a huge increase in its popularity as more and more organic farmers look for disease-resistant crops. Although it belongs to the same family as common wheat, it has a different gene structure so it is higher in protein and has a greater concentration of vitamins and minerals. It is low in gluten and often makes a digestible substitute for wheat flour for those who are gluten intolerant. We use organic wholemeal spelt flour from Dunany Flour in County Louth and Oak Forest Mills in County Kilkenny.

MAKES 1 LOAF

- olive oil, for greasing
- 450g spelt flour
- 9g salt
- 1 teaspoon black treacle or molasses
- 400ml tepid water
- 20g fresh yeast
- sesame seeds or a mixture of seeds, such as pumpkin, sunflower, sesame and/or kibbled wheat (optional)

Preheat the oven to 230°C/450°F/gas mark 8. Oil a 13cm × 20cm (450g) loaf tin.

Mix the flour with the salt in a large mixing bowl.

In a small bowl or Pyrex jug, mix the treacle or molasses with 150ml of the tepid water, crumble in the yeast and let it sit. After about 5 minutes, it should be creamy and slightly frothy on top. When it's ready, stir and pour it into the flour with all the remaining water. Mix with your hand in a full circular movement to make a loose, wet dough. The mixture should be too wet to knead. Put the mixture into the greased tin. Sprinkle the top of the loaf with sesame seeds or a mixture of seeds of your choice (if using).

Cover the tin with a clean tea towel to prevent a skin from forming. After 10–15 minutes, just as the bread comes to the top of the tin, remove the tea towel and pop the bread into the oven for 15 minutes. The bread will rise a little further in the oven – this is called oven spring.

After 15 minutes, reduce the oven temperature to 200°C/400°F/gas mark 6 and bake for a further 40–45 minutes, until it looks nicely browned and the base sounds hollow when tapped. Cool on a wire rack.

Ballymaloe Cookery School White Yeast Loaf

We use Doves Farm organic white bread flour, so the water quantity may vary for other brands. This bread can be baked in loaf tins or made into plaits or rolls.

MAKES 2 LOAVES

- 20g fresh yeast (or 10g dried yeast)
- 20g granulated sugar
- 400g tepid water (weigh the water for accuracy)
- 700g organic strong white flour
- 16g pure dairy salt
- 25g butter, diced
- oil, for greasing

Crumble the yeast into a bowl, then add the sugar and tepid water (remember, anything above 50°C (122°F) will kill yeast). Mix and allow to stand for a couple of minutes. After 4–5 minutes, it should be creamy and slightly frothy on top.

Meanwhile, put the flour in a wide mixing bowl and stir in the salt, then rub in the butter until it resembles coarse breadcrumbs.

Add all the liquid ingredients to the flour and mix to a dough with your hand. Turn out onto a clean work surface (no flour), cover with the upturned bowl and allow to rest for 5–10 minutes.

Uncover the dough and check it – if it feels a little dry and tough, wet your hand, rub it over the dough and knead by hand for approx. 10 minutes, until silky smooth. Return the dough to the bowl and cover with a clean tea towel. Allow to rise in a warm, draught-free place for 1½–2 hours, until doubled in size.

Preheat the oven to 230°C/450°F/gas mark 8. Oil two 13cm × 20cm (450g) loaf tins.

Turn the dough out onto the work surface. Knead for a minute or two and shape as desired (see the variations for a plait, rolls, knots or snails). For loaves, divide the dough in half. Working with one half at a time, fold it over and knead it with the heel of your hand into a roll. Tuck in the ends and pop into the oiled tins.

Cover the tins with a clean tea towel to prevent a skin from forming. After 10–15 minutes, just as the bread comes to the top of the tin, remove the tea towel. The bread will rise a little further in the oven – this is called oven spring. The bread is ready for baking when a small dent remains if the dough is pressed lightly with your finger. Spray with a water mister and dust with flour for a rustic-looking loaf and slash the surface with a baker's knife (lame) or sharp blade.

Pop the bread into the preheated oven and bake for 25–35 minutes, depending on size. When baked, the bread should sound hollow when tapped underneath. Cool on a wire rack.

Ballymaloe Plait

Take half the quantity of white yeast dough after it has been knocked back after the first rise and divide it into three equal pieces. Use both hands to roll each piece into a rope – the thickness depends on how plump you want the plait to be. It will shrink at first, so re-roll each piece a second time. Pinch the three ends together at the top. Bring each outside strand into the centre, alternating to form a plait. Pinch the ends and tuck in neatly. Transfer to a baking tray and leave to double in size. Spray with a water mister and either dust with flour or brush with egg yolk before baking for a rustic-looking plait.

Pinch the ends together at the top

Bring each outside strand into the centre

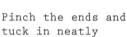

Repeat until the end

Pinch the ends and tuck in neatly

Bread Rolls

Divide the dough into 50g pieces, then shape into balls on a clean, unfloured work surface with the palm of your hand. Transfer to a baking tray, cover with a clean tea towel and allow to rise in a warm, draught-free place until the rolls have doubled in size. Moisten with a water mister and dust with flour, then bake in the preheated oven for 15–20 minutes. Cool on a wire rack.

Ballymaloe Knots

Roll a piece of dough into a rope, then into a knot. Allow to rise in a warm, draught-free place, then glaze and bake as above for the plait. Make one large knot or many small knots, as you please.

Roll

Twist

Knot

Ballymaloe Snails

Roll the dough into a rope, then wind into a snail shape(s). Seal the end with water and sprinkle with poppy seeds if you fancy. You could use a clove for an eye.

Batch Loaf

Using 600g of dough, divide the dough into thirds. Roll each piece into a ball on a lightly floured board and slip them side by side into an oiled loaf tin. Cover and allow to rise in a warm, draught-free place for 45–60 minutes, until the dough has risen above the top of the tin. Bake in the preheated oven for 25–35 minutes. You can remove the bread from the tin for the last few minutes to crisp up the base. The loaf should sound hollow when tapped underneath. Cool on a wire rack, then pull apart.

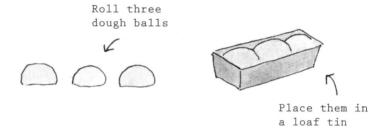

Roll three
dough balls

Place them in
a loaf tin

Bean Can Bread

Originally this might have been done when people were short of loaf tins or cake tins, but it's a brilliant way of using what you have to bake bread. Plus it makes round slices! Choose tins (bean or tomato cans) that don't have a deep lip on top and open the tin with a tin opener that takes the entire top off the tin. Follow the white yeast dough recipe, but bake the dough in the well-greased tins. Fill the tins only about half full to allow for rising. Tins work best if they've been seasoned in the oven a few times before the dough is inserted (see page 6), but if in doubt, line your tins with parchment paper. Cool on a wire rack. We use one 400g tin or a big 2.5kg tin from tinned tomatoes.

Breadsticks

Crusty breadsticks make a delicious nibble. The more rustic looking, the better. These are great with soups, salads or salami.

MAKES 10-20

- Ballymaloe Cookery School white yeast loaf dough (page 52) or sourdough (page 86)
- coarse sea salt, chopped fresh rosemary, crushed cumin, coriander or caraway seeds, sesame seeds, poppy seeds, ground black pepper, chilli flakes, grated Parmesan cheese …

Make the dough as per the recipe on page 52. When the dough has been knocked back, preheat the oven to 220°C/430°F/gas mark 7. Sprinkle the work surface with coarse sea salt or your chosen flavouring.

Pull off small pieces of dough, 10–25g. Roll into very thin, medium or fat breadsticks with your hands, but remember that they will double in size when they bake. Roll in your chosen 'sprinkle' (you may need to brush the breadsticks lightly with cold water first) and place on a baking sheet. Repeat until all the dough has been used. Breadsticks are usually baked without a final rising, but for a slightly lighter result, let the shaped dough rise for about 10 minutes before baking.

Bake in the preheated oven for 8–15 minutes, depending on size, until golden brown and crisp. Cool on a wire rack.

Wiggly Worms

Shape a very thin breadstick that has been rolled in finely grated Parmesan cheese into a wiggly worm. Serve with a green salad.

Parma Sticks

Breadsticks wrapped in a slice of Parma or Serrano ham make a delicious nibble to serve with an aperitif.

Chocolate Breadsticks

Make plain breadsticks as above. When cool, dip half of each stick in melted dark chocolate. Allow to set on parchment paper. Serve as a snack.

Sgabei

These deep-fried breadsticks, a traditional recipe from the Lunigiana area of Italy, are completely addictive and utterly irresistible.

MAKES 30-32
....

- 450g Ballymaloe
  Cookery School white
  yeast loaf dough
  (page 52)
- olive or sunflower
  oil, for deep-frying
- sea salt
....

TO SERVE:
- garlic butter (page
  309), chilli oil (page
  322) or sweet chilli
  sauce
- prosciutto

Make the dough as per the recipe on page 52. When the dough has been knocked back, allow it to rest for 5–10 minutes, covered.

Heat the oil in a deep-fryer to 190°C/375°F.

Pull off 7g pieces of the dough and roll into thin breadsticks with your fingertips. Cook a few at a time in the hot oil. After 1 minute, when they are puffed and golden on one side, turn over onto the other side and continue to cook for another 1½ minutes approx., until cooked through. Drain on kitchen paper and sprinkle with sea salt.

Eat as soon as possible with hot garlic butter, chilli oil or sweet chilli sauce to dip or wrapped with prosciutto.

Sgabei with Cheese

Pull off 50g pieces of bread dough and roll into fat breadsticks. Deep-fry in hot oil or lard for 4–5 minutes, turning halfway through. Drain on kitchen paper, then slit along the side and fill with Taleggio or Stracchino cheese and eat as the cheese melts – yummy!

Anchovy Breadsticks

Break off 15g pieces of bread dough, roll out and flatten. Lay one or two anchovies along one side, pinch to cover and roll again. Deep-fry in hot oil for 2–3 minutes, turning halfway through. Addictive.

Pretzels

There are three options here. The first produces dark brown pretzels because of the alkalisation process. The plain or sea salt and caraway baked options are simpler but also delicious, and the last, a sweet version, is rolled in cinnamon sugar – what can I say ...

MAKES 10-12

....

— 1.2kg Ballymaloe
  Cookery School white
  yeast loaf dough (page
  52)
— 3.8 litres cold water
— 200g bicarbonate of
  soda

Make the dough as per the recipe on page 52 and leave it to rise in a warm, draught-free place for 2–2½ hours, until doubled in size.

Knock back the dough and divide it into approx. 100g pieces. Roll each piece into a thin rope, about 60cm long × 1cm thick.

To shape the pretzels, form each piece of dough into a loose horseshoe shape with the ends pointing towards you. Take hold of the ends and cross them over twice, then rest both ends on the edge of the loop of dough to make a pretzel shape.

Transfer the pretzels as they are shaped onto a well-floured clean cloth or baking sheet. Cover and allow to rise in a warm, draught-free place for approx. 10 minutes.

Preheat the oven to 200°C/400°F/gas mark 6.

Meanwhile, pour the cold water in a deep saucepan, add the bicarbonate and bring to the boil. Slide one pretzel at a time into the liquid and poach for 25–30 seconds, splashing it with water all the time. Remove with a slotted slice, shake off the excess drops of water and transfer to parchment-lined baking trays.

Brush with egg wash and bake in the preheated oven for approx. 15 minutes, until golden brown. Transfer to a wire rack and serve warm or cold.

Baked Pretzels with Sea Salt and Caraway Seeds	When the shaped pretzels have risen, glaze gently with a light egg wash, sprinkle with coarse crystals of sea salt and a few caraway seeds. Bake as above.
Baked Pretzels with Cinnamon Sugar	Bake as above. Meanwhile, mix together 225g caster sugar and 4 teaspoons ground cinnamon. Whisk 1 egg yolk with a little cold water and use this to glaze the pretzels. Melt some butter. When the pretzels come out of the oven, brush both sides with melted butter, then dip in the cinnamon sugar and enjoy.

Ballymaloe Quick White Yeast Bread (One Rising)

A brilliant recipe for those who would like to make a white yeast bread but don't have the time to knead and double rise the dough. It's a riff on the Ballymaloe brown yeast bread (page 48) made with white rather than brown flour, a perfect bread for sandwiches or toasting.

When making yeast bread, remember that yeast is a living organism. In order to grow, it requires warmth, moisture and nourishment. The yeast feeds on the sugar and produces bubbles of carbon dioxide, which expand in the heat of the oven and rise the dough.

Once again there is no kneading involved in this recipe and only one rising, so it's a brilliant introduction to using yeast.

MAKES 1 LOAF

....

- 450g strong white flour
- 9g salt
- 1 teaspoon honey
- 325ml tepid water
- 20-25g fresh yeast
- sunflower oil, for greasing
- sesame seeds (optional)

In a wide, roomy bowl, mix the flour with the salt. The ingredients should all be at room temperature.

In a small bowl or Pyrex jug, mix the honey with the tepid water, then crumble in the yeast and allow to sit for a few minutes. After about 5 minutes, it will have a creamy, slightly frothy appearance on top.

When ready, stir and pour it into the flour to make a loose, wet dough. The mixture should be just too wet to knead.

Meanwhile, brush the base and sides of a 13cm × 20cm (450g) loaf tin with a good-quality sunflower oil. Scoop the dough into the greased tin. It will look uneven, but don't worry, it will become smoother as it rises. Sprinkle the top of the loaf with sesame seeds if you like. Cover with a clean glass cloth to prevent a skin from forming and put the tin in a warm place – somewhere in your kitchen close to the cooker or near a radiator, perhaps.

Preheat the oven to 230°C/450°F/gas mark 8.

After about 30 minutes, when the bread has risen just over the top of the tin, remove the tea towel (this bread takes considerably longer to rise than brown yeast bread). The bread will rise a little further in the oven – this is called oven spring.

Pop the loaf in the preheated oven and bake for 20 minutes, then turn the temperature down to 200°C/400°F/gas mark 6 and bake for another

40–50 minutes, until it looks nicely browned and the base sounds hollow when tapped. We usually remove the loaf from the tin about 10 minutes before the end of the cooking time and put it back into the oven to crisp all round, but if you like a softer crust there's no need to do this. Cool on a wire rack.

Richard's Super-Easy 'No Knead' Yeast Bread

A brilliant, super-easy recipe, with no need for a food mixer.

MAKES 2-3 LOAVES

....

- 20g granulated sugar
- 740g tepid water
  (weigh the water for
  accuracy)
- 10g fresh yeast
- 1kg strong white flour
- 16g dairy salt

Stir the sugar into the tepid water, then crumble in the yeast. Allow to sit for a few minutes. After about 5 minutes, it will have a creamy, slightly frothy appearance on top.

Sieve the flour and salt into a large bowl, then add all the liquid. Mix well using a spatula or dough scraper until the mixture is very well combined. The dough will be wet and shaggy looking. Cover with a light cloth and allow to rest for 15–20 minutes.

It's time to start the folding process. With the dough still in the bowl and starting at the 12 o'clock position, lift and pull the dough towards you using a dough scraper or spatula. Repeat this technique at the one o'clock position, 2 o'clock position, and so on until you return to your original starting point, giving it 12 folds in total. Turn the bowl as required to ease the process.

Cover and allow to rest again for 30 minutes, then repeat the folding process. Do this process six times, every 30 minutes – this will take 3 hours in total.

Shape the dough into two or three loaves or a combination of a loaf, plait and bread rolls (see page 53). Cover and allow to rise at room temperature for 1–2 hours, until doubled in size.

Preheat the oven to 220°C/430°F/gas mark 7.

Bake in the preheated oven for 15 minutes, then reduce the oven temperature to 200°C/400°F/gas mark 6 and bake for a further 15–20 minutes, until fully cooked and the base sounds hollow when tapped. Cool on a wire rack.

Lift and pull the dough towards you

Repeat at the one o'clock position, two o'clock position, etc.

Ballymaloe Burger Buns

Homemade buns transform a burger – it's so easy to make your own, plus they freeze brilliantly. Brioche burger buns are also a game-changer (see the brioche recipe on pages 198–9).

MAKES APPROX. 15
....

- 20g fresh yeast
- 225ml tepid milk
- 600g strong white flour
- 12g salt
- 1¼ level tablespoons caster sugar
- 50g butter
- 1 small egg
- 100ml organic natural yogurt
- egg wash (page 325)

Stir the yeast into the tepid milk (remember, anything above 50°C (122°F) will kill yeast). After about 5 minutes, it should be creamy and slightly frothy on top.

Sieve the flour and salt into the bowl of a stand mixer, then add the sugar and rub in the butter. Whisk the egg and add it to the yogurt. Finally, add the milk and the yogurt to the flour. Knead with the dough hook for 5–6 minutes, until the dough is smooth and elastic. Cover with a clean tea towel and allow to rise at room temperature for about 1 hour, until doubled in size.

Knock back the dough and divide it into three pieces. Shape each piece into a roll, then cut into five pieces about 50g each. Roll each piece into a ball, then flatten with the heel of your hand. Transfer to one or two baking trays, cover and allow to rise again at room temperature for about 1½ hours (they won't rise too much). Brush them gently with egg wash.

Preheat the oven to 230°C/450°F/gas mark 8.

Open the door and quickly spray the inside of the oven wall using a water mister. Close the door for a few seconds, then put the tray in at once and bake for 10 minutes. Spray with water twice more during the total baking time – around the oven bottom, sides and over the buns.

Reduce the temperature to 200°C/400°F/gas mark 6 and bake for a further 8–10 minutes. When fully cooked, the buns will sound hollow when tapped on the base. Cool on a wire rack.

Butter and Milk Bread

This bread has a tender crumb. Like most white yeast bread, this dough is suitable for making loaves, plaits or rolls of any shape or a tear-and-share. If you like, you can divide the dough in half and make one loaf and then have fun with a batch of clusters or swirls.

MAKES 2KG OF DOUGH OR
2 × 900G LOAVES OR
ABOUT 15 ROLLS
....

– 30g fresh yeast (or
  15g dried yeast)
– 750g tepid milk
  (approx.)
– 1.1kg strong white
  flour
– 22g salt
– 100g butter, diced
– light olive oil, for
  greasing
....

TO GLAZE:
– 1 beaten egg mixed
  with 1 tablespoon
  cream
....

DECORATION (OPTIONAL):
– poppy seeds, caraway
  seeds, fennel seeds,
  pumpkin seeds or
  sunflower seeds

Dissolve the yeast in the tepid milk (if you are using dried yeast, stir it into the tepid milk and leave it in a warm place for about 10 minutes to activate).

Sieve the flour and salt into a bowl, then rub in the butter.

Pour most of the liquid into the flour and mix to a soft dough, using more liquid if necessary. Cover and allow to rest in the bowl for 10 minutes.

Turn the dough out onto a floured board and knead for 8–10 minutes, until the dough is elastic, smooth and glossy (or knead for 5 minutes using a stand mixer fitted with a dough hook). The dough should be fairly firm, so add a little more flour if necessary.

Put the dough into a lightly oiled bowl, cover and leave the dough to rise in a warm, draught-free place for 1½–2 hours (depending on the temperature and humidity), until it has doubled in size. The dough is ready when a finger pressed into it leaves a dent that does not immediately smooth itself out.

Knock back the dough and knead it again just for a few minutes, then form it into the required shapes or put it into 2 × 900g loaf tins. Cover the bread with a cloth and leave it to rise for about 30 minutes, until doubled in bulk again or until it has risen to the rim of the tins. The bread will rise a little further in the oven – this is called oven spring. However, if the bread rises over the top of the tin before it goes into the oven, it will continue to rise as it bakes and will flow over the edges.

Preheat the oven to 230°C/450°F/gas mark 8.

Brush the top of the shapes or loaves with the egg and cream glaze and sprinkle with seeds if desired. Bake the bread in the preheated oven for 20 minutes if you are making rolls or 45 minutes for loaves. The bread is ready when it looks golden brown and sounds hollow when the base is tapped. It may be necessary to remove the bread from the tin about three-quarters of the way through the baking time to cook the bottom properly. Cool on a wire rack.

Milk Dough Clusters	We often make this dough into a cluster of small rolls (25g of dough each) that can be pulled apart at the table as required. Use a 23cm round tin with 4cm sides (of course, you can make slightly larger rolls).

Make the dough, let it rise and knock it back as in the master recipe. Divide the dough into 15 × 25g pieces, shape into rolls and arrange side by side in a well-oiled tin. Leave a little space between each one to allow for expansion. Cover and allow to rise, then brush with egg wash or spray with a water mister, dust with flour and bake in the oven for 20–25 minutes. Remove from the tin and cool on a wire rack.

Sun-dried Tomato or Caramelised Onion Bread or Swirls	This makes 12 swirls. Knead 225g of caramelised onions into half of the dough before shaping into a loaf, log or rolls (450g of raw onions will result in 225g caramelised onions). Alternatively, roll the white yeast dough into a rectangle. Spread a layer of caramelised onion or chopped sun-blush tomatoes and a drizzle of basil pesto (page 312) evenly over the surface, then shape into a roll. Brush with olive oil and allow to rise until doubled in size. Sprinkle with sea salt and bake in the oven at 200°C/400°F/gas mark 6 for 20–25 minutes. Alternatively, cut into 5cm rounds and cook, cut side down, on an oiled baking sheet or in a tin so they form a loaf of rolls. Cool on a wire rack.

Carta Musica

This traditional Sardinian flatbread is irresistible to nibble. It's great with roasted vegetables or just to serve with pre-dinner drinks. The beauty of this recipe is that it is so quick and easy, as using fast-acting yeast does away with the first rising. It's also a brilliant way to use up a little leftover dough.

MAKES 8-16

- 680g strong white flour
- 14g salt
- 15g caster sugar
- 1 × 7g packet of fast-acting dried yeast
- 2-4 tablespoons olive oil
- 450-510ml tepid water, plus more if needed
- extra virgin olive oil, for brushing
- pinch of flaky sea salt
- one fresh herb, such as rosemary, sage, thyme or marjoram, or a mixture, finely chopped (optional)

Sieve the flour and salt into a large, wide mixing bowl. Add the sugar and fast-acting yeast, then mix all the ingredients thoroughly.

Make a well in the centre of the dry ingredients. Add the oil and most of the tepid water. Mix to a loose dough. You can add more water or flour if needed.

Turn the dough out onto a floured worktop, cover and leave to relax for about 5 minutes. Knead the dough for 8-10 minutes, until smooth and springy. (If kneading in a stand mixer fitted with a dough hook, 5 minutes is usually long enough.)

If you have time, chill the dough at this point for about half an hour – it will make it easier to handle. Otherwise, leave the dough to relax again for about 10 minutes.

Preheat the oven to 230°C/450°F/gas mark 8. Put a baking tray in the oven to heat.

Divide the dough into eight or more pieces. (If you do not want to make this much bread in one go, the dough freezes perfectly at this stage.) Keep the other pieces covered while you work on one.

Roll out the piece of dough as thinly as possible into a large, paper-thin square, rectangle or round (or you can cut the dough into large triangles, squares or strips). It will shrink back, so let it rest for a minute or two while you start to roll two or three of the others, then return to the first one and roll it even more thinly. Alternatively, roll the dough directly onto a baking tray (no need to preheat the tray), let it rest, then roll it again until it is as thin as possible.

Brush with extra virgin olive oil, then sprinkle lightly with flaky salt and some finely chopped rosemary or other gutsy herbs if you fancy. Cut into squares or rectangles with a pizza cutter and place on the heated baking tray.

Bake in the preheated oven for 2–4 minutes. They will shrink apart. Watch carefully – carta musica cooks very fast and sometimes unevenly, so you may need to take some out of the oven earlier than others. Cool on a wire rack.

Funny Faces

These are super fun to make with kids – each bread will have its own personality. Roll a piece of dough into a round, then stretch into an oval shape. Using a knife and an éclair pipe, mark out the eyes, nose and mouth. Brush with oil or water, then put on a baking tray and bake in the oven for 4–5 minutes, watching carefully to make sure they don't burn.

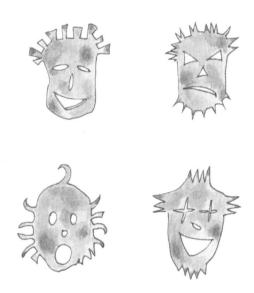

Ballymaloe Yeast Bread Buns

These are made like Ballymaloe brown yeast bread but baked in muffin tins. Sprinkle seeds on top or leave plain to serve with smoked salmon and cream cheese or with marmalade for breakfast.

MAKES 12
....

- sunflower oil, for greasing
- 15g fresh yeast
- 310g tepid water
- 1 teaspoon treacle
- 175g strong white flour
- 175g wholemeal flour
- 9g dairy salt

Lightly grease a muffin tin (approx. 25cm wide × 32cm long × 2.5cm deep) with sunflower oil.

Sponge the yeast in 150ml of the tepid water with the teaspoon of treacle. Leave in a warm place for about 5 minutes for the yeast to become active. It should be creamy and slightly frothy on top.

In a large, wide mixing bowl, combine the flours with the salt. Make a well in the centre.

Add the remaining water to the yeast and treacle mixture and stir together well. Pour into the dry ingredients and mix with an open hand, drawing the flour from the sides of the bowl. Mix to a wettish dough – it will be too wet to knead.

Divide equally between the holes in the oiled muffin tin. Cover with a light tea towel and allow to rise in a warm, draught-free place for about 20 minutes, until the buns have risen to twice their original size.

Preheat the oven to 230°C/450°F/gas mark 8.

Remove the tea towel and bake in the preheated oven for 25–30 minutes, until the buns look nicely browned and sound hollow when tapped on the bottom. We like to remove the buns from the tins about 10 minutes before the end of the cooking time and put them back into the oven to crisp all round. Cool on a wire rack.

Granary Loaf

Granary flour is a mixture of malted wheat and rye, with some whole wheat kernels. Some people find the malt flavour rather strong, so you can mix some plain or strong white flour with the granary flour. Homemade granary bread stays fresh and moist for an unusually long time.

MAKES 1 LARGE OR 2 SMALL
LOAVES
....

- 560g granary flour
  (or 450g granary flour
  plus 110g strong white
  flour)
- 11g teaspoon salt
- 20g fresh yeast
- 150g tepid water plus
  approx. 225g tepid
  water
- 2 tablespoons extra
  virgin olive oil
- 1-2 teaspoons treacle
- light olive oil, for
  greasing
- kibbled wheat

Mix the flour(s) with the salt in a large, wide bowl.

Mix the yeast with 150ml of tepid water along with the extra virgin olive oil and treacle. Leave in a warm place for about 5 minutes for the yeast to become active. It should be creamy and slightly frothy on top.

Add this to the flour and mix to a dough with the remaining 225ml water – it will be very pliable. Knead for 8–10 minutes in a stand mixer fitted with the dough hook (or for approx. 12 minutes if kneading by hand). Shape into a ball and place in a well-oiled bowl, cover with a clean tea towel and leave to rise in a warm, draught-free place for 2½–3 hours, until the dough has at least doubled in bulk and is puffy.

Knock back the dough and knead it for 2 minutes. Put the dough into a well-oiled 11cm × 29cm loaf tin or two smaller tins and brush lightly with olive oil. Cover and leave for approx. 30 minutes, until the dough is beginning to rise above the rim of the tin. The bread will rise a little further in the oven – this is called oven spring. However, if the bread rises over the top of the tin before it goes into the oven, it will continue to rise as it bakes and will flow over the edges.

Preheat the oven to 230°C/450°F/gas mark 8.

Brush lightly or spray with water and sprinkle with kibbled wheat. Bake in the preheated oven for approx. 25 minutes. Reduce the heat to 200°C/400°F/gas mark 6 and bake for 20 minutes more, until the bread sounds hollow when the base is tapped. Remove from the tin(s) and allow to cool on a wire rack.

Wholegrain Spelt Bagels

This recipe comes from Debbie Shaw, who contributed all the gluten-free recipes in the 'Gluten-Free Bread' chapter. Organic spelt is a highly nutritious grain with a low gluten content. Barley malt extract provides a natural sweetness and gives the bagels their traditional malty taste. Barley has a high mineral content, helps lower cholesterol and is soothing on the digestive tract and stomach.

MAKES APPROX. 8 LARGE
BAGELS

....

- 250g organic white
  spelt flour
- 250g brown spelt
  flour, sieved
- 11g salt
- 200g tepid water
- 1½ tablespoons barley
  malt extract
- 20g fresh yeast (or
  1 × 7g packet of fast-
  acting dried yeast,
  added to the dry
  ingredients)
- 1 large egg, whisked
- 2 tablespoons melted
  butter

....

TO FINISH:
- 2 tablespoons barley
  malt extract, for
  poaching
- 1 egg white, lightly
  beaten, for glazing
- sesame seeds or poppy
  seeds, for the top

Put the sieved flours and salt into a wide bowl. (If you are using fact-acting dried yeast, add it now too.)

Measure 100g of the tepid water into a Pyrex jug. Stir in 1½ tablespoons of barley malt extract, then crumble over the fresh yeast. Leave it in a warm place for about 5 minutes, until it's creamy and slightly frothy on top.

Make a well in the centre of the dry ingredients. Add the yeast mixture, the remaining 100g tepid water, the whisked egg and the melted butter.

Mix with your hand to make a soft, pliable dough. Cover and rest for 5 minutes, then knead for 10 minutes on a lightly floured surface until smooth and elastic. Transfer the dough to a large bowl, cover and allow to rise in a warm, draught-free place for approx. 1½ hours, until doubled in size.

Knead the dough lightly to knock the air out. Roll into a log and divide it into eight equal balls, cover with a towel and rest for 5 minutes.

Working with one ball at a time (keep the rest covered), flatten it slightly. Flour your index finger and push it through the centre of the ball and twirl to make the hole bigger – it needs to be quite big. Repeat with the rest of the dough. Arrange on a floured baking tray, spaced well apart, cover and allow to rise again for approx. 45 minutes, until doubled in size again.

Preheat the oven to 200°C/400°F/gas mark 6.

Bring a large, wide saucepan of water to the boil, then stir in the 2 tablespoons of barley malt extract. Drop the bagels gently into the water without overcrowding the pan. Poach for 30 seconds on each side. Drain the bagels thoroughly in a wide slotted spoon, then place on a baking tray lined with parchment paper. Brush each one with lightly whisked egg white and sprinkle with sesame or poppy seeds. Bake in the preheated oven for 20 minutes, until light and golden. Cool on a wire rack.

Enjoy with cream cheese, smoked salmon and dill or whatever you fancy.

Divide dough into eight equal balls

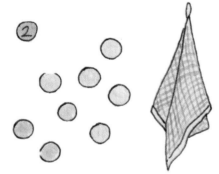

Cover with a towel and rest for five minutes

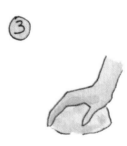

Flatten each ball slightly

Flour your index finger and push it through the centre of the ball

Twirl to make the hole bigger

Easy Rye and Caraway Seed Bread

This is particularly delicious with salami or cured meats. The quantity of caraway seed will depend on the freshness of the spice.

MAKE 1 LARGE LOAF OR
3 SMALL LOAVES

- 25g fresh yeast
- 400g tepid water
- 350g strong white flour
- 150g dark rye flour
- 20g caraway seeds
- 10g salt
- 45g butter, cut into cubes and softened
- light olive oil, for greasing
- 1 tablespoon approx. mixed caraway and poppy seeds

Crumble the yeast into the tepid water and leave it for about 5 minutes, until it's creamy and slightly frothy on top.

Mix the flours, caraway seeds and salt in a large, wide bowl. Add the liquid yeast with a little more tepid water if necessary to make a soft but not sticky dough. Add the butter gradually, kneading until smooth – this should take 8–10 minutes by hand or 5 minutes in a stand mixer fitted with a dough hook. Cover with a clean tea towel and allow to rise in a warm, draught-free place for 2–2½ hours, until doubled in size.

Grease the tin(s) well with oil. Knock back and shape into one 13cm × 20cm (450g) loaf tin or three smaller loaves (to fit 4cm × 13.5cm × 5cm tins). Cover and allow to rise again for about 1 hour, until doubled in volume.

Preheat the oven to 230°C/450°F/gas mark 8.

Brush or spray lightly with water, sprinkle with a mixture of caraway and poppy seeds and slash the top in a cross with a sharp knife. Bake in the preheated oven for 40–45 minutes for a large loaf or about 25 minutes for smaller loaves, until the bread sounds hollow when tapped underneath. Cool on a wire rack.

Rye and Caraway Breadsticks

Makes 64 × 12g or 96 × 8g breadsticks, but you could use a smaller portion of the dough and make fewer.

Preheat the oven to 220°C/430°F/gas mark 7. Divide the dough into 12g or 8g balls. Roll each ball into a piece 25cm or 12cm long and spray lightly with a water mister. Scatter some extra caraway seeds and flaky sea salt on the worktop and roll the breadsticks lightly in this. Transfer to a heavy baking tray and continue until the tray is full. Bake in the preheated oven for 7–8 minutes, until crisp and golden. Cool on a wire rack.

SOURDOUGH

For thousands of years, until the Industrial Revolution, the only type of bread that existed was sourdough. Commercial yeast (strains of *Saccharomyces*) is a relatively new phenomenon, introduced less than 200 years ago. This concentrated yeast produces masses of CO_2 quickly, hence the process could be speeded up, resulting in more profit but significantly less nourishment.

Who knows how sourdough was originally discovered, but an oft-repeated tale relates how an Egyptian woman, circa 3000 BC, was making a simple dough for flatbread on the banks of the Nile. She baked some, presumably on hot flat stones by the fire. Some interruption meant that she couldn't bake the rest, so the next day she scraped the remainder into fresh dough. To her delight, the resulting bread increased in volume and was lighter in texture, and so sourdough was born.

There has been a phenomenal revival of interest in sourdough bread, partly because the quality of many commercial breads has deteriorated so dramatically in the past couple of decades. The significant rise in allergies and gluten intolerance is being linked to the Chorleywood process and the chemical additives, enzymes and improvers used in industrial bread-making, many of which do not have to appear on the label because they are classed as processing aids.

Another reason to make your own is that at present there is no official definition of sourdough, so beware, there's a lot of 'faux sourdough' around. The 48–96 hour fermented natural sourdough from the Ballymaloe Bread Shed has a growing fan base.

The sourdough revival has not only brought joy and satisfaction (not to mention a degree of frustration!) to countless people but has also enabled many to enjoy bread without having to endure the painful indigestion and bloating they experience when they eat the 'speedy' bread. Natural sourdough bread is unquestionably more nutritious than a regular Chorleywood loaf. Sourdough contains vitamins, minerals, magnesium, B vitamins, iron, zinc and calcium plus fibre and protein, with lots of probiotics that enhance our gut health. This is because the fermentation process breaks down the gluten that can cause bloating and other digestive problems. It's interesting that one slice of sourdough seems more filling and satisfying to eat than several slices of sliced pan.

Lactobacillus is the beneficial bacteria found in yogurt, kefir, buttermilk, sour cream and so on, which helps the body to absorb more nutrients from the bread. *Lactobacillus* help to feed the good bacteria in our gut biome, enhancing both mental and physical health and boosting our immune system. Sourdough bread is also fermented by using gut-healthy *Lactobacillus* cultures. The bacteria don't survive baking, but the lactic acid imparts flavour to the bread, makes it easier to digest, and improves its keeping quality.

Nonetheless, many confident bread makers – even those who have been baking both soda and yeast bread for years – are intimidated by sourdough. They feel it's complicated, unpredictable and difficult to fit into a busy lifestyle. I want to take the mystery out of the process and show that anyone and everyone can make sourdough. You will get such a kick out of taking your first loaf of crusty sourdough bread from the oven.

In many ways, baking with sourdough can be a humbling experience. Unlike soda bread, sourdough is made with a living starter so it reacts to the environment, the baker's skills, the type of flour used, even the weather. The baker needs to be constantly observant, learning from each day's experience. Sourdough bread-making is a craft that not only produces a nourishing loaf but becomes a passion. You will become determined to keep trying over and over in pursuit of the perfect loaf.

Richard Hart of Hart Bageri in Copenhagen, one of the world's finest bakers, says that he only manages to make what he considers to be a perfect loaf a couple of times a year. But don't let that depress you! It's all part of the fun. Even if your loaf is not a stunner, it will still be nourishing and taste delicious and you will have learned something to apply to your next bake. Your sourdough will also be unique to you and reflect the microflora, wild yeasts and bacteria of your local environment. Hence the difference in flavour and texture of the loaves made in different artisan bakeries around the country and the world.

Can I Fit Sourdough into My Busy Life?

With a little planning, the sourdough process can be adapted to fit in with your work schedule. All bakers have different processes, depending on what suits their situation. Some ferment the bread for 8 hours, others for much longer. Here in the Ballymaloe Bread Shed we do a long, slow fermentation overnight in the fridge. From Wednesday to Saturday, our breads have a 48-hour ferment, whereas Monday's bread, made on Friday and fermented in the fridge over the weekend, will be a 72-hour fermentation and Tuesday's bread a 96-hour fermentation. One would expect that bread to be 'sourer', but this is not necessarily the case. There is much about sourdough and fermentation that we still don't fully understand.

Can I Refrigerate My Starter?

If you are making bread regularly, it's important to look after your starter carefully. However, despite what others may tell you, the starter does not have to be fed strictly on the hour. It can be stored in a fridge and refreshed to revive it later. The micro-organisms, yeasts and bacteria in the starter slow down rather than die. They can survive and be revived even after several years, rather like weed seeds buried in soil waiting for optimum conditions to grow. If you only want to make a loaf once or twice a fortnight, it's best to keep the starter in the fridge. You'll need to feed it two to three days ahead to reactivate it.

The fridge needs to be cold (3–5°C/37–41°F). If your fridge is being continually opened, it may be at a higher temperature for periods of time, which can affect the sourdough starter. In this case, it may be better to freeze the starter if you don't need it for a week or so. In the Ballymaloe Bread Shed, the starter is kept in a cold room where the temperature is a constant 2–5°C (36–41°F).

Can I Freeze My Starter?

Freezing does not kill yeast, so a sourdough starter can certainly be frozen for up to a year and maybe longer. The sourdough will go into hibernation.

Put the active sourdough into a robust plastic container or container with a tight-fitting clip-on lid. Allow a little space for the starter to expand as it freezes. Label and date the container.

To defrost your frozen starter, remove the container from the freezer and allow it to defrost in the fridge. When it has almost fully defrosted, feed it as you would when creating the starter originally by adding flour and water. It could be a good idea to feed it twice on the first day, depending on how active and bubbly it is. Keep it in a warm kitchen and continue to feed it for the next couple of days, until it's really active, then proceed to make the bread.

What Should I Do if My Starter Has a Layer of Grey Liquid on Top and Smells Vinegary?

The starter is still alive, but it will smell vinegary or has a whiff of stale beer. Pour off the liquid and any grey layer. Reduce to about 100g, add flour until it's the thickness of a cake batter and allow to stand for 2–3 hours, until it starts to bubble. Add another 100g of flour and 100g of water, cover and leave for a further 2–3 hours. Repeat this process twice more. By the following morning, you should have a lively starter but occasionally it may take longer depending on the state of the starter.

Can I Travel with My Sourdough?

Yes, indeed you can, whether overland, by sea or by air. Our students take their precious starters home to all four corners of the earth. Countries such as the US, Australia and New Zealand have different, stricter regulations, though, so check first.

Put a small blob of thick sourdough starter into an airtight container. Pop it into your carry-on or checked-in luggage, then feed and refresh when you arrive at your destination. Or here's another method shown to me by Richard Hart of Hart Bageri in Copenhagen. Take some active starter and add enough flour to make it into a dry, crumbly mixture. Reconstitute it with water when you arrive at your destination.

How to Dry Sourdough Starter

Spread about 100g of active sourdough onto a square of parchment paper. Lay another sheet on top and roll it as thinly as possible until it covers the entire surface of the paper. Allow to dry at room temperature for at least 48 hours, by which time it will be crisp and brittle. Break into little pieces and store in a small airtight box with a tight-fitting clip-on lid or in a glass jar. It can be preserved for months or even years if stored in a cool, dry place. You can even pop some in the mail. The starter may be transported in your carry-on or checked baggage.

To rehydrate your dried sourdough starter, transfer all the dried sourdough starter into a large jar. Add enough water to cover, stir gently and allow to soak for at least 1 hour. Stir again – the sourdough starter will begin to dissolve in the water. Rest and stir several more times, until the starter has fully dissolved. Then add equal quantities of water and flour, cover, mark the level on the side of the jar and leave for another 4 hours, by which time fermentation bubbles will be evident. Feed again with the same quantity of flour and water, cover and wait another 4 hours. Finally, feed it one last time and leave for 8 hours, until the sourdough starter doubles in size. Stir again. The starter will now be active, so you're ready to make a new loaf of sourdough.

SOME SOURDOUGH BAKING TERMS

Autolyse Method

This sounds complex, but it's basically just mixing a portion or all of the water and flour together, covering it and leaving for 20 minutes (or up to several hours) before adding the other ingredients. During this time, the glutenin and gliadin proteins will start to create bonds. The fermentation process in sourdough neutralises the phytic acid that locks up minerals such as calcium, iron, zinc and magnesium in fast-fermented breads. The final dough will be easier to handle and require less kneading. Some bakers use autolyse for every loaf, while others use the technique only occasionally.

Biga

A liquid starter or pre-ferment used to make many Italian breads, including ciabatta and pizza. It's made simply by mixing flour, water and a little commercial yeast together and allowing it to ferment until it's lively. This will add more flavour and result in a lighter, more open-textured bread with lots of holes.

Mix strong white or baker's flour (14–16% protein), water, ideally at 15–18°C (59–64°F), and yeast (any kind) until you have a rough dough, then cover and leave to ferment. For a short ferment leave it for 16–24 hours or for 36–48 hours for a long ferment.

Levain or Leaven

A sourdough starter made with naturally occurring yeast from the atmosphere. It's really easy to make a starter from scratch – it just takes time.

Levain is made by mixing flour and water together and letting it ferment over a period of time. It takes six or seven days to become active enough to rise the bread. It can live indefinitely when fed regularly.

Poolish

Poolish 'sponge' is a type of pre-ferment, frequently used in French bread-making, made with equal quantities of flour and water and a little baker's yeast (100% hydration). The technique was first developed in Poland in the 1880s by Baron Zang and brought to France by Polish bakers.

Just mix 100g strong white flour, 100g water and ½ teaspoon baker's yeast. Cover the bowl and allow it to ferment for 10–12 hours at room temperature or in the fridge, but it will take longer in the fridge.

The quantity of poolish should be about one-third of the overall recipe.

Ale may be substituted for water for a different flavour.

<table>
<tr><td>Sourdough</td><td>The term 'sourdough' refers to breads leavened with a wild yeast starter rather than commercial baker's yeast. Sourdough bread is a totally natural process, made from just three ingredients: flour, salt and water. Sourdough breads take longer to make than other types of bread, as the dough ferments naturally. Like many fermented foods, it has digestive benefits. The process increases the nutritional value and adds depth and complexity of flavour to bread. The texture of sourdough tends to be denser and chewier (in a good way) than breads leavened with commercial yeast.</td></tr>
</table>

<table>
<tr><td>What's the Difference between Poolish and Biga?</td><td>Both are starters or pre-ferments, but poolish is a liquid pre-ferment while biga is a more solid dough. Because it's a liquid dough, poolish ferments in a shorter amount of time with the same quantity of yeast. It results in a bread with extra crispness and smaller, more regular air bubbles, better flavour and a better keeping quality than bread made in an all-in-one process.

On the other hand, biga requires a longer time to ferment (12–16 hours). The bread will have larger, more irregular holes, taste less 'sour' and have an unmistakable aroma of freshly made bread, also with lots of flavour and good keeping quality.

Neither poolish nor biga need to be fed.</td></tr>
</table>

<table>
<tr><td>Pâte Fermentée (Old Dough)</td><td>This is simply a piece of dough held back and added to the next batch of bread. It's one of the oldest methods of making sourdough. It contributes to the flavour and makes a particularly interesting version of the Ballymaloe brown yeast bread (page 48).</td></tr>
</table>

Ballymaloe Sourdough Starter

Sourdough is an inconsistent medium of nature. Every loaf will be slightly different depending on the activity of the starter.

From Day 1 of making the starter to baking the loaf will take between 11 and 12 days. Once you've established the sourdough starter, making a loaf of sourdough bread from start to finish will take 48 hours, depending on how lively the starter is. Once the starter gets going, it can be used to make all kinds of breads, both savoury and sweet, using a variety of flours.

A few words of caution before you start:

+ Residues of washing-up liquid on your bowl can affect the starter, as do residues of fungicides in flour, which is why you should use organic flour when possible.
+ If your tap water is heavily chlorinated, pour it into a wide-mouthed open bowl or bucket and allow the chlorine to dissipate over 24 hours.
+ Your sourdough starter can become more active at different times of the year and you may need to feed it a little extra flour. This usually happens during warmer weather, but it's quite mysterious, really. Starter is not always predictable and has a mind of its own, as any baker will tell you. While writing this book, our starter was so active that we had to increase the flour by 20–30%.
+ If you re-do your kitchen – particularly if various glues and other building materials are used – it may affect your starter, which can take time to re-establish. Open the window to release trapped air.

Day 1
To make the starter from scratch (levain, leaven or natural sponge), put 60g cold water and 60g strong white flour into a 1-litre airtight Kilner jar. Mix well, then close the jar and leave it at room temperature for 24 hours.

Day 2, 3, 4 and 5

Add 60g cold water and 60g strong white flour into the Kilner jar. Mix well, close and leave for 24 hours at room temperature. Repeat this on days 3, 4 and 5.

As you are adding the flour and water to your starter, yeast from the air will enter the jar and feed on the sugars and starch in the flour. This will activate the starter. It will begin to bubble as it becomes a natural, homemade yeast.

As the yeast feeds on the flour, the starter will become softer and smell yeasty and fermented, like beer. It will be very bubbly and it may develop a layer of grey-ish liquid on top, but that's fine – just pour it off.

In warm climates, keep the starter at room temperature for the first three days, then refrigerate for the last two days.

In cool climates, keep your starter at room temperature for all five days. The optimum temperature is 25–28°C (77–82°F).

After five days of feeding your starter, you will now have a good, stable starter, ready to use in the next stage.

Day 6

The starter will need to be refreshed. Reduce the starter in the jar to approx. 200g. (Don't throw this out – you can share it with a friend, feed it to the hens, or use it to make the sourdough crackers on page 98). Thicken the starter with strong white flour until it has the consistency of a thick cake batter. Feed with 240g water and 240g strong white flour and stir well until combined. Allow to stand at room temperature for 2–6 hours to become active again – it should be thick and bubbly. Cover and put in the fridge overnight or up to 24 hours.

The more you use your starter, the stronger and more stable it gets. In fact, the first few loaves you bake may be disappointing, but please persevere.

You are now ready to make your dough. At this stage your starter should be thick enough for the dough to hold its shape. If it's too runny, your dough won't hold its shape and may be flat when baked.

Rye Starter

This same method can also be used to make a spelt starter.

Day 1

Put 50g cold water and 40g organic dark rye flour in a 1-litre airtight Kilner jar. Mix well, close the jar and leave at room temperature for 24 hours.

Day 2

You should begin to see some bubbles at this stage. Add 50g water and 40g organic dark rye flour. Mix well, close the jar and leave for 24 hours at room temperature.

Day 3

Add 50g water and 40g organic dark rye flour. Mix well, close the jar and leave for 24 hours at room temperature.

Day 4

More bubbles should have appeared today and the mixture should smell like yeasty beer. Add 50g water and 40g organic dark rye flour. Mix well, close the jar and leave for 24 hours at room temperature.

Day 5

Add 50g water and 40g organic dark rye flour. Mix well, close the jar and leave for 24 hours at room temperature.

Day 6

Add 50g water and 40g organic dark rye flour. Mix well, close the jar and leave for 24 hours at room temperature. Your sourdough starter will now be very runny and bubbly. It's hungry and ready to proceed to the next stage.

Reduce the starter in the jar to about 200g (the overall weight of the Kilner jar, including the remaining starter, will be about 1kg). Thicken it with 30g–40g organic dark rye flour and mix to a firm paste. Allow to stand at room temperature for 2–3 hours, then feed with of 100g water and 80g rye flour. Stir well. It should be thick and bubbly. You may leave the starter out at room temperature in the winter but it's best to refrigerate it in the summer.

The starter is now ready to use. Twenty-four hours before you want to use it, remove it from the fridge and refresh it with 100g water and 80g organic dark rye flour.

The more you use your starter, the stronger and more active it becomes. In fact, the first few loaves may be disappointing, but please persevere.

The longer the starter has been sitting in the fridge without being used, the more times it will need to be refreshed (i.e. pouring half the starter out and replacing it with new flour and water to reactivate). But don't waste a scrap of your leftover starter – use it to make the sourdough crackers on page 98.

Ballymaloe Sourdough Bread

Once you've established your starter, it's only a question of mixing the other ingredients and having patience. It does take time, but most of that time the bread is quietly rising or baking. Every loaf is an adventure. Each will be slightly different and every time you make a loaf you will learn more about the process. Enjoy experimenting and remember, people have been making sourdough bread for centuries.

MAKES 1 LOAF

....

- 340g sourdough starter
- 200g cold water
- 230g strong white flour
- 70g malted/granary flour
- 20g rye flour
- 5g wheat germ
- 11g salt

Put the starter, water, flours and wheat germ in the bowl of a stand mixer. Mix with a dough hook on a slow speed for a few seconds, until the dough has combined. Rest the dough for 5 minutes.

After resting, add the salt and turn the mixer on a slow speed – if you beat it too fast at this stage, you can break the gluten. When the dough is sticking to the sides of the bowl and coming away in strings, this is the gluten being developed. Increase the speed and continue to mix until it doesn't stick to the sides of the bowl and the dough hook lifts the dough cleanly out.

Place the dough in a bowl, cover and leave to rest in the fridge for 24 hours.

The next day, for the first shaping, pour the dough out of the bowl onto a clean work surface and knock it back. Stretch and fold the dough a few times, then shape it into a smooth, tight, round ball and leave to rest for 15–20 minutes in a cool kitchen or 5–10 minutes in a warm kitchen.

Stretch and fold the dough a few times

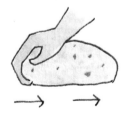

Turn and push to shape it into a smooth, tight, round ball

For the second shaping, flip your dough over, flatten and spread it out with your fingers. Pull all the edges into the centre of the dough – this helps to trap the CO_2 and gases in the dough to give it a nice airy crumb. Flip it back over with a dough scraper (or roll it over) and shape into a smooth, tight, round ball again. The tighter and less sticky the ball is, the better it will hold its shape and rise in the oven. If it's *too* tight, though, the surface will rip and become sticky again. If this happens, rest the dough again for 10–15 minutes and repeat.

Flip the dough over

Flatten and spread it out with your fingers

Pull all the edges into the centre of the dough

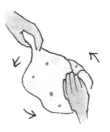

Put the dough upside down into a lined, floured banneton (or in a 16–20cm bowl lined with a clean linen tea towel and floured) and leave in the fridge, covered, overnight or for up to 24 hours.

The next day, put a casserole/Dutch oven with its lid on in the oven to preheat. (For this recipe, the lid must be flat. Alternatively, you could cook the loaf directly on a hot baking tray in the oven, but this is the least good option for home baking.) Preheat the oven fully to its maximum temperature or at least 250°C/480°F/gas mark 9. It is essential that the casserole/Dutch oven is fully preheated, overwise the bread will stick firmly to the base. It will take 30–35 minutes for the heat to penetrate completely.

Meanwhile, take the dough out of the fridge and allow it to sit at room temperature while the casserole/Dutch oven is preheating.

Using an oven mitt or thick tea towel, lift the hot casserole/Dutch oven out onto a pot rack. Lift off the lid and carefully turn the dough out of the banneton onto the upturned lid. Slash the top with a sharp serrated knife or baker's blade (lame) and mist lightly with water (optional).

Replace the casserole/Dutch oven base on top of the lid and quickly put it back in the hot oven. Reduce the temperature to 230°C/450°F/gas mark 8 and bake for 20 minutes. Remove the upturned base and continue to bake the bread on the lid for 10–15 minutes, until the crust is dark golden brown. When fully cooked, the bread will feel light and will sound hollow when tapped on the base. Cool on a wire rack.

Molly's Sultana and Cinnamon Sourdough

Thank you to Ballymaloe Cookery School alumna Molly Fink, who shared this recipe with us. Put 340g sourdough starter, 200g cold water, 325g strong white flour, 11g salt, 40g sultanas, 1 tablespoon caster sugar and 1 tablespoon ground cinnamon in the bowl of a stand mixer and follow the recipe as outlined above. The next day, after you've knocked back the dough when doing the first shaping, sprinkle 1 tablespoon caster sugar and 1 tablespoon ground cinnamon over the centre of the dough, then fold the dough in on itself and shape into a smooth, tight, round ball again. Finish and bake as in the master recipe.

Richard O'Connell's Saturday Morning Sourdough

My brother Richard O'Connell, who co-founded Mueller & O'Connell artisan bakery in Abbeyleix, County Laois, shared this recipe, which uses the folding technique. He says, 'When I was working in a nine-to-five job, I used a schedule that meant the bread was ready for baking first thing every Saturday morning. I maintained a jar with 450g of sourdough starter in the fridge that I fed once a week as part of this schedule.'

MAKES 2 × 900G LOAVES

....

Step 1: Thursday Evening

Take your Ballymaloe sourdough starter (page 82) from the fridge and feed it with 225g tepid water and 225g strong white flour. Mix well, cover and leave overnight at room temperature. (I never wash the starter jar – when I empty it into a bowl for the first feed, I just pop the jar back into the fridge.)

Step 2: Friday Morning, First Thing

For the second feed for the starter, add 225g water (use cooler water this time) and 225g strong white flour. Mix well, cover and leave at room temperature for the day.

Step 3: Friday Evening

Save 450g of the starter in the jar and pop it back in the fridge. Put the remainder (approx. 900g) in the bowl of a stand mixer fitted with the dough hook and add 225g tepid water, 700g strong white flour and 2–3 tablespoons of oat or wheat bran. Mix well, cover and allow to rest for approx. 30 minutes. Add 2½ teaspoons salt and knead on a slow speed for about 5 minutes.

I use the 'folding' method to develop the dough. In my opinion, sourdough doesn't like being handled too much, unlike yeast breads, which you can knead for 10–15 minutes with no ill effects.

So, let's say you mixed the dough at 6:30 p.m. on Friday. Allow the dough to rise for 3½–4 hours. During that time, you 'fold' the dough every hour. This gently stretches the dough and redistributes the yeast, allowing for better fermentation.

To fold, put your fingers down each side of the middle of the dough so that your fingers meet in the middle underneath. Gently lift the dough out of the bowl, allowing it to stretch for 5 seconds or so before putting it back in the bowl on its side. Leave it to settle for a minute or so, turn the bowl 180 degrees and do another fold. Repeat this process twice more, roughly on the hour. (YouTube has good demos of this technique that you can look up online.)

Lift the dough out of the bowl and allow it to stretch for 5 seconds

Around 10:30 p.m., divide the dough into two loaves, approx. 900g each. Shape the loaves using 'soft' hands. You must resist the temptation to overhandle the dough (which can be difficult because it just feels so good!). Handle it as little as possible to get a nice, smooth skin in the shape you want. (Again, YouTube has loads of demos.)

Put the loaves upside down in lined bannetons or bread baskets well dusted with flour. Slip each basket into a plastic bag and put in the fridge overnight.

Stage 4: Saturday morning
You have two options here.

First option: Take the loaves out of the fridge and leave for 1 hour at room temperature. Preheat the oven to 220°C/430°F/gas mark 7. Warm a baking tray in the oven, then lightly dust it with semolina before turning the dough balls onto it. Slash the loaves with a very sharp knife or razor blade. (A tricky manoeuvre, so it's back to YouTube again.) Spray with water and lightly dust with semolina before popping in the preheated oven to bake for 40 minutes. If not fully baked to your satisfaction, turn down the temperature to 200°C/400°F/gas mark 6 and bake for a further 5–10 minutes.

Second option: Bake on a rising heat. This will be more energy efficient and may well create a better oven spring, as the gentler heat of the oven at the start of the bake will encourage more yeast activity. Take the bread out of the fridge and allow to rest for about 15 minutes. Turn on the oven to 220°C/430°F/gas mark 7. Proceed immediately with the steps outlined above to get your loaves oven ready and put them in the oven even though the oven will not be fully preheated. You will need to add 5–10 minutes of extra baking time, depending on how quickly your oven preheats. The loaves will sound hollow when tapped on the base. Cool on a wire rack.

Ballymaloe Traditional Pan Loaf

Because of the inclusion of a little fresh yeast, the texture of this bread is softer than a natural sourdough. This bread freezes brilliantly.

MAKES 1 PAN LOAF OR
2 BAGUETTES

....

- 350g strong white flour
- 100g natural white flour starter sponge (page 82)
- 10g fresh yeast
- 10g granulated sugar
- 192g water
- 9g salt

Put all the ingredients except the salt in the bowl of stand mixer fitted with the dough hook. Mix on a slow speed for 5–10 minutes to bring together into a dough.

Sprinkle the salt over the surface of the dough and allow to stand for 5 minutes. Mix for 10 minutes at a medium speed and a further 10–15 minutes at a faster speed until the dough is smooth and shiny. Cover the bowl and allow to prove in the fridge for 3–4 hours, until doubled in size.

Knock back, fold and shape into a tight 'bun'. Cover and allow to rest and relax for about 15 minutes. Knock back a second time, fold into a tight oblong and tuck into an oiled 13cm × 20cm (450g) loaf tin. Slip the tin into a roomy plastic bag and put in the fridge to rise slowly overnight.

The next day, take the tin out of the fridge and allow it to stand at room temperature for 25 minutes.

Meanwhile, preheat the oven to 240°C/465°F/gas mark 9.

Use a mister or put a bowl of water in the oven to create steam. Dust the surface of the loaf with flour, then slash with a sharp knife. Bake in the preheated oven for 10 minutes, then reduce the heat to 220°C/430°F/gas mark 7 and bake for a further 10–15 minutes, until golden brown and fully cooked. The bread will sound hollow when tapped on the base.

Remove from the tin and cool on a wire rack.

Bread Shed Sourdough Rye Bread

A brilliantly versatile recipe. The uncooked dough can be stored in an airtight tub in the fridge for up to a week so that you can bake one or two small loaves as you need them. This bread has built up an enthusiastic following in our farm shop.

MAKES 5 MINI LOAVES

....

- 180g white sourdough starter (page 82)
- 375g rye starter (page 84)
- 75g black treacle
- 96g melted butter
- 675g tepid water
- 336g plain flour
- 336g rye flour
- 90g rye flakes
- 90g wheat flakes
- 54g sunflower seeds
- 54g poppy seeds, plus extra to decorate
- 54g flax seeds
- 33g salt

Put the white and rye starters and the treacle into a mixing bowl and mix to combine.

Melt the butter so that it is completely liquid, then add it to the tepid water and combine with the starter/treacle mixture in the mixing bowl.

Mix together all the flours, flakes, seeds and the salt, then add to the water and starter/treacle mixture and stir to combine. The dough should have the consistency of rather grainy porridge and when pressed with the tip of a finger it should leave an indentation that eventually closes on itself. Allow to ferment in a sealed container in the fridge for three days.

After three days, brush the sides and bases of five small loaf tins (13.5cm × 5cm) with sunflower oil. Divide the dough evenly between the five tins, cover and refrigerate overnight.

The following day, preheat the oven to 190°C/375°F/ gas mark 5.

The dough should have risen to the top of the tins. Sprinkle the loaves with poppy seeds. Bake in the preheated oven for 60–65 minutes, until risen and nicely coloured. Take the loaves out of the tins and allow to cool completely on a wire rack. The loaves will seem undercooked, but don't worry, they're fine.

Cut into thin slices and serve with pickled herring, Danish liver pâté, gravlax or just soft Jersey butter.

Some rye bread lovers claim that the rye bread should be at least a couple of days old before eating. If you're in this camp, then the bread should be stored in the fridge for a couple of days after baking.

Catherine Clark's Focaccia

We have several recipes for focaccia but this one, given to us by Catherine Clark, is our current favourite.

....

STEP 1:
- 670g tepid water
- 50g sourdough starter (page 82)
- 6g dry active yeast
- 780g strong white bread flour

....

STEP 2:
- 13g water
- 18g salt
- 15g extra virgin olive oil

Day 1

Mix the water, sourdough starter and yeast together in the bowl of a food mixer fitted with the dough hook. Set aside for 5 minutes, until the mixture looks creamy.

Add the flour and mix on a low speed for about 1 minute, until the dough starts to come together. Increase the speed to medium and continue to mix for a further 5 minutes. Cover the bowl with a clean tea towel and allow to stand at room temperature for 15 minutes to autolyse.

Dissolve the 13g of water in a small bowl with the 18g of salt (it won't dissolve completely, but don't worry). After the dough has rested for 15 minutes, add the saltwater and extra virgin olive oil to the dough. Turn the mixture back on to a medium-high speed and knead for 15–20 minutes, until the gluten has developed.

Pour the dough out onto a clean, damp worktop for its bench rest (see page 324). Gently fold the dough from each side into the centre like a parcel. Rest for 5–6 minutes. Repeat twice more.

With oiled hands or a flexible dough scraper, transfer the dough onto an oiled 23cm × 33cm baking tray or tin (no need to line it yet). Oil or wet your hands and perform the first coil fold by grabbing the dough in the middle and lifting up until the dough is completely off the tray. Fold the dough back onto itself and rotate the tray 90°. Perform one more coil fold, then cover the dough with an oiled piece of parchment paper. Perform a few more coil folds over the next 3 hours while the dough sits at room temperature. The coil folds help with gluten formation and build tension on top of the dough for a good rise.

Remove the dough from the tray. Put it on a damp work surface and line the tray with parchment paper. Put the dough in the lined tray, cover again with the piece of oiled parchment paper and put in the fridge to rise (bulk ferment) for 36–48 hours.

Day 3
After 36–48 hours, remove the tray from the fridge. Drizzle or brush a little olive oil over the surface of the dough, then dimple the dough with oiled fingers. Leave at room temperature for 2–3 hours.

Preheat the oven to 240°C/465°F/gas mark 9.

Bake in the preheated oven for 20 minutes, then reduce the temperature to 220°C/430°F/gas mark 7 and bake for a further 10–15 minutes, until cooked – it should sound hollow when tapped on the bottom. Cool on a wire rack.

Artisan Sourdough Baguettes

Halve the measurements if you are using a domestic food mixer and use one rather than two baking trays.

MAKES 4

....

- 20g fresh yeast
- 20g granulated sugar
- 385g cold water
- 200g sourdough starter (page 82)
- 700g strong white flour
- 18g salt

Put the crumbled yeast, sugar, water and sourdough starter in the bowl of a stand mixer. Stir and leave to sit for approx. 5 minutes to activate the yeast. It will have a creamy, slightly frothy appearance on top.

Mix the flour and salt together, then add to the wet ingredients. Mix with a dough hook on a medium speed for 15 minutes. Turn off the mixer and allow the dough to rest for 5 minutes. Knead for a further 15 minutes, until the dough is very smooth and silky. Cover, refrigerate and leave to rise for 2–3 hours, until doubled in size.

Knock back the dough and divide it into four pieces, each weighing approx. 335g. Shape into smooth, tight, round balls and rest, covered, for 10 minutes to relax. Shape each one into a small baguette, 30–35cm long.

Place each one on a tray lined with a floured tea towel, glass cloth or baker's couche with a pleat of fabric between each baguette to keep them separate. Cover loosely with cling film and put in the fridge overnight.

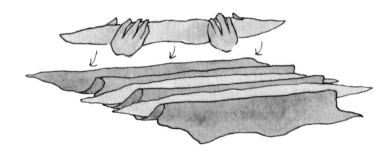

The next morning, preheat the oven to 250°C/480°F/gas mark 9. Use a mister or put an ovenproof bowl, half filled with hot water or ice cubes, in the oven to create steam to help the baguettes to rise and form a nice crust.

Remove the baguettes from the fridge and gently roll them off the tea towel or couche onto two baking trays. With a sharp knife, slash each baguette at an angle three or four times.

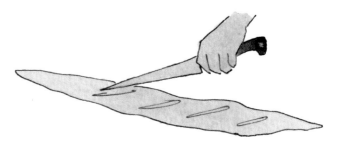

Bake in the preheated oven for 10 minutes, then reduce the temperature to 220°C/430°F/gas mark 7 and bake for a further 10–15 minutes, until golden brown. Cool on a wire rack.

Sourdough Crackers

Don't waste a scrap of sourdough starter – we use surplus to make these delicious crackers.

....

- 200g mature sourdough starter (100% hydration) (page 82)
- 60g plain flour
- 60g whole wheat flour
- 12g rye flour
- 32g extra virgin olive oil
- 6g salt
- flaky sea salt, for the topping
- 1 tablespoon thyme leaves or finely chopped rosemary (optional)

Put the sourdough starter, flours, olive oil and salt in a bowl. Mix and knead with your hands until it comes together into a dough.

Wrap the dough tightly in a lightly oiled plastic bag. Refrigerate for at least 30 minutes or, if time allows, up to 24 hours.

Preheat the oven to 200°C/400°F/gas mark 6.

Remove the dough from the plastic bag and divide it in half. Put one half back in the plastic bag and put it back in the fridge while you roll out the rest.

Cut the dough again into four smaller pieces. Roll each piece into an oblong rectangle. You can do this with a rolling pin on a lightly floured surface or use a pasta roller for super-thin crackers. If rolling by hand, just roll as thinly as you possibly can. Cut into eight crackers.

Lay the crackers side by side (not overlapping) on two baking sheets. Brush lightly with water and sprinkle with a little flaky sea salt and gutsy herbs (if using).

Bake in the preheated oven for 5–10 minutes, until light golden brown and crisp. Allow to cool on the sheets, then transfer the crackers to a wire cooling rack. Repeat with the remaining dough. Crackers will keep for up to a week in an airtight container at room temperature.

PIZZA AND FOCACCIA

Pizza is the ultimate fast food, universally loved. But here's a fun (or scary) fact: Ireland is one of the biggest consumers of takeaway pizza on the planet. Unfortunately, all too often it's frozen pizza from the supermarket chill cabinet or a lukewarm, soggy pizza delivered to your door. These pizzas bear little resemblance to the real thing.

Pizza has come a long way since the 1960s, when I was super excited to learn how to make my first pizza. I slathered tomato sauce over the base, carefully arranged a lattice of anchovies on top and popped a black olive into every space.

Way back then, pizza was a very defined thing. It didn't even occur to me that one could deviate from the original until I first tasted Wolfgang Puck's designer pizzas in LA in the early 1980s. It was a eureka moment. Suddenly we had license to experiment, and what fun it's been. I could easily write a whole book on pizza and variations on the theme: calzone, sfinciuni, panzerotti and panuzzo (the love child of a pizza and a sandwich), not to mention Polish zapiekanka, crackly Roman pizza and irresistible trapizzino. In the US alone there are so many interpretations: New York style, Brooklyn style, New Haven style, Detroit style and Chicago-style deep dish.

We all love a really good pizza and of course there is no reason why it can't be nutritious as well as delicious. In this chapter, I want to get you excited about making your own. I'll show you how simple it is to make your own homemade dough and a delicious tomato sauce.

The toppings can vary from Italian classics like margarita, pepperoni or quattro formaggio to Moroccan, Japanese, Korean, Mexican, Nordic and Chinese flavours. I love adding a drizzle of something on top of a pizza when it comes out of the oven. It could be a beautiful extra virgin olive oil, chilli oil (page 322), chilli honey (page 321), pesto (page 312), aioli or any other flavoured mayo. A salad of seasonal or foraged leaves piled on top is another favourite.

Apart from the toppings, the secret of a fantastic pizza is a brilliant dough. You can of course vary the texture and flavour of the base by using different flours (wheat, rye, spelt) and leavens or sourdough.

The best pizzas are unquestionably baked in a wood-fired oven, where they will cook in just two or three minutes. We built one here at the school in 1997 after I went on a reconnaissance mission

to California, travelling from Elk and Point Reyes right down to
Berkeley to check out pizza ovens built by the legendary New
Zealand oven builder, the late Alan Scott.

Handy DIY-ers can build brilliant pizza ovens from kits or one of
the many books of designs. Otherwise, you can make very good pizza
at home in a regular domestic oven or in one of the new outdoor
Ooni-type ovens. Barbecued pizza is also brilliant, but a Weber-
style covered barbecue with a flat grid is essential. Children love to
make pizza – they can help to roll out the dough and add their own
toppings.

TIPS FOR COOKING PIZZA
IN A DOMESTIC OVEN

+ Preheat the oven fully to its maximum temperature or at least
  250°C/480°F/gas mark 9.
+ Use a combo or fan and grill if that's an option in your oven.
+ Sprinkle the pizza paddle with cornmeal or semolina. This helps
  the pizza to slide easily off the paddle and gives it a crunchy base.
+ Heat a heavy, upturned baking tray or a pizza stone to maximum
  heat. Slide the pizza directly onto it from the paddle so that the
  base is cooked really well.
+ Wipe any burnt flour, semolina or cornmeal off the baking tray or
  stone each time between pizzas.

HOW TO STRETCH PIZZA DOUGH BY HAND

Divide your dough into 250g pieces. Cover and rest overnight – it will be easier to stretch.

The next day, dip the ball of dough in strong white flour. Flour the countertop.

Lay the floured dough on the floured counter. Press it into a round with your fingers and palm until it's about a finger thick – approx. 12.5cm across. Pick up by the top edge, pinch and turn to form an edge, then lay it back down on the counter. With both hands, turn and stretch the dough until it's about the size of a dinner plate – approx. 25.5cm. Using the knuckles of both hands, lift it up in the centre and rotate so it hangs down and stretches naturally. It will be about 35.5cm in diameter. Transfer to a pizza paddle dusted with semolina (if cooking in a domestic oven) or flour (if cooking in a wood-fired oven). It will contract to about 25.5cm.

Lay the dough on counter and press it into a round

Lift and pinch the edges as you turn the dough

Lay it back down on the counter and continue to stretch

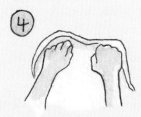

Lift and rotate so it stretches

Transfer to a pizza paddle

HOW TO ROLL OUT PIZZA DOUGH

Lay the ball of floured dough on a lightly floured countertop. Roll
and turn, roll and turn until the pizza is approx. 35.5cm. Transfer to a
floured or semolina-dusted pizza paddle. Brush the edges with extra
virgin olive oil if you like, then top as you fancy.

Roll and turn
the dough

HOW TO USE A PIZZA PADDLE

Sprinkle a pizza paddle with semolina or cornmeal if using a
domestic oven or flour if cooking in a wood-fired oven. Roll or
stretch the pizza, then transfer it to the paddle. Arrange the toppings
on the base. Hold the paddle over where you want to place it in
the oven, then flick the pizza into position with a sharp forward
movement. Use a short-handled pizza paddle for a domestic oven
and a long-handled pizza paddle for a wood-fired oven so that the
pizza can be placed anywhere inside the oven. To remove it from the
oven, slide the pizza paddle under the cooked pizza.

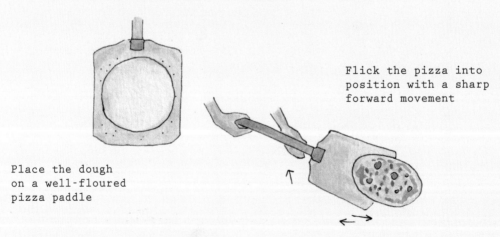

Flick the pizza into
position with a sharp
forward movement

Place the dough
on a well-floured
pizza paddle

Garden Café Pizza Dough

The beauty of this recipe is that it is so quick and easy, as using fast-acting dried yeast does away with the first rising. By the time your tomato sauce is bubbling, your pizza bases will be ready for their toppings!

MAKES 8 × 25CM PIZZAS

- 680g strong white flour (or 600g strong white flour plus 110g rye flour)
- 15g caster sugar
- 2 level teaspoons salt
- 50g butter, cut into cubes
- 1 × 7g packet of fast-acting dried yeast
- 3 tablespoons olive oil
- 450-500ml tepid water (more if needed)

Sieve the flour, sugar and salt into a large, wide mixing bowl. Rub in the butter and sprinkle in the fast-acting yeast, then mix all the ingredients thoroughly.

Make a well in the centre of the dry ingredients. Add the oil and most of the tepid water. Mix to a loose dough. You can add more water or flour if needed.

Turn the dough out onto a lightly floured worktop, cover with a clean tea towel and leave to relax for about 5 minutes, then knead the dough for about 10 minutes, until smooth and springy (or if you're kneading the dough in a stand mixer fitted with a dough hook, 5 minutes is usually long enough).

Leave the dough to relax again for about 10 minutes, then divide into eight equal balls of dough, each weighing approx. 150g. Shape into balls and lightly brush each one with olive oil.

If you have time, put the oiled balls of dough on a tray, cover and chill in the fridge. The dough will be easier to handle when cold, but it can be used immediately. Stretch into a round or roll each ball into a 25cm disc on a well-floured work surface. It's brilliant to pop a few rolled-out, uncooked pizza bases in the freezer. You can take one out, put the topping on and slide it straight into the oven. What could be easier? This dough also makes delicious white yeast bread, which we shape into rolls, loaves and plaits (see pages 53–4).

Baked Dough Balls

A way to use a little dough deliciously.

- 2 teaspoons chopped
  fresh chives
- 2 teaspoons chopped
  fresh marjoram
- 140g Garden Café pizza
  dough (page 105)
- olive oil, for
  greasing
- garlic butter (page
  309), melted, to serve

Preheat the oven to 230°C/450°F/gas mark 8.

Knead the finely chopped herbs into the dough, then roll out until it's 1cm thick. Stamp out the dough with a small round dough cutter (2cm).

Put the dough balls on an oiled baking sheet, cover with a clean tea towel and allow to rise again for about 10 minutes. Remove the towel and bake in the preheated oven for 5–10 minutes.

Serve straight from the oven with a ramekin of melted garlic butter.

Deep-fried Dough Balls

Roll little bits of dough into balls about the size of a large marble. Deep-fry in hot oil for 3–4 minutes, splashing with oil as they cook, until golden. Remove and drain on kitchen paper. Serve hot with a ramekin of melted garlic butter.

Pizza Margherita

Everyone's favourite! Possibly the most traditional and universally popular pizza in Italy – the green, white and red are the colours of the Italian flag. As this pizza is only tomato, mozzarella and fresh basil, it's crucial that each element is of superb quality.

MAKES 1 PIZZA

- 250g Garden Café pizza dough (page 105)
- semolina or extra flour, for dusting the pizza paddle
- 3 tablespoons extra virgin olive oil
- 4 tablespoons Isaac's roasted tomato sauce (page 304)
- 175g mozzarella cheese, grated and drizzled with extra virgin olive oil
- 1 × 125g ball of fresh buffalo mozzarella, torn into pieces
- 6-7 fresh basil leaves
- flaky sea salt

This is best made in a wood-burning oven, but otherwise, preheat the oven fully to its maximum temperature or at least 250°C/480°F/gas mark 9.

Slide a heavy baking tray into the oven (turn it upside down if it has edges). Alternatively, put a pizza stone on the floor of the oven and preheat for 1 hour.

Stretch or roll the pizza dough into a 27.5cm disc. Sprinkle a little semolina (if cooking in a domestic oven) or flour (if cooking in a wood-fired oven) over the surface of the pizza paddle, then put the pizza base on top. Brush the edges with extra virgin olive oil. Spread the well-flavoured tomato sauce evenly over the dough, keeping in from the edge. Sprinkle the grated mozzarella evenly over the tomato sauce, then add the torn buffalo mozzarella and a few fresh basil leaves. Season well with flaky sea salt.

Bake in the fully preheated oven for 7– 9 minutes, until the base is crisp and the top is bubbly and golden. (It takes 3–4 minutes in our wood-fired oven and we use flour rather than cornmeal or semolina on the paddle. The pizza is cooked when it's golden and bubbling around the edges.) Add the remaining basil leaves, drizzle with extra virgin olive oil and serve immediately.

Turkish Pizza with Tahini, Yogurt and Sumac

If I could choose only one pizza, this might have to be it. I love the spiciness and the combination of flavours.

MAKES 6

SAUCE:
- 2 tablespoons extra virgin olive oil, plus extra for drizzling
- 1 onion, finely chopped
- 1 × 400g tin of whole plum tomatoes, chopped
- 1 teaspoon sugar
- salt and freshly ground black pepper

TOPPING:
- 1 red onion, thinly sliced
- 225g minced beef
- 225g minced lamb
- 3 teaspoons Aleppo pepper (or 1 teaspoon dried chilli flakes)
- 3 teaspoons roasted and ground cumin
- 2 teaspoons roasted and ground coriander
- ½ teaspoon paprika
- ½ teaspoon salt
- ½ teaspoon freshly ground black pepper

DOUGH:
- 1 batch of Garden Café Pizza Dough (page 105)

TO FINISH:
- tahini
- natural yogurt
- sumac
- flaky sea salt
- sprigs of fresh flat-leaf parsley
- lemon wedges

To make the sauce, heat the oil in a frying pan over a gentle heat. Add the onion and cook for 5 minutes, until soft but not coloured. Add the chopped tomatoes and their juices. Cook for 5 minutes, until reduced by half, then add the sugar, salt and freshly ground black pepper. Taste and correct the seasoning. Cool completely.

For the topping, drizzle the sliced red onion with a little extra virgin olive oil and toss to coat.

Mix the meat, spices and salt and pepper in a bowl. Add the cooled tomato mixture to the spiced mince and mix well. Keep cool while you roll out the dough.

Preheat the oven to 250°C/480°F/gas mark 9. Put an upside-down baking tray in the oven to heat up too.

Weigh the pizza dough into 150g portions for each pizza. Working with one ball at a time, stretch or roll out the dough to a 25.5cm disc. Transfer to a floured pizza paddle.

Brush the edges with extra virgin olive oil. Spread 125g of the spiced mince over the base, then scatter some sliced red onion over the meat. Slide onto the hot baking tray in the preheated oven and bake for 6 minutes.

To serve, slide the pizza onto a hot plate. Drizzle with tahini and then with natural yogurt. Sprinkle with sumac and a few flakes of sea salt, then scatter lots of flat-leaf parsley sprigs on top. Serve as soon as possible with a wedge of lemon.

Chargrilled Pizza Margherita

Pizza is brilliant for a barbecue, though you'll need a Weber-type grill with a cover and a flat grid. Top with seasonal flavours of your choice.

MAKES 1 PIZZA

- 175g mozzarella cheese, grated
- 3 tablespoons olive oil
- 225g Garden Café Pizza Dough (page 105)
- 4 tablespoons Isaac's roasted tomato sauce (page 304) or tomato fondue (page 306)
- 1 tablespoon freshly grated Parmesan (Parmigiano Reggiano is best)
- salt and freshly ground black pepper
- 1 dessertspoon coarsely chopped fresh parsley or annual marjoram OR pesto and fresh basil leaves

Preheat the barbecue.

Put the grated mozzarella in a bowl and drizzle with some of the extra virgin olive oil.

Shape or roll the pizza dough into a 30cm rectangle or a large circle about 5mm thick (see page pages 103–4 for tips on how to stretch or roll the dough). Brush the edges with extra virgin olive oil.

Gently place the dough on the grid in the centre of the barbecue, directly over the medium heat. Cover with the lid and cook for 2–4 minutes, until the bottom of the crust is well marked and browned. Flip over and spread the tomato sauce or tomato fondue over the grilled side, then quickly sprinkle on the grated mozzarella to within 2.5cm of the edge. Sprinkle with the freshly grated Parmesan. Season well with salt and freshly ground black pepper.

Cook with the lid tightly shut for 5–6 minutes, until the base is well browned, the toppings are warm and the cheese is bubbly.

Transfer the cooked pizza to a chopping board. Sprinkle the coarsely chopped fresh herbs on top.

Alternatively, drizzle with pesto and scatter a few whole basil leaves on top. Cut into wedges and pass around immediately.

Pizza Stromboli

Stromboli is a small island off the north coast of Sicily with an active volcano, hence the name. Stromboli is a stuffed pizza roll, an Italian-American creation often served with a tomato dipping sauce. It's an Italian bread and a sandwich all in one. The dough is baked with a cheese and sausage filling inside, but it can of course be vegetarian. It's served in thick slices and is perfect picnic food. You can vary the fillings with any combination of cheeses. Sometimes we add crispy bacon or 'nduja instead of the spicy sausage or even a little fresh chilli if you want an extra kick. Serve alone or with Isaac's roasted tomato sauce (page 304) or tomato fondue (page 306) as a dipping sauce. Alternatively, use basic pizza dough.

MAKES 1

- 15g fresh yeast
- 225ml tepid water
- 1 teaspoon honey
- 1 egg
- 2 tablespoons extra virgin olive oil
- 1 teaspoon salt
- 70g fine (or sieved) wholemeal or rye flour
- 350g strong white flour

FILLING:

- 175g grated mozzarella
- 50g grated Parmesan cheese, plus extra
- 50g fennel salami or chorizo, chopped
- 1 egg, beaten
- 2 large garlic cloves, crushed
- 2 tablespoons chopped fresh flat-leaf parsley
- 2 tablespoons chopped fresh chives or marjoram
- 1 teaspoon salt
- pinch of freshly ground black pepper

FOR BRUSHING:

- olive oil or egg wash (page 325)

Crumble the yeast into the tepid water with the honey, then leave in a warm place. After about 5 minutes, it will have a creamy, slightly frothy appearance on top.

Put the egg, oil, salt and the wholemeal or rye flour in the bowl of a stand mixer fitted with the dough hook. Add 4 tablespoons of the strong flour and the yeast mixture, then beat on a high speed for 4–5 minutes, until smooth. Rest for 10 minutes, then add the remaining strong flour a few spoonfuls at a time, continuing to knead until the dough is smooth and elastic.

Turn out onto a lightly floured work surface and knead by hand for about 3 minutes. Put the dough in a lightly oiled bowl and cover with a clean tea towel. Allow to rise in a warm, draught-free place for about 1 hour, until doubled in size.

Meanwhile, to make the filling, mix all the ingredients together and set aside until needed.

Gently knock back the dough, then turn it out onto a lightly floured work surface. Roll into a 30.5cm × 40.5cm rectangle (alternatively, you could make two smaller stromboli). Spread the filling over the dough, leaving 2.5cm clear around the edge. Roll up from the long side as you would a Swiss roll, brushing the edge with water. Pinch along the seams to seal in the filling.

Carefully transfer to a lined baking sheet, seam side upwards. Cover and allow to rest for 30 minutes.

Preheat the oven fully to 220°C/430°F/gas mark 7.

Brush the stromboli with olive oil or egg wash and prick here and there with a skewer. Sprinkle with a little extra Parmesan.

Bake in the centre of the preheated oven for 15 minutes, then reduce the temperature to 190°C/375°F/gas mark 5 and cook for a further 25–30 minutes.

Cool on the baking tray for 10 minutes, then transfer to a wire rack. Best served warm.

Variation

Spread a layer of tomato sauce over the base. Cover with overlapping layers of salami, prosciutto and pepperoni. Sprinkle with grated mozzarella or thin slices of provolone cheese. Season with salt and freshly ground black pepper, then sprinkle with fresh marjoram, basil or thyme leaves. Roll, seal and cook as above.

Pizza Bianca

This simple pizza just seems to be addictive. It's one for all you garlic lovers out there.

MAKES 1 PIZZA

- 140g Garden Café Pizza Dough (page 105)
- 2 tablespoons approx. garlic butter (page 309), melted
- semolina, for dusting if using a pizza paddle
- 75g Gruyère cheese, grated
- salt and freshly ground black pepper
- garlic flowers and leaves, when in season, or chopped fresh parsley

Preheat the oven fully to its maximum temperature or at least 250°C/480°F/gas mark 9.

Slide a heavy baking tray into the oven (turn it upside down if it has edges). Alternatively, put a pizza stone on the floor of the oven and preheat for 1 hour.

Roll or stretch the pizza dough to a 25cm disc (see pages 103–4 for tips on how to stretch or roll the dough). Brush with melted garlic butter.

Sprinkle a little semolina all over the surface of the pizza paddle and lay the pizza base on top, then sprinkle with the grated Gruyère. Season well with salt and freshly ground black pepper.

Bake in the fully preheated oven for 8–10 minutes, until the base is crisp and the top is bubbly and golden. Sprinkle the garlic flowers and leaves or chopped fresh parsley on top, cut into wedges and serve immediately.

Garlic Butter Pizza   Omit the Gruyère and proceed as above.

Goat's Cheese and Fresh Herb Calzone

Calzone originated in Apulia, the high heel of Italy. It's basically a covered pizza baked in the shape of a turnover or half-moon. There are many fillings you can use, but here is one we enjoy.

SERVES 1 VERY HUNGRY
PERSON OR 2 PEOPLE WHO
FEEL SHARING IS FUN!

- 110g fresh goat's cheese (use one of the Irish artisan goat cheeses)
- 200g grated mozzarella cheese
- 25g Parmesan cheese
- 3 slices of prosciutto, julienned (optional)
- 2 garlic cloves, crushed
- 1 tablespoon chopped fresh chives
- 1 tablespoon chopped fresh parsley
- 1 teaspoon fresh thyme leaves
- 1 teaspoon fresh annual marjoram leaves
- salt and freshly cracked black pepper
- 200g approx. Garden Café pizza dough (page 105)
- semolina, for dusting
- extra virgin olive oil, for brushing

TO SERVE:
- rocket and a tomato salad

Preheat the oven fully to its maximum temperature or at least 250°C/480°F/gas mark 9.

Slide a heavy baking tray into the oven (turn it upside down if it has edges). Alternatively, put a pizza stone on the floor of the oven and preheat for 1 hour.

Crumble the goat's cheese into a bowl, then add the grated mozzarella and Parmesan, prosciutto (if using), crushed garlic and chopped fresh herbs. Mix it all together and season with salt and freshly cracked black pepper.

Roll the dough very thinly into a 30.5cm round. Sprinkle the pizza paddle with semolina, put the dough on top and spoon the filling over the bottom half to within 3cm of the edge. Brush the edge with water, fold over the rest of the dough and seal the edge by crimping with your fingers. Brush the top with cold water and slide onto the hot baking tray or pizza stone in the fully preheated oven.

Bake for 20–30 minutes. Brush with olive oil and serve with rocket and a delicious tomato salad. A steak knife is a good idea for cutting this.

Sfinciuni

This speciality of Palermo is what one might call a pizza pie – dough on the top and bottom and a chosen filling in the centre. There's nothing to prevent you from experimenting, but this is one of the many versions that we enjoy. There's also a Sicilian version of sfinciuni that's more like a focaccia with a tomato- and anchovy-based topping.

SERVES 1-2

- 110g roughly grated mozzarella cheese
- 2 tablespoons olive oil, plus extra for brushing
- 15g freshly grated Parmesan cheese
- 3 tablespoons tomato fondue (page 306)
- 1 dessertspoon chopped fresh parsley
- 1 dessertspoon chopped fresh basil
- 2-4 anchovies or 6-8 stoned and halved black olives (optional)
- 200g approx. Garden Café pizza dough (page 105)
- semolina, for dusting

TO SERVE:
- green salad

Preheat the oven fully to its maximum temperature or at least 250°C/480°F/gas mark 9.

Slide a heavy baking tray into the oven (turn it upside down if it has edges). Alternatively, put a pizza stone on the floor of the oven and preheat for 1 hour.

Put the grated mozzarella in a large bowl, drizzle over the olive oil and allow to soak for 1 hour while the oven preheats. When the time is up, add the Parmesan, tomato fondue, fresh herbs and the anchovies or olives (if using) and mix together.

Divide the dough in half. Roll out one piece as thinly as possible. Sprinkle semolina over the pizza paddle and arrange the dough on top. Spread the filling on the dough base to within 2cm of the edge. Dampen the edges with cold water. Roll out the rest of the dough, lay it on top, seal and crimp the edges. Brush with cold water and slide onto the preheated baking tray or pizza stone in the fully preheated oven.

Bake for 20 minutes, until crisp and golden. Brush with olive oil and serve immediately with a salad of seasonal leaves.

Ham and Cheese Sfinciuni

An Italian riff on a ham and cheese sandwich. A slick of mustard is also good here.

- 350g Garden Café pizza dough (page 105)
- extra virgin olive oil
- 1-2 tablespoons Dijon mustard (optional)
- 175-225g cooked ham, thinly sliced
- 110g grated mozzarella cheese
- 50g grated Parmesan cheese
- 2 tablespoons chopped fresh parsley or rocket leaves
- salt and freshly ground black pepper
- egg wash (page 325)

Preheat the oven fully to its maximum temperature or at least 250°C/480°F/gas mark 9.

Divide the dough in half. Roll one piece into a rectangle to fit a 30.5cm × 20.5cm rectangular tin. Brush the tin with olive oil and spread the dough over the base. Cover with a slick of mustard (if using), slices of ham, sprinkle with a mixture of mozzarella and Parmesan cheese and the chopped parsley or rocket. Season with salt and freshly ground black pepper.

Spread the filling right out to the edges and corners. Roll out the remainder of the dough and cover the filling, pressing it down gently at the edges. Brush with egg wash.

Bake in the preheated oven for 15–20 minutes, then reduce the temperature to 200°C/400°F/gas mark 6 and bake for a further 5 minutes. Cut into squares and serve warm.

Piadina Romagnola

Super-easy to make – no oven needed, just cook the thin dough on a griddle or heavy cast iron frying pan. They are delicious spread with cream cheese mixed with fresh herbs, perhaps a slice of prosciutto, smoked salmon or cooked ham, some charcuterie or slivers of hard cheese or a few slices of ripe tomato. Roast aubergine and red peppers also make a delicious topping either on their own or with cream cheese. Piadina sandwiches are much loved in Italy, particularly in Florence.

MAKES APPROX. 10
....

- 225ml tepid milk
- 225ml tepid water
- 20g fresh yeast
- 1 teaspoon caster sugar
- 985g strong white flour
- 2 generous teaspoons salt
- 200g butter, cubed, or lard (or a mixture)

Mix the tepid milk and water together. Mix the yeast with a little of the tepid liquid and the teaspoon of sugar, then leave in a warm place. After about 5 minutes, it will have a creamy, slightly frothy appearance on top.

Sieve the flour and salt onto the worktop or into a bowl, then rub in the butter or lard.

Mix the dissolved yeast with the rest of the tepid milk and water. Make a well in the centre of the flour, pour in the liquid and mix to a pliable dough. Knead for a few minutes, until smooth. Cut the dough into small pieces 50–75g in weight. Roll out each piece very thinly – it shouldn't be more than 5mm thick.

Preheat a griddle or heavy cast iron frying pan. Cook one piadina at a time, moving it every few seconds so it doesn't stick. When it is brown and speckled on one side, flip it over and continue to cook on the other side. It should still be pliable. Fill with your chosen filling, fold over and eat warm or cold.

Gnocco Fritto

From the Emilia-Romagna region of Italy, these puffy little deep-fried pillows are an irresistible and traditional accompaniment to prosciutto, salami and cheese.

MAKES APPROX. 30

- 1 teaspoon dried yeast
- 160ml tepid water
- 350g plain white flour
- generous pinch of salt
- 50g lard
- light olive oil, for deep-frying

Mix the yeast with the tepid water, then leave in a warm place. After about 5 minutes, it will have a creamy, slightly frothy appearance on top.

Put the flour into a bowl, then add the yeast and water. Sprinkle in a pinch of salt, then rub in the lard. Mix to a soft dough, then knead for 4–5 minutes, until the dough is smooth and springy. Put the ball of dough in an oiled bowl, cover and allow to rise in a warm, draught-free place for about 2 hours, until doubled in size.

Knock back the dough, then tip out onto a lightly dusted worktop. Roll the dough to a thickness of 3mm. Cut into 5–6cm squares, approx. 15g.

Heat the oil in a deep-fryer to 180°C/350°F.

Working in batches, fry the gnocchi for 3–4 minutes on each side, until they puff up and are golden. Turn over and splash with oil while cooking. Remove with a slotted spoon and drain on kitchen paper.

Ballymaloe Cookery School Focaccia

The secret of super-light focaccia, an Italian flatbread, is to incorporate enough water into the dough. The original was simply sprinkled with some flakes of sea salt, but we also add rosemary, thyme or sage. This is delicious for sandwiches, or use a larger tin for a thinner focaccia.

MAKES 1 FOCACCIA

- 20g fresh yeast
  (or 10g dried yeast)
- 15g caster sugar
- 600g tepid water
- 2-4 tablespoons olive
  oil
- 700g strong white
  flour
- 2 level teaspoons salt
- extra virgin olive
  oil, for brushing
- pinch of flaky sea
  salt
- small sprigs of fresh
  rosemary

Mix the yeast and sugar with 150g of the tepid water, stir and leave in a warm place. After about 5 minutes, it will have a creamy, slightly frothy appearance on top. Add the olive oil (how much you add is up to you – some people prefer to add all 4 tablespoons and others prefer to add less) and another 300g of water.

Sieve the flour and salt into the bowl of a stand mixer fitted with the dough hook. Make a well in the centre and pour in the yeast mixture. Mix for approx. 5 minutes, until the dough is loose and smooth.

Add another 75g water and continue to mix. It will be very runny, but the dough will develop. Knead for 5–6 minutes, then add the remaining 75g water. It will look like soup, but hold your nerve! Continue to knead for another 5–8 minutes, until the dough becomes soft, silky and stretchy.

Pour the dough out onto a clean, damp worktop for 10 minutes for its bench rest (see page 324). Gently fold the dough from each side into the centre, like a parcel. Rest for 5–6 minutes. Repeat twice more.

Fold the dough from each side into the centre, like a parcel.

Transfer to an oiled bowl (we use the bowl of the stand mixer). Cover and allow the dough to rise in a warm, draught-free place for 1–2 hours, until doubled in size. Yeast dough rises best in a warm, moist atmosphere, so the rising time will depend on the ambient temperature.

Brush a large rectangular tin (32cm long × 23cm wide × 5cm deep) evenly with extra virgin olive oil.

When the dough has doubled in size, pour it gently into the oiled tin. Drizzle with a little more extra virgin olive oil, then dimple the dough with your fingertips. Allow to rise for 15–20 minutes (no need to cover).

Dimple the dough with your fingertips

Preheat the oven to 230°C/450°F/gas mark 8.

Sprinkle the top of the dough with flaky sea salt and a few sprigs of rosemary. Bake in the preheated oven for 10–15 minutes. Reduce the temperature to 200°C/400°F/gas mark 6 and bake for a further 10–15 minutes, until almost cooked.

Remove the focaccia from the tin and return it to the oven directly on the oven rack to crisp the base. Bake for approx. 5 minutes, until fully cooked. It will feel light and should sound hollow when the base is tapped. Cool on a wire rack.

Focaccia with Roasted Red Onions, Gruyère and Thyme Leaves

Fresh rosemary also works well here instead of thyme.

MAKES 1 FOCACCIA

....

- 1 batch of focaccia dough (page 118)
- 4-6 red onions, cut into quarters (or eighths if very large)
- 4 tablespoons extra virgin olive oil
- flaky sea salt and freshly ground black pepper
- 4-5 sprigs of fresh thyme (2-3 tablespoons leaves)
- 175g Gruyère cheese, grated

Make the dough as per the recipe on page 118. When the dough has almost finished its first rise, preheat the oven to 230°C/450°F/gas mark 8. Brush a 28cm × 40cm baking tray generously with oil.

Put the onion chunks in a bowl, drizzle with some of the oil, season with salt and pepper and toss quickly. Spread out on a baking tray in a single layer, sprinkle with half the thyme and roast in the preheated oven for 10–15 minutes, until the edges of the onions are beginning to brown. Allow to cool, then transfer to a bowl.

When the dough is fully risen and puffy, knock it back, cover and rest for 4–5 minutes. Roll it out into a rectangle to fit your well-oiled baking tray. Drizzle with extra virgin olive oil and gently dimple the dough with your fingertips.

Add the grated Gruyère and the remaining thyme leaves. Spread this evenly over the dough. Season with salt and pepper and drizzle with a little extra virgin olive oil. Allow to rise again for 5–10 minutes.

Bake in the oven for 20–25 minutes, until golden on top. Check underneath to make sure the base is cooked. Cut into squares and serve warm.

Late Summer Cherry Tomato and Pesto Focaccia

Halve a few handfuls of cherry tomatoes, put them in a bowl and season well with salt, pepper and sugar. Arrange in a single layer on top of the focaccia instead of roast onions. Drizzle with extra virgin olive oil and proceed as above. Drizzle with basil pesto (page 312) before cutting into squares.

Potato and Rosemary Focaccia

I just love this delicious combination. I sometimes scatter diced chorizo between the cheese and potato slices for extra oomph.

SERVES 10-12

- 1 batch of focaccia dough (page 118)
- extra virgin olive oil
- 2-3 tablespoons chopped fresh rosemary or thyme leaves
- flaky sea salt and freshly ground black pepper
- 175-225g Fontina or raclette or a combination of mozzarella and grated Parmesan
- 6-8 waxy potatoes (approx. 1kg), boiled until almost cooked, then peeled and thinly sliced
- pinch of flaky sea salt
- fresh rosemary sprigs and flowers, when in season

Make the dough as per the recipe on page 118. When it's almost done with its first rise, preheat the oven to 230°C/450°F/gas mark 8. Brush a 28cm × 40cm baking tray generously with oil.

Knock back the dough and allow to rest for 4–5 minutes.

Sprinkle the base of the well-oiled baking tray with most of the chopped rosemary or thyme. Gently roll the dough into a rectangle to fit the tray, then lay the dough on top of the herbs on the base of the baking tray. Drizzle with extra virgin olive oil and gently dimple the dough with your fingertips.

Season with salt and freshly ground black pepper. Cover with thin slices of Fontina cheese. Season the slices of cooked potato well with salt and pepper, add the remaining chopped rosemary or thyme and toss. Arrange in overlapping slices over the dough and cheese. Drizzle with extra virgin olive oil.

Bake in the preheated oven for 20–25 minutes, until the base is crusty and the potatoes are beginning to crisp. Remove from the oven and sprinkle with some flaky sea salt and some rosemary flowers when in season. Drizzle with extra virgin olive oil, cut into squares and eat warm.

FLATBREADS

Flatbreads are a staple in many cuisines and have been made for centuries in homes and on street stalls all over the world, from India, Morocco and Australia to Mexico, the Arctic and Nordic regions and the Middle East.

Originally they were peasant breads, made with locally available grains, but nowadays they are made with a wide variety of flours, most commonly wheat but also barley, rye, oats, maize, rice, chestnut, chickpea, almond or a mixture. Initially they were cooked directly over an open fire and later a clay tava, comal, plancha or an iron griddle. Some Indian flatbreads, such as naan, are cooked in a tandoor oven, while lavash was traditionally baked in an underground clay oven called a tonir. One could fill several volumes with recipes for flatbreads.

Initially made by simply mixing flour with water to make a thick, malleable, unleavened dough, these days flatbreads often include a little yeast or other leavenings as well as fat, yogurt, herbs, spices and/or other flavourings.

Flatbreads are a much-loved street food but chefs and enthusiastic home cooks have also 'discovered' them, so they are really having a moment. I've included a variety of flatbreads to whet your appetite to get you started. Many flatbreads are made in minutes, are fun to cook and super versatile. Everyone should have a few flatbreads in their repertoire. Get started and experiment.

Pitta

This recipe for pitta, or pocket bread, is easier to make than you might imagine. It was originally given to us by a past student, Arnaud Leopold de Volder, who spent some time with us at Ballymaloe Cookery School in 1997.

MAKES 8-10
....

- 25g fresh yeast
- 310ml tepid water
- 450g strong white flour
- 1 teaspoon dairy salt
- pinch of caster sugar
- 1 tablespoon extra virgin olive oil

Crumble the yeast into 100ml of the tepid water and leave in a warm place. After about 5 minutes, it will have a creamy, slightly frothy appearance on top.

Sieve the flour, salt and sugar into a bowl. Add the yeast mixture, the oil and the rest of the tepid water. Stir by hand until well mixed. The dough should not be too dry. Knead the dough until it's smooth and elastic, about 4–5 minutes. If it's too sticky, add flour while kneading. Transfer the dough to an oiled bowl and oil the whole surface of the dough too. Cover and leave to rise for 1–1½ hours at room temperature, until more than doubled in volume.

Knock back the dough and knead it again until smooth. Roll into a thick log and cut with a floured knife into 8–10 equal-sized pieces. Roll each piece into a smooth ball. Gently place on a floured surface, cover and leave to rise for about 30 minutes, until doubled in size again.

Preheat the oven fully to its maximum temperature or at least 250°C/480°F/gas mark 9. Put two baking sheets in the oven to preheat as well.

Roll the dough balls into circles about 5mm thick. Don't worry about a perfect shape, but it's important to roll the discs thinly. Rest for a couple of minutes, then transfer two at a time onto a hot sheet. Bake on the middle rack of the preheated oven for 5–7 minutes, until they are just beginning to brown and have puffed up. Occasionally one will not puff up enough to make a pocket, but it will still be delicious. Wrap in a clean tea towel to keep soft or cool on a wire rack if not using immediately.

Stuff with salad, spicy mince, ragu, cheese – whatever takes your fancy. Pitta can be frozen, but it's not quite as good as fresh.

Sesame Pitta

Roll each ball of dough in 1 teaspoon of sesame seeds before rolling it into circles.

Yufka (Turkish Flatbread)

This is a version of the yufka (similar to lavash – see page 126) that Sarit Packer and Itamar Srulovich from Honey & Co. in London showed us how to make when they taught at Ballymaloe Cookery School in 2015. You could use 275g plain flour instead of the mix of three flours called for here. Yufka is perfect for wrapping shawarma or as a side. Traditionally it's baked on a large convex iron griddle on an outdoor wood-burning stove, but a griddle or non-stick pan works perfectly. The size of the flatbread can vary – I have eaten a yufka almost as large as a bicycle wheel in Turkey.

MAKES 8

- 110g strong white flour
- 110g plain flour
- 50g wholemeal flour, sieved
- 1 scant teaspoon salt
- 200-225ml tepid water

Mix all the flours (or see the intro) and the salt in a bowl. Add 200ml of the tepid water, mix to a dough and knead well for just 3–4 minutes. Add the remaining water if needed to bring it together into a dough. Shape into a roll, then divide into eight pieces, about 50g each. Cover and leave to rest for at least 1 hour, though 3–4 hours would be better.

When the dough has rested, roll each piece into a thin round, approx. 23cm.

Heat a griddle or large iron or non-stick frying pan over a medium to high heat. Working with one at a time, cook the yufka quickly on both sides until light golden and puffed in spots, about 2 minutes on each side. Transfer to a plate. Cooked flatbreads steam as they stack.

Eat immediately or the yufka can be stacked for several days, weeks or even months in a dry place. Yufka may also be frozen. To reheat before eating, mist or sprinkle a yufka with warm water. Fold it in half or into quarters, wrap it in a clean cloth and allow to soften for about 30 minutes.

Enjoy with butter, honey, cheese or a Turkish stew. Alternatively, if you fill yufka with roasted vegetables, cured meat and salads, they are then called dűrűm, which means 'roll'. We save stale yufka to serve with a cheeseboard.

Lavash (Armenian Flatbread)

Lavash is an ancient flatbread that is still made all over the Caucasus. It is traditionally cooked in a tandoor or tonir oven (an underground clay oven) or on a convex metal griddle known as a saj.

Some versions are unleavened but most contain yeast or 'old dough', where a little ball of each batch is kept aside and added to the next dough to inoculate it (a form of sourdough).

Traditionally they are rectangular (approx. 36cm × 24cm), stretched over a long convex cushion and slapped onto the walls of the oven. The intense heat of the oven causes the dough to bubble in seconds. It can be eaten fresh but also allowed to dry completely. It keeps well for weeks on end and can be rehydrated by sprinkling it with water to soften at home.

Lavash is soft and perfect for wraps and sandwiches. Children love to help make these little flatbreads.

MAKES APPROX. 20

- 150g tepid water
- 150g warm milk
- 1 tablespoon light olive oil or vegetable oil
- 10g granulated sugar
- 6g dairy salt
- 1 × 7g sachet of instant yeast
- 500g plain white flour

Mix the tepid water, milk, oil, sugar, salt and yeast in a large bowl. Slowly add the flour, mixing by hand or using a stand mixer fitted with a dough hook until the dough comes together. This will take 8–10 minutes. The dough should be supple but it will still be a bit sticky.

Sprinkle a little oil over the surface of the dough and pop into a large bowl. Cover and allow to rise for 40–50 minutes at room temperature.

When it's risen and puffy, knock it back and shape into a roll. Divide into 20 pieces. Shape each piece into a ball, approx. 45g. Cover all the balls with a glass cloth so they don't form a skin.

Heat a non-stick frying pan over a medium heat. Flour the work surface and your rolling pin very well. Working with one at a time, roll a ball of dough into a very thin round, approx. 18cm diameter and 1–2mm thick.

Slap it onto the hot pan and cook for 45–60 seconds. There will be bubbles. Flip and cook on the other side for 30–45 seconds. Transfer to a plate and cover with a clean tea towel.

Repeat with the remaining dough. Eat soon or store in a ziplock bag. It's not very traditional, but it works well.

Penny's Ethiopian Injera

Injera is an Ethiopian and Eritrean spongy flatbread made from teff, the world's smallest grain. Teff flour is highly nutritious and naturally gluten-free. You can get teff flour in health food shops, but if you can't find it, buckwheat flour works well. Teff has a slightly sour flavour that becomes addictive. Traditionally injera is made in 40cm rounds, but it can be cooked on any griddle or non-stick pan. It's also used as an eating utensil to scoop up meat and vegetable stews or as a 'tray' to serve them on so that the juices soak into the bread deliciously.

MAKES APPROX. 6
....

- 140g teff flour or buckwheat flour
- 225ml water
- ¼-½ teaspoon salt (optional)
- ghee or clarified butter (page 307), for greasing

Put the flour in a bowl and gradually whisk in the water. Cover the bowl with a cloth and leave at room temperature for 36–48 hours, until it starts to ferment. It will be covered with bubbles and have a thin watery layer on top. The batter will keep, covered, for several days but it gradually gets sourer. You could put it in the fridge if you wish to keep it for longer than a day or two. Whisk in salt to taste (if using). The batter should be the consistency of crêpe batter.

Heat a griddle or non-stick frying pan on a medium heat. Grease it very lightly with ghee or clarified butter.

Pour a small ladleful onto the pan or griddle to cover the base to a thickness of a scant 3mm. Cook for 3–4 minutes, until the edges of the injera start to come away from the edges of the pan. The surface will be covered with bubbles – the injera is cooked when the bubbles burst.

Eat with sambals, vegetable curry or relishes or for breakfast with bacon and maple syrup.

Lovisa's Swedish Crispbread

On our 12-week course at the Ballymaloe Cookery School, we have students of many different nationalities. We always encourage them to make their own ethnic bread. Some students, like Lovisa, a young Swedish girl, often get homesick for the breads of their own country and are thrilled to get the chance to make them. We made these super-light and crunchy crispbreads with Lovisa and she was surprised to see that we had a traditional Scandinavian knäckebröd rolling pin. The wood on the pin has a criss-cross scored pattern on the surface. When you roll out the dough, it pricks the surface and gives it a textured finish, but an ordinary rolling pin works well too – just prick the dough with a fork.

These crispbreads are irresistible to nibble with cheese. They keep for weeks if stored in an airtight container.

MAKES 10

- 1 teaspoon caraway seeds
- 300ml barely warm milk
- 150ml tepid water
- 25g fresh yeast
- 310g rye flour
- 310g strong white flour
- 1 teaspoon salt

Preheat the oven to 180°C/350°F/gas mark 4. Put two baking sheets in the oven to preheat too.

Toast the caraway seeds for 2–3 minutes in a dry pan over a medium heat, then grind the seeds finely.

Mix the barely warm milk and tepid water together in a large bowl, then crumble in the yeast. Leave to sponge for 5 minutes – it will have a creamy, slightly frothy appearance on top.

Mix the flours with the salt and ground caraway seeds, then sprinkle onto the liquid. Bring together to form a soft dough, then turn out onto a lightly floured work surface and knead for 5 minutes. Roll into a cylinder and divide into 10 equal pieces. Shape each piece into a ball, cover and leave to rise for 20 minutes.

Sprinkle a work surface lightly with rye flour. Roll out each ball with a smooth rolling pin to 20cm, turning the dough as you roll to keep it round. Prick all over with a fork (or if you have a traditional knäckebröd rolling pin, use this instead). Stamp out a little hole in the centre of each circle with 2.5cm cutter.

Place the dough on the hot baking sheets and bake in the preheated oven for 10–12 minutes. (There's no need to waste the little centre pieces of dough! Cook them as well, they make super-tiny cheese biscuits.) Eat warm or cold.

Tunnbröd (Swedish Flatbread)

Tunnbröd translates as 'thin bread' and is sometimes called polar or Arctic bread, as it was originally made in the Nordic region. It can be rolled into a rectangle, pricked, then cut into smaller rectangles or squares rather than rounds. Use to make sandwiches with fillings of your choice. Tunnbröd also freezes well and defrosts quickly.

MAKES 8-10

- 300g strong white flour
- 150g rye flour
- 1 teaspoon salt
- 1 teaspoon fennel or aniseed, lightly crushed
- 12g fresh yeast
- 200ml tepid water
- 2 tablespoons honey
- 4 tablespoons natural yogurt or crème fraîche

Sieve the white flour into a bowl and mix thoroughly with the rye flour and salt. Add the lightly crushed fennel or aniseed and mix well.

Dissolve the yeast in the tepid water, stir in the honey and leave in a warm place. After about 5 minutes, it will have a creamy, slightly frothy appearance on top.

Gradually stir the yeast and yogurt or crème fraîche into the flour and mix until it comes together into a dough that almost comes away from the sides of the bowl. Knead for about 10 minutes (or 5 minutes in a stand mixer with the dough hook). Shape the dough into a ball and pop into a lightly oiled bowl. Cover with a shower hat or a slightly damp cloth and allow to rise for 1 hour.

Knock back the dough and divide it into 8–10 small balls. Cover and rest again for 20–30 minutes.

Heat a heavy frying pan (25cm) on a medium heat.

On a lightly floured work surface, roll each ball of dough into a round about 1–2cm thick. Prick the surface all over with a fork.

Cook on the preheated pan for 3–4 minutes, until speckled and bubbly. Flip over and cook on the other side for 3–4 minutes more, then transfer to a plate or wire rack. Wipe out the pan with a dry cloth. Continue with the other flatbreads, piling them on top of each other as they finish cooking.

Msemen

This square, flaky, flat, slightly chewy bread is eaten for breakfast in Morocco, Tunisia and Algeria, where it's available from both bakeries and street food carts. It's easy and fun to make at home. Eat freshly cooked off the pan or enjoy with honey (or a syrup of honey and butter) and a glass of mint tea – so delicious. Msemen also freeze well.

MAKES 20

- 2 teaspoons granulated sugar
- 350ml tepid water
- ¼ teaspoon dried yeast
- 465g plain white flour
- 90g durum or fine semolina
- 1 teaspoon salt

FOR FOLDING:
- 225-300ml vegetable oil
- 50g butter, softened
- 90g semolina

Stir the sugar into 50ml of the tepid water, sprinkle in the yeast and allow to sit for 4–5 minutes. It will have a creamy, slightly frothy appearance on top.

Put the flour, durum or semolina and the salt in the bowl of a stand mixer fitted with the dough hook. Add the yeasty liquid and the rest of the water. Knead for about 6 minutes (or 10 minutes by hand), until the dough is smooth and elastic but not sticky. Flours vary, so it may need a little more water.

Turn out onto a worktop. Divide the dough into 20 pieces and roll into smooth balls. Transfer to oiled baking trays, cover and allow to rest for 15 minutes.

Clear the worktop (granite or stainless steel are best). Have three separate bowls of the oil, semolina and soft butter and semolina. Oil the work surface and your hands generously.

Dip a dough ball in the oil and put it on the work surface. Using your fingers, using light, tucking movements, gradually spread the dough into a paper-thin round, roughly 20.5cm. Oil your fingers as necessary. Dot the dough with butter and sprinkle with semolina.

Using light, tucking movements, gradually spread the dough into a paper-thin round

Fold into three to form an elongated rectangle, like a letter. Dot again with soft butter and sprinkle with semolina and fold again, but this time make a square. Repeat with the rest of the dough.

Fold into a rectangle, and then a square

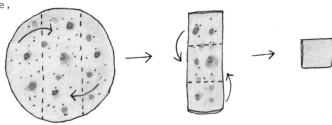

Meanwhile, heat a griddle or large frying pan. Lay a square of folded dough on the oiled work surface, oil your hands and spread out once again until the square is double the original size (10cm–12.5cm).

Transfer to the hot griddle and cook until flecked with golden spots. Flip over and cook on the other side, flipping several times, until crisp and golden. Repeat with the rest of the dough. When the msemen has cooked, pick it up from the opposite ends and flex it slightly – this helps to separate the layer. These are best eaten as soon as they come off the pan.

Pick the msemen up from the opposite ends and flex it slightly

Enjoy as is or slather with a mixture of honey and butter. Warm equal quantities of honey with butter, turning off the heat as soon as it bubbles. Dip the msemen in the honey butter so both sides are coated. It will be sticky but delicious.

Khobz (North African Flatbread)

Khobz, or kesra, is a soft yeasted flatbread eaten across North Africa. It puffs up when baked and can be filled with vegetables, used as a wrap for shawarma or as a dip with hummus (page 317). The name means 'home bread', as it's commonly homemade or cooked in a street oven, called a ferrane, and is eaten at virtually every meal.

MAKES 2 × 15CM
ROUND LOAVES

....

- 1 × 7g packet of fast-acting dried yeast or 15g fresh yeast
- 1 teaspoon granulated sugar
- 2 tablespoons plus 275ml tepid water (approx.)
- 510g plain flour
- 150g whole wheat flour, sieved
- 2 teaspoons salt
- 1 tablespoon aniseed (optional)
- 1 teaspoon sesame seeds
- 100ml tepid milk
- cornmeal or semolina

Put the yeast and sugar in a small bowl with the 2 tablespoons of tepid water. Stir and leave in a warm place. After about 5 minutes, it will have a creamy, slightly frothy appearance on top.

Mix the flours with the salt, aniseed (if using) and sesame seeds in a large mixing bowl. Make a well in the centre. Add the yeast mixture, then pour in the tepid milk and enough of the remaining 275ml tepid water to form a stiff dough. Flours vary in their capacity to absorb moisture, so you may need to add a little more water.

Turn the dough out onto a lightly floured board and knead it well. In Morocco they knead with clenched fists. It will take anywhere from 10 to 12 minutes to knead this dough thoroughly – it should be smooth and elastic. Or if you're using a stand mixer fitted with a dough hook, 7–8 minutes on a slow speed will be adequate. When the dough is smooth and elastic, shape it into two balls and rest for 5 minutes on the board.

Flour a baking tray lightly with cornmeal or semolina. Shape the first piece of dough into a roll approx. 40.5cm long. Curl it into a snake that is a little raised in the middle so that it's a slightly conical shape. Repeat this with the second piece of dough.

Shape a piece of dough into a roll

Curl it into a snake that is a little raised in the middle

Turn out onto a baking sheet that has been sprinkled with cornmeal or semolina. Repeat with the second ball of dough. Cover loosely with a clean damp towel and let the dough rise for about 2 hours in a warm, draught-free place. To check if the bread has fully risen, poke your little finger gently into the dough – the bread is ready for baking if it doesn't spring back.

Preheat the oven to 200°C/400°F/gas mark 6.

With a fork, prick the bread around the sides three or four times. Bake in the preheated oven for 12 minutes, then lower the heat to 180°C/350°F/gas mark 4 and bake for 40–50 minutes more. The bread will sound hollow when tapped on the bottom when fully cooked. Cool on a wire rack and cut into wedges just before serving.

Griddle Khobz Mikla

Flatten a ball of dough into a circle. Traditionally this is cooked over an open fire, on a dry earthenware griddle called a mikla, until browned on both sides, but you can use a griddle or heavy-based frying pan. Cook for 3–4 minutes on each side, depending on the thickness. Absolutely delicious with fresh butter and crystallised honey. Best eaten fresh but can be stored in an airtight container for a few days or can be frozen for a month.

How to Revive Flatbread

Wrap the khobz in a clean, damp tea towel and pop into a low oven for a few minutes. The steam will help soften the khobz.

Baghrir

These soft lacy pancakes are beloved for breakfast in Morocco and other North African countries. Kids love them too. The fermented batter is cooked on one side only. These Moroccan crêpes are also called thousand-hole pancakes because of their honeycomb appearance. This recipe comes from L'Hôtel Marrakech in Morocco, one of my favourite places to stay in the whole world.

MAKES 6

....

- 200g fine semolina
- 400ml tepid water
- 1-1½ tablespoons orange blossom water
- 1 teaspoon vanilla extract
- ½ teaspoon baking powder
- ½ teaspoon caster sugar
- pinch of salt
- ½ teaspoon dried yeast
- 2 × 7g sachets of instant yeast

Put all the ingredients except the yeast in a blender and whizz for 5 minutes, until bubbles appear. Add the dried yeast and blend for a further 2 minutes. Allow the mixture to stand for about 5 minutes, until the mixture looks foamy, before starting to cook.

Heat a 12cm pan over a medium heat. Fill a 75ml ladle with batter, pour it into the pan and gently tilt to cover the base. Cook for 3–4 minutes, until all the bubbles burst and the surface looks dry.

Serve three or four baghrir on a warm plate with a mixture of equal quantities of melted butter and honey.

Fremantle Flatbread

The recipe for this delicious flatbread comes from a trip to Australia in the late 1990s.

MAKES 10 OR MORE

- 500g strong white flour
- 60g butter, melted and cooled
- 250ml water
- 1 teaspoon salt
- pinch of caster sugar
- rice flour, for dusting
- olive oil, for brushing
- flaky sea salt and freshly ground black pepper

Put the flour, melted butter and water in the bowl of a stand mixer fitted with the dough hook. Add the salt and sugar and mix on a slow speed for about 5 minutes, until the dough is smooth and shiny.

Turn out onto a lightly floured work surface and knead gently for a couple of minutes. Shape the dough into a roll, wrap it in greaseproof paper and refrigerate overnight.

The next day, divide the dough into 10 equal pieces, cover and allow to rest for 5–6 minutes.

Dust a work surface with rice flour. Roll each portion out into a very thin disc. Don't worry too much about the shape of the disc as long as it's thin. Place the breads on baking trays, cover and leave to rest for about 20 minutes.

Preheat the grill to its highest setting.

Brush the breads with olive oil and sprinkle with flaky sea salt and freshly ground black pepper.

Grill one or two flatbreads at a time, first one side, then the other. Alternatively, cook on a preheated heavy pan on a high heat for just a couple of minutes on each side. They will puff up almost immediately. Be careful not to overcook or they will become brittle and crisp. Serve immediately or wrap in a warm tea towel until ready to eat. Dip in extra virgin olive oil; maybe sprinkle with flaky sea salt; enjoy with prosciutto, salami or cold meat; or serve as an accompaniment to all manner of good things.

Paratha

India has a myriad of flatbreads. These roughly triangular flaky breads are eaten all over the country. They are easy to make at home – all you need is a cast iron frying pan. In India, ghee is often used instead of oil. The paratha can be round or square rather than a rectangle. Laccha paratha, Kerala paratha or porotta are made from maida or plain flour and are much flakier.

MAKES 16

....

- 185g plain flour
- 175g sieved wholemeal flour (weigh the flour after sieving - put the bran back in the bag)
- ½ teaspoon salt
- 2 tablespoons ghee or vegetable oil (or clarified butter - see page 307), plus extra for frying and brushing
- 200ml water

Put the flours and the salt in a bowl. Add the 2 tablespoons of ghee or oil over the top and rub it in with your fingertips. The mixture will resemble coarse breadcrumbs. Add the water and gradually mix to form a softish ball of dough.

Knead on a clean work surface for about 10 minutes. Rub the ball of dough with a little oil, put it on a plate, cover and allow to rest for 30 minutes.

Heat a cast iron frying pan on a medium-low flame. Knead the dough again, shape into a roll and cut into 16 equal pieces.

Keep 15 pieces covered while you work with one. Flatten this ball of dough, then dip both sides in a bowl of plain flour. Roll into a 15cm round. Brush a little melted ghee or oil over the surface of the paratha and fold it in half. Brush again, then fold to form a triangle. Roll this triangle towards the point into a larger triangle with 18cm sides approx. Dust with flour if necessary.

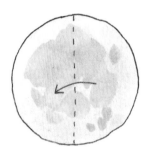

Fold in half

Fold again to form a triangle

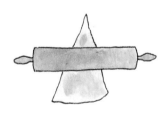

Roll this triangle towards the point into a larger triangle

When your frying pan is really hot, slap the paratha onto it. Let the paratha cook for a minute or so. Brush the top generously with ghee or oil, turn it over and cook the second side for a minute or so. Both sides should have brownish spots. Move the paratha around the pan and press it down as you cook so all the surface is exposed evenly to the heat, flipping it backwards and forwards until it's fully cooked through. Keep warm in a clean tea towel or on a covered plate. Cook all the parathas in the same way. Serve warm.

Parathas can be wrapped in parchment and reheated in an oven preheated to 180°C/350°F/gas mark 4 for 5–10 minutes.

Madhur Jaffrey's Naan

Naans and other similar flat leavened breads are eaten all the way from the Caucasus down through north-western India. In India, the baking is done in very hot clay ovens or tandoors. The breads are slapped onto the inside walls and cook quite happily alongside skewered chickens.

Madhur Jaffrey showed us how to make this flatbread when she was a guest chef at Ballymaloe Cookery School in May 2013. Few of us have tandoors at home, so Madhur suggested that naans can be baked by using both the oven and the grill – ideally you'll need two ovens.

Naans can be made both with and without egg. If you decide not to use the egg, just increase the yogurt by about 4 tablespoons. Naans may be enjoyed with almost any Indian meat or vegetable.

MAKES 6 LARGE BREADS

- 150ml hand-hot milk
- 2 teaspoons caster sugar
- 2 teaspoons dried yeast
- 450g plain flour
- 1 teaspoon baking powder
- ½ teaspoon salt
- 150ml natural yogurt, lightly beaten
- 1 large egg, lightly beaten (or see the intro)
- 2 tablespoons vegetable oil, plus a little extra

Put the milk in a bowl. Add 1 teaspoon of the sugar and all of the yeast. Stir to mix. Set aside for 10–15 minutes – it will have a creamy, slightly frothy appearance on top.

Sieve the flour, baking powder and salt into a large bowl. Add the remaining teaspoon of sugar along with the yeast mixture, yogurt, egg and vegetable oil. Mix and form into a ball of dough.

Tip out onto a clean work surface and knead for 10 minutes or more, until smooth and satiny. Shape into a ball. Pour about ¼ teaspoon oil into a large bowl and roll the ball of dough in it. Cover the bowl and set aside in a warm, draught-free place for 1 hour, until the dough has doubled in size.

Preheat the oven fully to its maximum temperature or at least 250°C/480°F/gas mark 9.

Heat the heaviest baking tray you own in the oven. Preheat the grill.

Knock back the dough, then divide into six equal-sized balls. Keep five covered while you work with the sixth. Roll this ball into a tear-shaped naan, about 25cm in length and about 13cm at its widest. Remove the hot baking tray from the oven, slap the naan onto it and put it back in the preheated oven to bake for 3 minutes. It should puff up.

Then put the baking tray and naan under the grill, about 7.5–10cm away from the heat, for about 30 seconds, until the top of the naan browns slightly.

Wrap the naan in a clean tea towel to keep it pliable. Continue with the remainder and serve hot.

Spring Onion Naan	Add 2 tablespoons chopped green spring onions or garlic chives to the dry ingredients.
Butter Naan	Brush the hot naan with melted butter or garlic butter (page 309).
Naan with Nigella Seeds	We harvest our own nigella seeds from the seed heads of nigella or love-in-a-mist, but you can source them easily in shops. Sprinkle the surface of each uncooked naan with nigella seeds, roll lightly and cook as above.

Corn Tortillas (Tortillas de Maíz)

I yearn for fresh tortillas, the quintessential taste of Mexico. Of course the best are made with freshly ground maize, but you can make good ones with masa harina, either white or yellow. Rick Bayless gave us the recipe and showed us how to make corn tortillas when he was a guest chef at the Ballymaloe Cookery School in 2000. Practice makes perfect, but it's useful to have a tortilla press.

MAKES APPROX. 16

- 450g freshly ground corn masa or 450g powdered masa harina (such as the Maza Real brand (non-GM))
- 600ml hot tap water

Heat a heavy rectangular griddle or two cast iron pans over two different temperatures: one side of the griddle or one pan over a medium to medium-low heat and the other side or pan over a medium-high heat. Line a tortilla press with two squares of plastic that just cover the plates (the thicker plastic from food storage bags is easier for beginners to work with).

Knead the masa (either fresh or reconstituted) with just enough of the warm water to make it soft, like soft cookie dough, but not sticky. The softer the dough, the more moist and tender the tortillas will be, but don't make it so soft that more than a bit sticks to your hands.

Open the tortilla press. Scoop out a walnut-sized piece of dough weighing approx. 70–75g, roll it into a ball and centre it in the middle of the plastic on the base. Cover with the second sheet of plastic. Close the press and use the handle to flatten the ball into a 13–15cm disc. Turn the plastic-covered disc 180° and press gently to even the thickness.

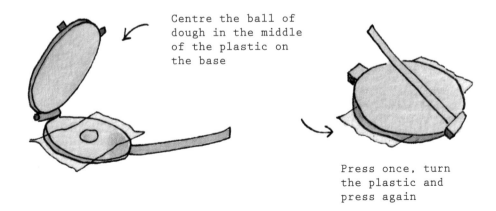

Centre the ball of dough in the middle of the plastic on the base

Press once, turn the plastic and press again

Open the press and peel off the top piece of plastic. Flip the uncovered side of the tortilla onto your palm, lining up the top of the tortilla with the top of your index finger. Starting at the top, peel off the remaining sheet of plastic. A portion of the tortilla will be dangling off the bottom of your hand. Quickly lay the tortilla on the cooler side of the griddle or the cooler pan. Don't flip it off your hand – that always results in rumpled tortillas. Instead, as you slowly sweep the tortilla away from you, let the dangling part catch on the hot surface, then roll your hand out from under the tortilla. The movement looks a little like you're sweeping something off the griddle with the back of your hand.

Cook for 15–30 seconds, just until the tortilla releases itself from the griddle or pan. It will look just a tiny bit dry around the edges, but don't leave it too long or it will turn out dry and heavy. Flip onto the hotter side of the griddle or the hotter pan and cook for 30–45 seconds, until splotchy brown. Turn once again, still leaving it on the hot side or hot pan, and cook another 30–45 seconds to brown.

During these last few seconds of cooking, a perfectly made tortilla will puff up like pitta. If yours doesn't, it may have been cooked for too long on the first side, it may not have been pressed evenly (or it may be too thin or too thick) or it may not have cooked on a hot enough surface. Though an unpuffed tortilla won't be as light, it will still be good.

Transfer to a cloth-lined basket and continue making tortillas, stacking one on top of another and keeping them covered. As the cloth traps the steam, the tortillas will complete their final little bit of cooking.

Flour Tortillas

Wheat flour tortillas are usually larger than corn tortillas and they come from northern Mexico, where maize does not grow so easily. They are made with plain flour, salt and lard, though butter also gives a good result. Cooked on a hot griddle, they must be very pliable and soft for storage. For most purposes flour tortillas can be used in place of corn tortillas and many people prefer them. They should be treated in the same manner as corn tortillas, though, and never eaten cold. Rick Bayless showed us how to make his tortillas when he taught at Ballymaloe Cookery School in July 2000.

MAKES APPROX. 25

- 450g plain flour
- 1 dessertspoon salt
- 75g lard, vegetable shortening or butter (reduce the salt to 1 teaspoon if using salted butter)
- 225ml tepid water

Heat a heavy-based frying pan (without greasing it) on a moderate heat until a drop of water will sizzle in it.

Sieve the flour and salt together in a bowl, then rub in the lard, shortening or butter as you would for shortcrust pastry. Add the tepid water slowly – the amount may vary with the type of flour used. Knead the dough on a floured board with floured hands until it is no longer sticky. Keep the dough covered with a warm, damp cloth.

Using approx. 25g dough at a time, knead it by folding it back on itself to trap air for a few seconds. Now make it into a little ball and flatten it. Place the flattened ball on a floured board and roll it out with a floured rolling pin until it is so thin that you can see the board through it. Cut into a 18–23cm round.

Slap the tortilla straight onto the hot pan. Cook for 30 seconds on one side, then turn it over and cook for 15–30 seconds on the other side. Slide the tortilla off the pan, cover with a clean tea towel and keep them warm or store them in a tortilla basket if you have one. If you need to warm up a lot of tortillas together, make a small parcel of 12 tortillas each, wrapped securely in aluminium foil. Place the parcels in a moderate oven (180°C/350°F/gas mark 4) for 15 minutes.

To Shallow-fry Tortillas	Cover the base of a heavy-based frying pan with 2.5cm cooking oil. When the oil is hot, fry one corn or flour tortilla at a time for about 20 seconds. Remove from the oil and drain on kitchen paper until required.
To Deep-fry Tortillas	Heat at least 10cm of oil in a deep-fryer to 200°C/400°F. Immerse the corn tortilla in the hot oil and fry for 1–1½ minutes. Remove from the oil when it's pale golden – be careful, as they keep browning after they have been removed from the fryer. Drain on clean absorbent kitchen towels. Use as a base for tostadas.
Tortilla Chips	Cut the raw or cooked corn tortilla into six pieces and deep-fry for a few seconds.
To Freeze Flour Tortillas	Put greaseproof or silicone paper between the tortillas, otherwise they may stick together, especially when frozen. They defrost easily if left at room temperature for 30 minutes.

Fougasse (Provençal Flatbread)

This crisp Provençal flatbread resembles a leaf with ragged holes. Serve alone or with anchoïade (page 316) and tapenade (page 315).

MAKES 4-6

- 1 batch of Ballymaloe Cookery School white yeast bread (page 52)
- extra virgin olive oil, for brushing
- flaky sea salt
- chopped fresh rosemary (optional)

Make the dough as per the recipe on page 52. After it's had its first rise, knock back the dough and divide it into 4–6 equal-sized pieces.

Gently roll each piece of dough into an oval shape at least 18cm long and 10cm wide. Using a very sharp knife or a razor blade, make a cut down the centre, then make three or five angled cuts on either side of the dough.

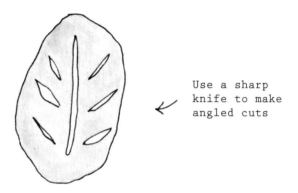

Use a sharp knife to make angled cuts

Brush two baking trays with olive oil. Transfer the fougasse onto the trays, pulling the cuts apart to create holes. Brush the top of the fougasse with olive oil before rising so that it doesn't form a skin. Allow to rise again in a warm, draught-free place for about 30 minutes, until doubled in size.

Preheat the oven to 230°C/450°F/gas mark 8.

Brush the top surface again with olive oil, then sprinkle with sea salt and rosemary (if using). Bake in the preheated oven for 5 minutes, then reduce the temperature to 200°C/400°F/gas mark 6 and bake for 20–25 minutes more, until golden. Cool on a wire rack.

Chapatis

It's fascinating to watch chapatis being cooked in India – it looks so easy. Originally chapatis were cooked over charcoal but you'll need a gas hob for this.

....

- 250g sieved chapati flour or wholemeal flour
- pinch of salt
- 175m water (quantity will vary with flour)

Put the flour in a bowl and add a pinch of salt. Pour in the water and gradually bring in the flour to form a soft dough. Knead the dough for 5–6 minutes, until it's smooth. Put the dough in a bowl, cover with a damp cloth and leave for 30 minutes to relax.

Heat an Indian tava or a cast iron frying pan over a medium-low gas heat for 10 minutes. When it's very hot, turn the heat to low.

Knead the dough again and divide it into roughly 15 pieces. It will be fairly sticky, so rub your hands with a little flour when handling it.

Take one piece of dough and shape it into a ball. Flour the work surface generously and roll the ball in it, pressing down to flatten. Now roll it out, dipping frequently in flour, until it's about 14cm in diameter. Pick up this chapati, pat it between your hands to shake off any excess flour, then slap it onto the hot tava or frying pan. Let it cook on the low heat for about a minute. The underside should develop white spots. Turn the chapati over (we use our hands to do this, but you could use a pair of tongs) and cook for about 30 seconds on the second side.

Now for the exciting bit: take the pan off the heat and put the chapati directly on top of the low flame. It should puff up in seconds. Turn the chapati over and let the second side sit on the flame for a few seconds. Put the chapati in a deep plate lined with a large cotton napkin and cover the chapati fully. Make the rest this way. Chapatis take practice to reach perfection, but even if they look a bit odd, they will still taste good.

Ideally chapatis should be eaten as soon as they are made, but if you want to eat them later, wrap the whole stack in parchment and either refrigerate for a day or freeze. The chapatis may be reheated, still wrapped, in an oven preheated to 220°C/430°F/gas mark 7 for 15–20 minutes, depending on how many you're reheating.

BREADS OF
THE WORLD

Bread is a staple food all over the world and every country has its specialties. There is an infinite variety of flatbreads and leavened breads and thousands of variations on the theme, made with a myriad of different grains.

Each has its own story and many bring back happy memories of trips to faraway places or the people who originally shared the recipe with me. The Chinese steamed bread, for example, came about after a chance conversation with a Chinese-American woman while visiting the Mayan ruins at Tikal in Guatemala. She was wistful as she reminisced about helping her grandmother when she was little while she made bread and steamed it over a wok. She described the flavour and texture as best she could, and the recipe for this soft, spongy bread that everyone loves is the result.

Brotherly Love will always remind me of our late neighbour, Rene Hague, son-in-law of the renowned typographer, Eric Gill. He took up baking in his later years and cooked his way through several books on bread. He made many memorable loaves, but this traditional Suffolk bread was one of his specialties.

Madhur Jaffrey, the much-loved Indian cook and actress, shared many delicious recipes with us during the classes she taught at the Ballymaloe Cookery School. She showed us how to reproduce several of the breads that I enjoy so much on visits to India.

Len Lipitch from Schull shared his recipe for the challah he brought to a Sabbath supper at a mutual friend's house in West Cork after I had waxed lyrical about how delicious it was – the best I've ever tasted.

There are many recipes for Russian borodinsky, but I was first introduced to this bread by Andrew Whitley of Bread Matters, co-founder of the Real Bread Campaign and Scotland The Bread, who has been responsible for introducing so many people to real bread over several decades.

My daughter-in-law, Penny, shared the recipe for her beloved Perthshire butteries, and a past student from the US, Kelley Ryan-Bourgoise, shared her favourite cornbread recipe, which we continue to pass on to each batch of students at the Ballymaloe Cookery School.

Damper reminds me of trips to Australia, where I was astonished to find a bread that closely resembled Irish soda bread. Presumably it was brought to Australia by the many Irish people who got a free passage there from the late 1700s. And on and on it goes ...

Kelley's Sweet Cornbread

This delicious cornbread was first baked for me by Kelley Ryan-Bourgoise, a past student from Los Angeles.

SERVES 12 APPROX.

....

- 375g plain flour
- 350g medium cornmeal
- 110g caster sugar
- 1½ tablespoons baking powder
- 1½ teaspoons salt
- 350ml buttermilk
- 110ml milk
- 110g butter, melted
- 2 eggs, beaten
- Tabasco, to taste
- 110g corn kernels (tinned is fine)
- 75g grated Cheddar cheese
- 50g chopped spring onions
- 2 tablespoons chopped fresh coriander

Preheat the oven to 220°C/430°F/gas mark 7. Line a 20.5cm × 20.5cm × 5cm square tin with parchment paper.

Combine all the dry ingredients in a bowl. In a separate large bowl, whisk together the buttermilk, milk, melted butter, beaten eggs and Tabasco, then add the dry ingredients and mix well to combine. Fold in the corn kernels, grated cheese, chopped spring onions and coriander.

Pour the batter into the lined tin. The mixture should come two-thirds of the way up the sides of the tin.

Put the tin in the preheated oven, reduce the oven temperature to 200°C/400°F/gas mark 6 and bake for 35 minutes. Cover the top with parchment paper and bake for a further 10 minutes, until golden brown and a skewer inserted into the centre comes out clean. Cut into squares, spread with butter and enjoy.

Arepas

These delicious round savoury cornbreads are made from masarepa, a pre-cooked maize meal. They have been eaten in South America since before the arrival of Christopher Columbus. They are similar to Mexican gorditas and Salvadoran pupusas. They are loved all over South America but are now sought after and greatly enjoyed in this part of the world too.

MAKES 8

FOR THE DOUGH:
- 350g white masarepa (pre-cooked cornmeal)
- 1 generous teaspoon salt
- 3 egg yolks
- 1 tablespoon olive or sunflower oil
- 500ml tepid water

FOR THE FILLING:
- 260g queso fresco, grated (or 130g Cheddar, grated, plus 130g mozzarella, grated)
- 3 tablespoons chopped fresh coriander
- 1-2 teaspoons toasted and ground dried ancho chilli
- 1 teaspoon cumin seeds, toasted and ground
- ½ teaspoon paprika
- ½ teaspoon salt
- freshly ground black pepper
- olive oil, for cooking

TO SERVE:
- guacamole (page 319) or tomato and coriander salsa (page 320)

Put the masarepa and salt in a large bowl and mix well. Make a well in the centre, then add the egg yolks, oil and enough tepid water to form a stiff but wet paste. Mix well, cover and allow to rest for 10 minutes.

Put the queso fresco (or the Cheddar and mozzarella) in a bowl with the coriander, ground chilli, ground cumin, paprika, salt and some freshly ground black pepper. Mix well, taste and correct the seasoning.

Knead the dough briefly in the bowl, then divide it into eight equal pieces and roll into balls. Dip your hand in cold water and press each ball into a round on the palm of your hand, approx. 10cm wide. Put a good spoonful of the cheese filling in the centre of each round and bring the edges up to fully encase the filling. Flatten once again until the arepa is a generous 1cm thick. Repeat with the remainder of the dough.

Heat 1 tablespoon of olive oil in a heavy pan over a medium heat. Add three or four arepas, cover and cook for 6–8 minutes, until golden brown underneath. Uncover, flip over the arepas and continue to cook, uncovered, until the other side is golden brown. Transfer to a wire rack and keep warm while cooking the rest.

Eat as is or serve with guacamole or salsa.

Borodinsky Bread (Russian Village Bread)

If you are starting from scratch, this bread will take six days to make. It takes time, but not your time. If you already have a sourdough starter, this takes just two days to make. Either way, it's worth the effort.

For accuracy this recipe is best made by weighing ingredients in metric measurements, including the water.

MAKES 1 LOAF

....

STEP 1: RYE SOURDOUGH
STARTER (MADE OVER 4
DAYS):
- 100g dark rye flour
- 200g tepid water
  (28°C/80°F)

....

STEP 2: PRE-FERMENT:
- 50g rye sourdough
  starter
- 150g dark rye flour
- 300g very warm water
  (40°C/104°F)

....

STEP 3: MAIN DOUGH:
- olive oil or melted
  butter, for greasing
- 10-15g coarsely
  cracked whole
  coriander seeds, to
  sprinkle in the tin
- 270g rye sourdough
  (the rest can be used
  for another loaf or
  made into crackers -
  see page 98)
- 230g rye flour (light
  or dark)
- 90g tepid water
  (35°C/95°F)
- 20g molasses or
  treacle
- 15g barley malt
  extract
- 5g sea salt
- 5g coriander seeds,
  coarsely ground
- 2g caraway seeds
  (optional)

Step 1

On day 1, mix 25g dark rye flour with 50g tepid water (28°C/80°F) in a large Kilner jar or plastic tub. Cover and keep at room temperature overnight.

On day 2, 3 and 4, add another 25g rye flour and 50g tepid water. It should become bubbly, a sign of fermentation, although it won't expand significantly. Allow the starter to ferment for a further 24 hours after the last feed on day 4 before making the bread.

Step 2

Put 50g of your rye sourdough starter in a large bowl. Stir in 150g dark rye flour and 300g warm water (40°C/104°F). Cover and allow to ferment in a warm kitchen for 12 hours or overnight. The rest of the starter can be stored in the fridge and fed with 25g rye flour and 50g warm water 24 hours before making the next rye loaf.

Step 3

Brush a 13cm × 20cm (450g) loaf tin thoroughly with olive oil or a little melted butter. Sprinkle coarsely cracked coriander seeds over the base of the tin, reserving some for the top.

To make the final dough, add all the remaining ingredients to the base from step 2 and mix well. It won't look like ordinary bread dough. Turn it out onto a wet worktop and shape it into a rough loaf with wet hands. Lift it into the loaf tin, cover with a damp tea towel and allow to rise for up to 6–8 hours in a warm, draught-free place, until it has at least doubled in size.

Preheat the oven to 220°C/430°F/gas mark 7.

Sprinkle the rest of the crushed coriander seeds over the top. Bake the loaf in the preheated oven for 10 minutes, then reduce the heat to 200°C/400°F/gas mark 6 and bake for a further 30 minutes. The loaf will have shrunk in from the sides of the tin.

Remove from the oven and turn out onto a wire rack. Cool completely before wrapping in parchment paper. Rye bread is best after a day or two, as it slices more easily and it keeps really well. It's delicious with thinly sliced cheese or salami.

Chinese Steamed Buns

Sitting on the steps of a café late one evening in Guatemala while visiting the Mayan ruins of Tikal, I got chatting to a Chinese-American woman who had fond memories from when she was little of helping her grandmother make Chinese bread in a bamboo steamer over a wok. Her family had long since lost the recipe, but as we sat talking, she explained how they made the dough. It seemed similar to our white yeast dough but cooked in a steamer over a wok. So here is my version of Chinese steamed bread for you, wherever you are.

MAKES 7 SOFT BUNS

- 20g fresh yeast
- 200ml tepid water, plus more as needed
- 450g strong white flour
- 30g butter, diced
- 15g caster sugar
- 1 teaspoon dairy salt

Sponge the yeast with 150ml of the tepid water and set aside. After about 10 minutes, it will have a creamy, slightly frothy appearance on top. Add the remaining tepid water.

Sieve the flour into a large bowl. Stir in the butter, sugar and salt, then make a well in the centre and pour in most of the tepid liquid. Mix to a loose dough, adding the rest of the liquid, or more flour or liquid, if necessary.

Turn the dough out onto a floured board, cover and leave to relax for 5 minutes approx. Knead for about 10 minutes, until smooth, springy and elastic (if kneading in a stand mixer fitted with a dough hook, 5 minutes is usually long enough).

Put the dough in a pottery or delph bowl. Cover the top tightly with cling film (yeast dough rises best in a warm, moist atmosphere). The rising time depends on the temperature, but the bread will taste better if it rises more slowly. When the dough has more than doubled in size, knock it back and knead again for 2–3 minutes, until all the air has been forced out. Leave to relax again for 10 minutes.

Shape the bread into seven balls of dough. Transfer to the middle section of a large bamboo steamer that's been dusted well with flour. Cover with a light tea towel. Allow to rise again in a warm, draught-free place, though this rising will be shorter, about 20–30 minutes. The bread is ready to be steamed when a small dent remains when the dough is pressed lightly with your finger. Sprinkle with a little more flour.

Position a wok on a high gas flame or high heat. Fill with water so that the water level reaches up over the base of the bamboo steamer. Put the middle of the bamboo steamer gently into the wok. The bread will take exactly 1 hour to cook. **DO NOT under any circumstances lift the lid off the steamer or the bread will collapse!**

The beauty of this bread, and what my Chinese-American friend recalled loving so much, is the way you can peel it layer by layer. You can eat the buns just as they are, as an accompaniment or fill them as you would a sandwich.

Ciabatta

A light, airy, rustic Italian bread. You'll need to start the recipe a day or two ahead.

MAKES 4-10
....

FOR THE BIGA:
- 7g fresh yeast
- 400ml tepid water
- 500g plain flour
....

FOR THE CIABATTA:
- 7g fresh yeast
- 100ml tepid milk
- 300ml tepid water
- 1 tablespoon olive oil
- 500g plain flour
- 15g salt

Make the biga by stirring the yeast into 50ml of the tepid water and set aside. After about 10 minutes, it will have a creamy, slightly frothy appearance on top. Stir in the remaining tepid water and then the flour. Put the biga in a lightly oiled bowl, cover with cling film and allow to rise at room temperature for 12–24 hours. It will more than double in volume and it will be wet and sticky. It will also have a strong fermented smell when it's ready. This is the starter. (See page 80 for more about bigas.)

To make the ciabatta, measure out 600ml of the biga. (Save the rest for the next batch – cover and refrigerate or freeze the biga until ready to use. If refrigerating the biga, use it within two or three days. If using frozen biga, allow it to come back to room temperature for about 3 hours, until it's bubbly and active again.)

Stir the yeast into the warm milk in the bowl of a stand mixer. Let it stand for about 10 minutes, then add the water, oil and biga. Mix with the paddle attachment until blended.

Add the flour and salt and mix for 10 minutes, still with the paddle attachment. Change to the dough hook and beat for 15–25 minutes at high speed, until the dough is stringy and pulling away from the sides of the bowl. Getting the dough to this stage is essential for the final shaping of the dough.

Put the dough in an oiled bowl, cover and leave to rise for 1–1½ hours, until it has doubled in size. The dough should be full of air bubbles and it should be supple, elastic and sticky when fully risen. **DO NOT knock the dough back.**

Turn the dough out onto a well-floured work surface. Cut the dough with a dough scraper into 4–10 pieces depending on what size you want and what occasion you are making the bread for. Generously flour two baking trays. Lift the soft pieces of dough onto the trays. Gently dimple the loaves with the tips of your fingers.

Cover with tea towels and leave to rest for 30–45 minutes, until puffy. The loaves will not have risen much and when pressed with a finger will still be quite active.

Preheat the oven to 220°C/430°F/gas mark 7.

Dust the loaves lightly with flour before baking. Bake in the preheated oven for 20–25 minutes, until they are pale golden and sound hollow when tapped on the base. Cool on wire racks.

Pooris

Pooris look like puffed-up balloons. They are crisp, soft and delicious and may be eaten with almost all Indian meats, vegetables and pulses. They are also easy to make. Rolled-out discs of dough are put into hot oil and they cook magically in just a few seconds.

As pooris are best eaten hot, I have taught my entire family how to make them. I make three pooris per person. Then, if anyone wants more, they are told to go to the kitchen and make their own. And they do! Our poori dinners invariably turn into a 'happening', with flour-covered children and husbands wandering in and out of the kitchen, rolling pin in hand and looks of great achievement on their faces.

However, a word of caution: as the cooking oil for pooris is very hot, care should be taken not to splash it around and of course children should be supervised. An Indian karhai is the safest and most economical utensil for deep-frying. If you don't have one, use a domestic deep-fryer or a high-sided frying pan. If you take these simple precautions (which are necessary for any deep-frying), poori-making can be fun.

MAKES 12

- 110g wholemeal flour
- 110g plain flour
- ½ teaspoon salt
- 2 tablespoons vegetable oil, plus more for deep-frying
- 100ml water

Sieve the flours and salt in a bowl (put the wheat bran back into the flour bin). Drizzle 2 tablespoons of oil over the top and rub it in with your fingers so the mixture resembles coarse breadcrumbs. Slowly mix in the water to form a stiff dough.

Turn the dough out onto a clean work surface. Knead it for 10–12 minutes, until smooth. Rub about ¼ teaspoon oil on the ball and slip it into a plastic bag. Set it aside for 30 minutes to rest.

Knead the dough again, form it into a roll and divide it into 12 equal balls. Keep 11 covered while you work with the twelfth. Flatten it, then roll it out into a 13–14cm round. Roll out the remainder and keep them covered.

Heat the oil in a deep-fryer to 190°C (375°F). The oil must be very hot or the pooris will not blister and puff. If you don't have a deep-fryer, heat 2.5cm of oil in a small, high-sided frying pan. Meanwhile, line a large plate with kitchen paper.

Lay a poori carefully over the surface of the hot oil. Do not drop the poori into the oil from a great height or it will splash you with hot oil. It might sink a little, but it will rise in seconds and begin to sizzle. Use the back of a slotted spoon to push the poori gently into the oil and splash it. Within seconds, the poori will puff up. Turn it over and cook the second side for about 10 seconds. Remove it with a slotted spoon and put it on the kitchen paper.

Make all the pooris in the same way. These are best served hot, but if some are left over they are also delicious cold.

Penny's Perthshire Butteries

A special thank you to our Scottish daughter-in-law, Penny, for this delicious recipe.

MAKES 20

....

- 680g strong white flour
- 15g salt
- 25g fresh yeast
- 1 tablespoon caster sugar
- 450ml tepid water
- 240g butter, softened

Sieve the flour and salt together into a large, wide mixing bowl. Make a well in the centre.

Crumble the yeast into the sugar in a measuring jug, Add the tepid water and mix to a smooth liquid. Pour this yeast liquid into the flour and work it to a soft but not sticky dough.

Turn the dough out onto a lightly floured work surface and knead for about 10 minutes, until it's smooth, shiny and springy to the touch. Put the dough in a large, clean bowl. Cover with a tea towel and leave in a warm, draught-free place to rise for 1½–2 hours, until the dough has doubled in size.

Knock back the dough, then roll it out on a lightly floured work surface to a rectangle approx. 45cm × 15cm. Divide the softened butter into three equal portions. Spread the top two-thirds of the dough rectangle with one portion of the butter. Fold the unbuttered part of the dough up over half of the buttered dough, then fold the other half of the buttered dough over to make a three-layered sandwich. Seal the edges by pressing down on them with a rolling pin. Wrap the dough in cling film and chill for 30 minutes.

Spread the top two-thirds of the dough rectangle with butter

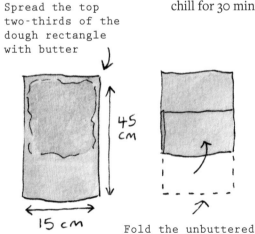

45 cm

15 cm

Fold the unbuttered part of the dough up over half of the buttered dough

Seal the edges by pressing down on them with a rolling pin

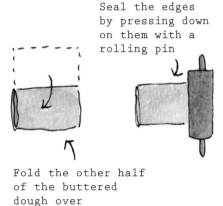

Fold the other half of the buttered dough over

Remove from the fridge and repeat the rolling, folding and chilling twice more. Always roll the dough out with the enclosed side to your left. This helps to capture and keep the precious air that gives these butteries their light texture.

Take the dough out of the fridge again, turn onto a floured work surface and roll to about 2cm thick. Leave to rest, uncovered, for 5 minutes. Using a metal dough cutter lightly dusted with flour, cut the butteries into 20 squares.

Lightly dust three baking sheets with flour. Place the butteries on the sheets upside down, spaced well apart. Cover with a tea towel and allow to prove for a further 20 minutes.

Preheat the oven to 200°C/400°F/gas mark 6.

Bake the butteries in the preheated oven for 20–25 minutes, until golden brown and crisp on top. Cool on a wire rack. Serve warm for breakfast with homemade raspberry jam (page 294) and whipped cream.

Faux Pumpernickel Bread

Reminiscent of pumpernickel but a fraction of the work and still delicious.

Dried yeast may be used instead of fresh yeast. Follow the same method but use only half the weight as given for fresh yeast and give it more time to rise.

MAKES 1 LOAF

....

- 450g wholemeal flour
- 1 teaspoon salt
- 1 tablespoon lightly crushed caraway seeds, plus extra whole seeds
- 100ml black treacle
- 185ml tepid water
- 25g fresh yeast (or see the intro)
- oil, for greasing

Mix the flour with the salt and lightly crushed caraway seeds in a large bowl.

In a small bowl, mix the treacle with 140ml of the tepid water, crumble in the yeast and set aside. After about 5 minutes, it will have a creamy, slightly frothy appearance on top.

Meanwhile, oil a 13cm × 20cm (450g) loaf tin.

When the yeast looks creamy and slightly frothy, give it a stir and add it to the flour with most of the remaining water to make a wettish dough. The mixture should be too wet to knead. Pour into the greased tin and sprinkle with some extra caraway seeds if you like.

Cover and allow to rise for 15–20 minutes, until it's risen almost to the top of the tin. The bread will rise a little further in the oven – this is called oven spring. However, if the bread rises over the top of the tin before it goes into the oven, it will continue to rise as it bakes and will flow over the edges.

Preheat the oven to 230°C/450°F/gas mark 8.

Remove the tea towel and bake the loaf in the preheated oven for 45–50 minutes, until the bread sounds hollow when tapped. We usually remove the loaf from the tin about 10 minutes before the end of the cooking time and put it back into the oven to crisp all around, but if you like a softer crust there's no need to do this. Cool on a wire rack.

Brotherly Love

Rene Hague, the son-in-law of the renowned typographer Eric Gill, was virtually our next-door neighbour for many years. In his later years, he loved to bake and particularly enjoyed making yeast dough. We loved to be invited to tea, as one of his specialities was this traditional Suffolk bread called Brotherly Love.

Do not attempt to make this unless you have fine lard from a well-reared pig – it's one of my favourite things. Try making your own using the recipe on page 323.

MAKES 1 LOAF

- 450g Ballymaloe Cookery School white yeast bread dough (page 52)
- 75g soft pork lard (page 323), plus a little extra for the tin (see the intro)
- 75g granulated sugar

Grease a 13cm × 20cm (450g) loaf tin with lard. Roll the dough into a 40cm × 25cm rectangular strip. Spread or dab lard all over the surface, then sprinkle generously with most of the sugar. Roll up, pop into the greased tin and leave to rise for 40–50 minutes, until doubled in size.

Preheat the oven to 220°C/430°F/gas mark 7.

Brush the loaf with water, then sprinkle with the remaining sugar. Bake in the preheated oven for 10 minutes, then reduce the heat to 200°C/400°F/gas mark 6 and bake for a further 25–30 minutes, until the loaf is sticky and golden and sounds hollow when you tap the base. Turn the bread upside down in the tin for the last 10 minutes, until fully cooked. Cool on a wire rack.

Serve freshly baked and still warm, cut into slices and buttered.

Rachel Allen's Bagels

Bagels are twice-baked. They get their dense chewiness from being poached first in water and then baked. My daughter-in-law Rachel makes these in a stand mixer using the dough hook, but you can make them perfectly well by hand too.

When cold, slice the bagels in half and freeze (for up to three months) so they can be popped into the toaster straight from the freezer without defrosting.

MAKES 7
....

- 450g strong white flour
- 2 level teaspoons salt
- 1 × 7g sachet of fast-acting yeast
- 250ml tepid water (use 125ml just-boiled water from the kettle and 125ml cold tap water to achieve slightly warmer than blood temperature)
- 2 tablespoons runny honey
- 1 tablespoon vegetable oil
- 3 tablespoons treacle or molasses
- maize or cornmeal, for sprinkling
- 1 egg, beaten
- sesame seeds, sea salt, poppy seeds or a savoury topping of your choice (optional)

Sift the flour and salt into the bowl you are making the bread in (I use the bowl of a stand mixer fitted with the dough hook), then add the yeast and mix well.

Measure the water in a measuring jug, then stir in the honey and oil. Using the lowest setting on your mixer, slowly add all the liquid to the dry ingredients. Knead on the lowest setting for 10 minutes, checking to make sure the dough is not wet and adding more flour if it does look too sticky. It is stiffer than a normal bread dough but will still have elasticity.

If making by hand, make a well in the centre of the flour and pour the liquid in gradually, bringing the dough together with your hands.

Turn the dough onto a clean, dry and floured work surface. Using more flour if necessary, start kneading the dough, stretching it away with the palm of one hand and folding it back again with the other, keeping this up for 10 minutes (great muscle builder!). You may need to use more flour as you go to avoid a sticky dough, which you don't want.

Put the dough in a lightly oiled large bowl and turn it in the oil to coat. Cover with cling film or a plastic bag to create a draught-free environment and put in a warm (not hot) place for 1–3 hours, until doubled in size.

When the dough is nearly ready – doubled in volume – bring a large saucepan of water (about 4 litres) to the boil and add the treacle or molasses. Cover and turn off the heat while you shape the bagels.

Lightly oil two baking trays and sprinkle with maize or cornmeal.

Remove the dough from the bowl, then punch it down and knead it briefly. Roll into a rough sausage shape and divide into seven chunks. As you work with one, keep the others covered with a clean tea towel.

There are two ways to shape the bagels. One is to firmly roll out each chunk into a long snake-like shape, then looping the 'snake' and sealing the ends together with a tiny splash of water and squeezing it. The other method is to roll each chunk into a ball. Piercing a hole in the centre with your finger, pull the dough open until you can fit your hand inside, stretching it wide, turning it around and squeezing it to keep it even, like a steering wheel. Put on the prepared baking trays and repeat with the rest of the dough.

Cover and allow to stand for 10–20 minutes to allow the dough to bounce back again.

Preheat the oven to 220°C/430°F/gas mark 7. Heat the saucepan to a gentle simmer.

Working with no more than three at a time, gently lower the bagels into the water and poach, turning gently with a couple of slotted spoons, for about 1½ minutes on each side. Remove the bagels from the water, allowing them to drain first, and place on the prepared trays, spacing them 3–4cm apart. Brush with the beaten egg and sprinkle with sesame seeds, sea salt, poppy seeds or a savoury topping of your choice, or just leave them plain.

Bake in the preheated oven for 15 minutes, then turn them upside down and bake for a further 10 minutes to cook the bases. Cool on a wire rack.

Challah

Challah is a rich, brioche-like bread of Ashkenazi Jewish origin. It is usually braided and typically eaten on ceremonial occasions such as Shabbat and important Jewish holidays.

Thank you to Len Lipitch for sharing the recipe for your delicious challah – the best I've ever tasted. Len advises allowing the challah to rise long and slowly. Don't rush the process, so the challah will be light and tender.

MAKES 2 MEDIUM OR 1
LARGE CHALLAH
....

- 100ml tepid water
- 15g fresh yeast or
  1 × 7g packet of dried
  yeast
- 560g strong white
  flour
- 75g honey
- 60g sunflower oil,
  plus extra for
  greasing
- 4 egg yolks
- 2 eggs
- generous pinch of salt
- egg wash (page 325)
- poppy seeds (optional)

Pour the tepid water into the bowl of a stand mixer and crumble in the yeast. After about 5 minutes, it will have a creamy, slightly frothy appearance on top. When it does, add all the remaining ingredients except the egg wash and poppy seeds.

Using a dough hook and with the machine on a low speed, mix together until it forms a dough. Turn the dough out onto a floured work surface. Knead by hand for 5–6 minutes, until the dough is smooth. Transfer to a large oiled bowl, cover and allow to rise in a warm, draught-free place for about 1 hour, until doubled in size.

Turn the dough over in the bowl, cover and allow to rise again for a further hour.

Remove the dough from the bowl, knock it back gently and cut into six equal-sized pieces. Roll each piece into a rope approx. 45cm long. Take three lengths for each challah and plait together. Alternatively, you can make one six-strand challah following the instructions as shown in the diagram

Lay the challahs on two baking sheets lined with parchment paper and brush gently all over with the egg wash. Leave to rise for 40 minutes, then carefully brush with egg wash again. Repeat this two more times (2 hours in total). Sprinkle the surface of each challah generously with poppy seeds (if using).

Preheat the oven to 190°C/375°F/gas mark 5.

Transfer the challahs to the oven, immediately reduce the temperature to 160°C/320°F/gas mark 3 and bake for 35–45 minutes, until they are beautifully golden and sound hollow when tapped underneath. Cool on a wire rack.

Gather six strands of
dough and pinch the
tops together

Move the right strand
to cross over to the
left

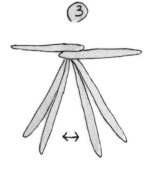

Take the second
strand from the left
and cross over to the
right. Leave a gap in
the centre.

Move the left strand
down to the centre
gap

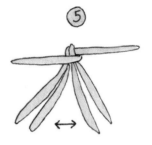

Take the second
strand from the right
and move to the left.
Leave a gap in the
centre.

Move the right strand
to the centre gap

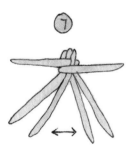

Take the second
strand from the left
and cross over to the
right. Leave a gap in
the centre.

Move the left strand
down to the gap in
the centre

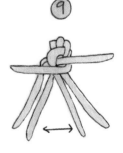

Take the second
strand from the right
and cross to the
left. Leave a gap in
the centre.

REPEAT FROM STEP 6 UNTIL THE PLAIT IS COMPLETE

Australian Damper

Damper, also called bush bread, was the staple bread of the Australian settlers, made from just three ingredients and usually cooked over an open campfire, either in the embers or in a pot oven with hot coals on top as well as underneath. It was eaten slathered with butter and golden syrup (called Cocky's Joy in Australia).

MAKES 1 LOAF

- 400g self-raising flour (or 400g plain flour plus 1 tablespoon baking powder)
- 1 teaspoon salt
- 300ml cold or tepid milk (or 150ml milk mixed with 150ml water - originally this was made with water)

Preheat the oven to 220°C/430°F/gas mark 7.

Sieve the flour and salt into a wide bowl. Make a well in the centre, pour in the milk (or milk and water) and mix until it comes together into a dough. Turn out onto a floured board. Tidy around the edges to form a round, then flip it over and flatten slightly to about 5cm. Transfer to a baking tray. Score the top deeply to make four, six or eight wedges or leave unscored.

Bake in the preheated oven for 20 minutes, then reduce the temperature to 180°C/350°F/gas mark 4 and bake for a further 10–15 minutes, until the loaf is golden brown and the base sounds hollow when tapped. (Alternatively, you can cook the bread in a bastible or casserole – see page 43). Enjoy slathered with butter and golden syrup.

Simit

These crunchy, braided, ring-shaped breads are the most famous street food in Turkey. The texture is soft and chewy inside, crunchy but nutty on the first bite. They are sometimes referred to as Turkish bagels in the US.

MAKES 6

....

- 500g strong white flour
- 2 tablespoons instant yeast
- 1 teaspoon dairy salt
- 300ml warm water

....

COATING:
- 110ml molasses or date or grape pekmez
- 50ml water
- 1 tablespoon plain flour
- 300g sesame seeds

Sieve the flour into a large mixing bowl, then sprinkle in the yeast and salt. Combine well. Gradually add the water and mix to a dough. Allow to sit for 2–3 minutes, then knead until smooth and elastic, about 5 minutes. Alternatively, use a food mixer with a dough hook. Cover and allow to rise in a warm, draught-free place for 1–1½ hours, until doubled in size.

Meanwhile, prepare the coating. Whisk the molasses, water and flour in a medium-sized bowl and keep aside.

Toast the sesame seeds over a medium heat in a wide pan for a few minutes, stirring occasionally, until they begin to smell toasty. Turn into a wide bowl.

When the dough has risen, knock it back and knead for 1–2 minutes. Shape into a log, cut into four, then divide each piece into three.

Take two pieces and cover the rest. Roll each into a 50cm length. Pinch the ends together, then twist to make a braid. Form into a coil and pinch the ends together to seal. Repeat with the rest of the dough.

Pinch the ends →

Twist

Form into a coil and pinch the ends

Dip the simit into the coating thoroughly. Shake off the excess, then coat with the toasted sesame seeds. Transfer to a parchment-lined baking tray. Allow to rise for a further 20–30 minutes.

Preheat the oven to 220°C/430°F/gas mark 7.

Bake in the preheated oven for 15–20 minutes, until golden and crusty. Cool on a wire rack.

Shokupan (Japanese Milk Bread)

My daughter-in-law Rachel kindly shared this recipe with me from her cookbook *Soup, Broth, Bread*, published by Penguin Random House (Michael Joseph). This is a Japanese tear-and-share bread with the most wonderful pillowy, soft texture. It's inspired by the yudane and tangzhong method, where a little bit of flour and water or milk (both, in this case) are cooked together to make a white sauce before mixing in the remaining ingredients. This method pre-gelatinises the starch in the flour, allowing it to absorb more liquid and giving you a super-light bread that stays fresh for longer, as it retains its moisture.

I weigh all the ingredients for this bread, including the liquid, as it's very precise. It is also divine with cinnamon, dried fruit and/or candied peel added as a sweet treat.

MAKES 1 × 23CM
TEAR-AND-SHARE LOAF
OR 2 × 450G LOAVES
....

TANGZHONG:
- 50g water
- 50g milk
- 15g strong white flour
....

DOUGH:
- 375g strong white flour
- 25g caster sugar
- 15g milk powder
- 1 teaspoon salt
- 115g milk
- 1 egg, beaten
- 25g fresh yeast (or 12g dried yeast)
- 50g butter, melted, plus extra for greasing
....

EGG WASH:
- 1 egg, whisked, for brushing the top
- a pinch of salt

To make the tangzhong, pour the water and milk into a small saucepan and bring to the boil. Add the 15g of strong white flour and cook, whisking all the time, over the heat for a couple of minutes, until the liquid has thickened to a white sauce. Tip every bit out of the saucepan into a bowl and set aside to cool.

To make the dough, put the 375g of strong white flour in a mixing bowl, or the bowl of a stand mixer fitted with the dough hook, along with the sugar, milk powder and salt. Mix these ingredients so that the yeast doesn't go directly on the salt, as this can kill the yeast.

Now put the milk (no need to heat it) in a separate bowl or a jug and add the beaten egg, the yeast, the melted butter and the cooled tangzhong mixture. Stir, then pour all this liquid into the dry ingredients and mix to a dough. Knead the mixture for 8–10 minutes by hand or for 5–6 minutes in the machine, until you have a smooth, almost springy dough. It's not necessary to add flour while you're kneading, as the dough is supposed to be slightly sticky. If you're kneading by hand and the dough is sticking to your hands, just gather it up into a ball and clean the work surface with the help of a dough scraper or a palette knife, then flour your hands and continue to knead. When I'm using a stand mixer for this, I scrape down the sides of the bowl a couple of times during kneading.

When the dough has been kneaded enough, it will be smooth on the outside. Press it with a floured finger and the dent that you make with your finger should spring back a little bit.

Put the dough in a bowl that's large enough to take it when doubled in size (or leave it in the stand mixer bowl) and cover the bowl with a clean tea towel, cling film or a plate. Put it somewhere warm, not above 45°C/113°F, or just stand it on the counter in your kitchen and allow the dough to double in size – this may take 2 hours. If you wish, you can put the covered bowl of dough in the fridge overnight.

When the dough has doubled in size, punch the dough down to knock it back using a floured fist, then knead it for just 1 minute. Now it's time to shape the dough into either a tear-and-share loaf or two 450g loaves.

If you're making a tear-and-share loaf, brush the inside of a 23cm or 25cm springform tin with melted butter, then dust it with flour. Divide the dough into eight equal pieces, each weighing about 90g. Keep all the dough covered with a clean tea towel while you work with one piece at a time.

Put one ball of dough on a very lightly floured work surface. Fold the edges all the way round into the centre of the ball of dough, squashing it down in the centre as you go. Turn the ball over so that the folded side is on the bottom and the smooth side is on top. Roll the ball gently under the palm of your hand to make a round roll, then put it in the prepared tin. Repeat with all the other balls of dough so that you end up with seven around the sides, spaced apart, and one ball in the centre.

If you're making two loaves of bread, brush the inside of the loaf tins with melted butter and dust with flour. Divide the dough into six equal pieces, each weighing about 120g. Keep all the dough covered with a clean tea towel while you work with one piece at a time.

Put one ball of dough on a very lightly floured work surface. Fold the edges all the way round into the centre of the ball of dough, squashing it down in the centre as you go. Roll the ball of dough, with a light dusting of flour to stop it sticking, into an oval about 20cm long. Fold in the left side and the right side (of the long sides) into the centre so that it looks like an envelope. Starting at one of the short ends, roll the dough away from you or towards you to make a short roll. Place this smooth side up in the loaf tin, with the 'swirled' sides next to the long sides of the tin. Repeat with two more balls of dough, placing them next to each other in the tin. Repeat with the remaining three pieces of dough to make the second loaf.

Cover the tins with a tea towel again and place on the work surface or somewhere a little warmer, but again not above 45°C/113°F, and allow to rise again for 35–45 minutes, until almost doubled in size.

Preheat the oven to 200°C/400°F/gas mark 6.

The dough is ready when you make a little dent with a floured finger and it doesn't spring back. Also, the balls of dough should have joined together at this stage.

Whisk the egg with a pinch of salt and brush it gently over the top of the risen bread. Put the bread in the lower part of the preheated oven to bake for 30–40 minutes. The bread should sound hollow when you tap it on the base. If you wish, you can bake the bread out of the tin for the last 5 minutes of the cooking time. Cool on a wire rack.

Conchas

These are sweet fluffy rolls with a scallop pattern on top – the word *concha* means shell. Recipes vary, but this one is based on Diana Kennedy's version, which she told me about when we visited her at her home in Michoacán, Mexico. Conchas are the most iconic of the Mexican pan dulce that are such a beloved part of a Mexican breakfast. I still dream of the delicious fluffy conchas I ate at Le Cardinale in Mexico City with nata de leche (milk skin) and a foamy cup of Mexican hot chocolate. Toppings vary in Mexico but I've included my favourite cinnamon flavour here.

MAKES 16

STARTER:
- 15g fresh yeast or 6g dried yeast
- 50g tepid water, approx.
- 225g strong flour, plus extra for the bowl
- 2 large eggs, lightly beaten

DOUGH:
- 450g strong white flour, plus extra for kneading
- 125g + 50g caster sugar, kept separate
- 40g unsalted butter, softened
- 4 large eggs, lightly beaten
- 75ml tepid water, approx.
- ½ teaspoon sea salt

TOPPING:
- 110g plain flour
- 110g icing sugar
- 15g ground cinnamon
- 100g unsalted butter, softened

Grease and flour a baking tray.

To make the starter, crumble the yeast into a small bowl with the tepid water, stir and allow to activate for 3–4 minutes.

Sieve the flour into the bowl of a food mixer. Add the yeast mixture and eggs to the flour and beat with a dough hook for about 2 minutes. The dough should be soft and sticky. Add a little more flour (5–10g) around the edge of the bowl and beat for 30–60 seconds longer so that the dough comes away from the sides of the bowl.

Sprinkle the work surface generously with flour, then scrape the starter out onto it and allow it to rest for a minute or two. Flour your hands and lightly pat the dough into a 10cm round. Transfer to the greased and floured baking tray and make three diagonal slashes on the top. Cover with dampened parchment paper, and set aside in a very cool oven (80°C/176°F is ideal) for 1–1½ hours, until doubled in size.

Divide the starter dough into two equal halves (weigh to make sure – it should be 180g approx.). Tear one part into pieces and put into the bowl of the mixer. Store the other half of the starter in a covered jar in the fridge or freeze it for another batch of conchas.

To make the main dough, add all the ingredients to the starter dough except for the 50g of sugar. Beat with a dough hook at medium-high speed for about 5 minutes. Add the rest of the sugar and beat for another 5–10 minutes, until the dough is soft and sticky with a shiny surface. It should form a cohesive mass on the dough hook. Sprinkle a little more flour (10g) around the edge of the bowl to help the dough come away from the sides.

Turn the dough out onto a floured surface and quickly pat it into a round cushion shape. Oil the bowl and put the dough inside it. Cover the bowl with a clean tea towel and set aside in a warm place for about 2 hours, until it has doubled in size. At the end of the rising period, put the covered bowl, with the towel, into the coolest part of your fridge and leave it to rise overnight (or up to 16 hours).

Shortly before the end of the proving period, prepare the topping. Sieve the flour, sugar and cinnamon together into a bowl. Cut the butter into small pieces and rub it into the mixture, then mix to a smooth dough. Set aside and cover so it doesn't dry out.

Turn the concha dough out onto a floured worktop and quickly form it into a roll. Divide into four equal portions, then divide each portion into four again so that you have 16 pieces in all (70g each approx.).

Line two baking trays with parchment paper and brush lightly with vegetable oil.

Roll each piece of dough into a ball (6cm diameter), then flatten it slightly onto the oiled tray. Allow 7.5cm of space between each ball to allow for expansion.

Roll out the topping and stamp into 7.5cm circles (use a tortilla press if you have one). Dust your palm again and press a piece of topping firmly onto each ball of dough. If you own a Mexican decorative concha cutter, mark the top of each one. Alternatively, trace a scallop pattern on each one with the back of a knife. Leave to rise for 2–2½ hours.

Press topping firmly onto each ball of dough

Trace a scallop pattern

Preheat the oven to 190°C/375°F/gas mark 5. Set two racks in the top part of the oven to preheat too.

When the conchas have risen, bake them in the preheated oven for 14–15 minutes, until they are browned slightly around the edge of the topping and are springy to the touch. Cool on a wire rack. These are best eaten on the day with a mug of hot chocolate.

SCONES

Considering how quick they are to make and bake, it can be surprisingly difficult to find a really delicious scone in a café or tea room. The basic recipe here for Grandma's sweet white scones is a gem, the one and only recipe you'll ever need. Once you master this, you can do endless variations on the original.

Stamp them into rounds, cut them into triangles, make teenie weenies or 'one-bite' scones; brush the tops with egg wash and dip the surface into chopped nuts or seeds, in coarse granulated or Demerara sugar, or sugar and spice for crunchy tops. Scones can be savoury or sweet, but in this chapter I have given lots of variations on sweet scones.

These scones are a big part of my childhood memories. There were nine of us children and we squabbled over the sugary tops as Mum took yet another tray of her delicious scones out of the oven when we dashed excitedly into the kitchen after school.

Many others around the country have similar memories of Mrs O'Connell's scones at The Sportsman's Inn, where mum cooked tray after tray of scones in our family pub in Cullohill – a perfect pit stop to look forward to on the original 'main road' from Dublin to Cork.

Because of the high baking powder content, scones stale quickly. They are best eaten fresh or within a few hours of being baked – or certainly on the same day. Leftover scones make a delicious scone and butter pudding (page 284).

A FEW TIPS

Scone mixture can be weighed ahead, even the day before. Butter may be rubbed in, but do not add the raising agent and liquid until just before baking.

When making a batch of scones, add all the liquid together and mix quickly. Turn the dough out on a floured worktop. Do not knead – just gently flatten to the precise thickness for the size of scone you are making. I don't want to sound prissy, but if the dough is too thick, the scones will topple over and be undercooked in the middle; too thin and they'll be out of proportion, all crust and not enough tender crumb in the centre.

Tempting as it is, don't use a food processor to 'rub' in the butter. The scones will be heavy rather than light and fluffy.

Scones made from the first rolling are always the best, so if you fancy traditional round scones, stamp them out with a plain or crinkled cutter so there is minimum dough left to re-roll. Alternatively, do what Mum did: shape the dough into a square or rectangle and just cut it with a knife so there's no dough to re-roll.

In the US scones are usually triangle-shaped, so if you like, form the dough into a couple of circles and cut into wedges so there's no waste and no need to re-roll here either.

Dried, fresh or candied fruit, nuts, spices or fresh herbs can also be added to the dry ingredients. It's also fun to drizzle or fully ice the tops, as they often do in the US with delicious results.

Grandma's Sweet White Scones

The trick to these sweet white scones is to make sure that the butter is really chilled so that it breaks and crumbles into the flour to give the scones their extra-special light texture.

MAKES 18-20 SCONES USING
A 7.5CM CUTTER
....

- 900g plain flour
- 50g caster sugar
- 3 heaped teaspoons
  (60g) baking powder
- pinch of salt
- 175g butter, cut
  into small cubes and
  chilled
- 3 eggs
- 450ml full-fat milk
  (approx.)
- egg wash (page 325)
- 75g crunchy Demerara
  sugar or coarse
  granulated sugar
  (approx.), for the
  tops of the scones
....

TO SERVE:
- homemade jam
- whipped cream or
  butter

Preheat the oven to 250°C/480°F/gas mark 9.

Sieve all the dry ingredients together into a large, wide bowl. Toss the chilled butter cubes in the flour and rub them in by hand until the mixture resembles coarse breadcrumbs.

Make a well in the centre. Whisk the eggs with the milk, then add to the dry ingredients in one go and mix to a soft dough.

Turn the dough out onto a floured worktop. Don't knead, but shape just enough to make a round. Roll out to about 2.5cm thick and cut or stamp into scones. Try to stamp them out with as little waste as possible, as the first scones will be lighter than the second rolling.

For the topping, brush the tops of the scones with egg wash, then dip each one in crunchy Demerara or coarse granulated sugar.

Put the scones on two baking trays – no need to grease. Bake on the middle shelf of the preheated oven for 10 minutes, until golden brown on top. Cool on a wire rack.

Serve split in half with homemade jam and a blob of whipped cream or just butter and jam.

Little Dotes

Mini anything seems to have a special appeal and these little dotes disappear like hot cakes! Follow the master recipe but roll out the dough until it's 2cm thick, then stamp out with a 4cm cutter and bake for 8–10 minutes.

Fruit Scones

Add 50g plump sultanas to the above mixture after the butter has been rubbed in.

Lexia Raisin and Rosemary Scones

Add 50g Lexia raisins and ½–1 tablespoon chopped fresh rosemary to the basic recipe.

Cherry Scones	Add 50g quartered natural glacé cherries to the basic mixture after the butter has been rubbed in.
Craisin Scones or Dried Cherry Scones	Substitute 50g craisins or dried cherries for cherries.
Crystallised Ginger Scones	Add 50g chopped crystallised or drained ginger in syrup to the dry ingredients.
Candied Citrus Peel Scones	Add 50g best-quality candied orange and lemon peel (or see the recipe for homemade peel on page 298) to the dry ingredients after the butter has been rubbed in. Coat the citrus peel well in the flour before adding the liquid.
Sugar and Spice Scones	Add 2 teaspoons freshly ground cinnamon to the dry ingredients in the basic mixture. Mix ½ teaspoon ground cinnamon with 25g granulated sugar. Dip the tops of the scones in the cinnamon sugar after brushing with egg wash instead of Demerara or granulated sugar before baking.
Poppy Seed Scones	Add 2 tablespoons poppy seeds to the dry ingredients after the butter has been rubbed in. Serve with coarsely crushed strawberries and cream.
Chocolate Chip Scones	Chop 50g best-quality chocolate and add to the dry ingredients after the butter has been rubbed in.
Strawberry, Raspberry or Blueberry Scones	Add 50g chopped fresh strawberries or whole raspberries or blueberries to the dry ingredients and increase the sugar by 10g.
Blackberry and Sweet Geranium Scones	Add 50–110g wild blackberries and 2 tablespoons chopped sweet geranium to the dry ingredients.
Peach Scones	Add 2 diced peaches and 1 tablespoon freshly chopped mint to the dry ingredients.
White Chocolate and Raspberry Scones	Add 40g roughly chopped white chocolate and 40g raspberries to the basic mixture after the butter has been rubbed in.

Rosemary and Ginger Scones	Add 1½ teaspoons chopped fresh rosemary and 2 teaspoons peeled and grated fresh ginger to the dry ingredients.
Christmas Mincemeat Scones with Brandy Butter	Add 225g mincemeat (vegetarian, no suet) to the dry ingredients and toss well to distribute evenly through the flour before adding the liquid. Serve warm with brandy butter (page 309). These can also be cooked as tear-and-share scones in a tin.
Christmas Tree Bread or Valentine's Day Heart	White yeast bread (page 52), white soda bread (page 26) or a scone mixture can be used to make a fir tree or heart shape. Make the dough as per the recipe but stamp out 24 scones from a 900g batch of dough. Brush with the egg wash and dip the tops in Demerara sugar, then arrange as shown below on a baking tray and bake for 10 minutes, until golden brown on top.

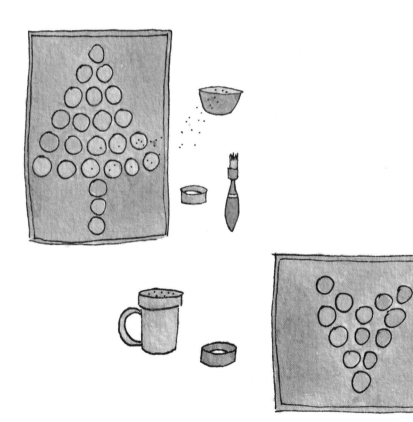

Shamrock Scones

We make these to celebrate St Patrick's Day. White yeast bread (page 52), white soda bread (page 26) or the sweet scone dough in the basic recipe above may be used here. Use three scones to make a shamrock shape plus a little stem. Glaze with egg wash and use green granulated sugar if available – naff but fun.

Iced Coffee Walnut Scones

These are inspired by US scones, which are often cut into rectangular wedges and iced. Walnut and coffee is a delicious combo, as is coffee and pecan, but how about lemon, pistachio and rose petals, perfumed with a little rosewater or orange blossom water? Or maybe roasted almonds and mint? Or Meyer lemon and blueberries?

Make a half batch of scones (don't forget the pinch of salt!). Add 50g coarsely chopped walnuts to the dry ingredients. Continue as in the master recipe. Roll into a rectangle approx. 20.5cm long × 18cm wide × 2.5cm thick. Cut in half lengthwise, then cut again into 10–12 rectangles. Brush with egg wash and bake as in the master recipe.

While the scones are cooking, make the coffee icing. Sieve 225g icing sugar into a medium-sized mixing bowl. Add 2–3 teaspoons Camp coffee essence and stir in 2 tablespoons (approx.) boiling water a little at a time, until the icing is silky-smooth but not too runny. When the scones have cooked, spread the top of each scone generously with the icing. Top with coarsely chopped walnuts or one walnut half.

Hot Cross Scones

I've taken a bit of liberty here – hot cross buns are normally made with a yeast dough, as on page 228, but this scone version gets rave reviews.

MAKES 9-10

- 450g plain flour
- 40g caster sugar
- 3 rounded teaspoons baking powder
- 2 teaspoons mixed spice
- 1 teaspoon freshly ground cinnamon
- ½ teaspoon freshly grated nutmeg
- pinch of salt
- 175g butter, cut into cubes and chilled
- 75g sultanas
- 50g currants
- 50g candied peel (page 298 or shop-bought), diced
- 2 medium eggs
- 200-225ml full-fat milk
- egg wash (page 325)
- Demerara sugar, for the tops of the scones

LEMON ICING:
- 110g icing sugar
- zest of ½-1 lemon
- 1 tablespoon (approx.) freshly squeezed lemon juice

Preheat the oven to 250°C/480°F/gas mark 9.

Put the dry ingredients in a large bowl. Rub in the cold butter cubes until the mixture resembles coarse breadcrumbs. Add the fruit and candied peel and mix well to distribute evenly.

Make a well in the centre of the dry ingredients. Whisk the eggs and milk together in a jug, then pour nearly all the mixture into the flour. Using one hand with the fingers open and stiff, mix in a full circle, drawing in the flour from the sides of the bowl, adding more milk and egg if necessary to bring the ingredients gently together into a soft dough.

Turn the dough out onto a floured work surface. Gently roll out the scone dough to about 2cm thick. Using a metal 8cm dough cutter lightly dusted with flour, stamp the dough into scones. Brush the tops of the scones with egg wash and dip in Demerara sugar.

Place the scones on a lightly floured baking sheet. Bake in the preheated oven for 10 minutes, until golden brown. Cool on a wire rack.

Meanwhile, to make the icing, sieve the icing sugar into a medium-sized bowl. Mix in the lemon zest and juice, being careful not to make it too liquid. Spoon the icing into a piping bag with a thin piping nozzle.

When the scones are almost cool, pipe a thickish cross over the top of each one. Enjoy while warm, split and slathered with butter.

Crunchy Orange Butter Swirls

We sometimes call these Oh My Gods – the reaction when people taste them, still warm from the oven.

If you wish, make 900g scone dough and make half into scones (cut into scones about 4.5cm thick), served with a little orange butter, and the remainder into these swirls. We love these swirls and continue to add to our repertoire of variations. Check out the suggestions at the end of this recipe and add more of your own.

MAKES 18

....

- 900g plain flour
- 50g caster sugar
- 60g baking powder
- pinch of salt
- rind of 1 orange
- 175g butter, cut into cubes and chilled, plus extra soft butter for greasing (optional)
- 3 eggs
- 450ml full-fat milk (approx.)
- egg wash (page 325)
- 50g Demerara sugar, for the tops of the scones

....

ORANGE BUTTER:
- 175g butter, softened, plus extra for greasing
- 3 teaspoons finely grated orange rind (I like to use organic oranges when available)
- 200g icing sugar, sieved

Preheat the oven 250°C/480°F/gas mark 9. If using tins, grease two rectangular tins (33cm × 23cm × 5cm) with soft butter.

First make the orange butter. Cream the butter with the finely grated orange rind. Add the sieved icing sugar and beat until fluffy.

To make the scone dough, sieve the flour into a large, wide bowl. Add the sugar, baking powder and a pinch of salt. Grate the orange rind on the finest part of the grater over the dry ingredients in the bowl. Mix the dry ingredients with your hands, lifting up to incorporate air and mix thoroughly.

Toss the butter cubes in the flour to coat. Using the tips of your fingers, rub in the butter until it resembles large flakes.

Make a well in the centre. Whisk the eggs with the milk, then pour this into the centre all at once. With the fingers of your 'best' hand outstretched and stiff, mix in a full circular movement from the centre to the outside of the bowl. This takes just seconds and hey presto! The scone dough is made.

Turn out the dough onto a lightly floured board or work surface. Scrape the dough off your fingers and wash and dry your hands at this point. Tidy the edges, flip the dough over and roll or pat gently into a rectangle about 2cm thick × 45cm long.

Slather most of the orange butter evenly over the scone dough, then roll the dough up tightly from the long side. Divide into six, then divide each piece again into three swirls to give 18 altogether.

Brush the tops of the swirls with the egg wash, then dip the tops in the Demerara sugar. Divide between the two greased baking tins, spaced fairly close together and cut sides up. Bake in the preheated oven for 10–12 minutes, until golden brown on top.

Alternatively, bake half of the dough in a rectangular greased or parchment-lined tin (33cm × 23cm × 5cm) and bake the rest on a baking tray. Arrange nine in each tin, allowing a little space between each one. Bake for 15–17 minutes. Cool in the tin for a few minutes.

Serve while still warm or at room temperature with a little extra orange butter. Pull apart gently if you've made these as a tear-and-share. The only problem is knowing when to stop eating …

Orange Blossom Swirls	Add 1–3 teaspoons orange blossom water (depending on intensity) to the orange butter.
Chocolate and Hazelnut Swirls	Substitute chocolate and hazelnut spread (page 295) for the orange butter. Brush the cut tops with egg wash and sprinkle with toasted hazelnuts.
Marmalade Swirls	Substitute marmalade (chop the peel finely first) for the orange butter.
Rhubarb and Ginger Swirls	Substitute new season rhubarb and ginger jam for the orange butter.
Jammy Swirls	Use any of your favourite jams and maybe a few fresh berries instead of the orange butter. Serve with a blob of softly whipped cream.
Sri Lankan Cinnamon Butter Swirls	Mix together 250g light brown sugar, 150g softened butter and 1 tablespoon Sri Lankan ground cinnamon. Make the dough and roll it out as in the main recipe but slather it with this cinnamon butter. Brush the cut tops with egg wash and dip in cinnamon sugar (25g granulated or Demerara sugar mixed with 1 teaspoon ground cinnamon).

SWEET BREADS

A little of what you fancy! This section includes many of my favourite sweet pastries and viennoiseries. It was such a challenge to decide what to include, but I certainly wanted to share our favourite croissant and brioche recipes as well as some cakes and a multipurpose laminated dough that can be used for a myriad of different delicious pastries.

The quality and freshness of the basic ingredients is always important, but more than ever in this chapter. Carefully source the best-quality butter, eggs, dried fruit, nuts and spices. Choose the type of flour that is best suited to each bread. Strong flour (sometimes referred to as baker's flour), with its high gluten content, is what you need for yeast breads, whereas cakes, biscuits and pastries are best made with plain (all-purpose) flour, which is lower in gluten. Self-raising flour already includes a raising agent, but make sure it's not stale, otherwise it may have lost its mojo and may produce a disappointingly heavy result.

If you're going to take the time to bake something, it ought to be delicious, so spend a few extra minutes to taste the nuts to ensure that they are fresh, not rancid, and that the dried fruit is plump and juicy. Use fresh spices and grind them yourself for extra deliciousness. Seek out really good-quality chocolate with a high cocoa butter content (at least 50%). Use freshly grated citrus zest and freshly squeezed orange or lemon juice rather than something that squirts out of a plastic container.

Butter is essential for flavour and texture rather than margarine or another hard white cooking fat. Here in Ireland we can grow grass like nowhere else in the world, so our dairy products, including our butter, which now contains less than 2% salt, is superb quality. We use salted butter unless stated otherwise in a recipe. If you are using unsalted butter you will need to add a pinch of salt to the recipe, otherwise the end result will be bland.

I'm also a big fan of lard, rendered from the fat of well-reared pigs. It gives a wonderful texture and flavour to some pastry and cakes. However, don't include it unless you have access to really good-quality lard (see page 323 on how to make it yourself).

Jen and Lili's All-Purpose Laminated Dough

This is a gem of a recipe. There is no end to the variations you can make once you have mastered the original. This recipe makes enough dough for six croissants, 10 pains au chocolat, 12 cinnamon swirls, 12 savoury swirls, 12 rhubarb and custard pastries, 12 kouign-amann or five cruffins.

MAKES 1KG

....

- 18g fresh yeast
- 50g granulated sugar
- 200g tepid water
- 50g butter, melted
- 425g strong white flour
- 8g salt
- 313g salted butter, cold but pliable

Crumble the fresh yeast into a small bowl. Add the sugar, tepid water and melted butter. Allow to sit for 8–10 minutes, until the yeast activates (bubbles slightly).

Put the flour and salt in a large bowl. Add the yeast mixture, then mix by hand to a soft dough. Rest for 10 minutes. Lightly bring the dough together with your hands to tighten it into a smooth, round ball. Cover and allow to rise in a warm, draught-free area in the kitchen until it doubles in size. This can take up to 1 hour.

Roll the cold butter between two sheets of greaseproof paper to approx. 20cm square.

Flour the worktop and roll the risen dough into a square approx. 40cm × 40cm. Place the square of butter in the centre of the dough and fold the dough over the butter. Press gently to seal the edges.

Make the first lamination. Flour the worktop lightly and roll the dough into a rectangle. Brush off any excess flour and fold in three lengthwise. Give the dough a 90° turn, then seal the open edges with a rolling pin. Re-roll the dough towards the open end into a rectangle. Fold in three once again. Cover tightly with parchment paper. Refrigerate for 1 hour. Repeat this process, cover and refrigerate the dough overnight.

The dough is now ready to use in any number of recipes.

Fold in three lengthwise

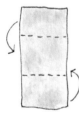

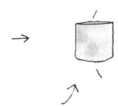

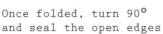

Once folded, turn 90° and seal the open edges

Re-roll the dough into a rectangle

Rhubarb and Custard Pastries

A gorgeous combination, but vary the fruit with the season – try green gooseberry and elderflower; plum, greengage or damson with bay; pear with cardamom and saffron …

....

- 1 batch of laminated dough (page 186)
- egg wash (page 325)
- 5 stalks of rhubarb, cut into 4cm pieces
- 70g caster sugar
- 490g crème pâtissière (page 301)
- icing sugar, for dusting

Roll the dough out until it's 0.75cm thick, 23cm wide and 30.5cm long. Use a ruler or a 7.5cm square cutter to cut out squares. You should get approx. 12 in total (three across and four down).

Flip over each square, brush off any excess flour and put it on a baking tray lined with greaseproof paper. Brush each square with egg wash. Stamp the centre of each square with a 4cm square cutter halfway through the dough.

Allow to rise for 30–60 minutes in a warm, draught-free place (above an oven is best), until at least doubled in size.

Meanwhile, toss the rhubarb in the caster sugar.

Preheat the oven to 220°C/430°F/gas mark 7.

When the pastries have risen, brush them with egg wash again. Using a piping bag, pipe approx. 10g of crème pâtissière (about the size of a large walnut) into the small square of each risen pastry. Arrange three pieces of sugared rhubarb on top of the crème pâtissière on each pastry.

Bake the pastries in the preheated oven for approx. 20 minutes. Consider dropping the temperature to 200°C/400°F/gas mark 6 once the pastries are golden brown. Cool on a wire rack before dusting lightly with icing sugar.

Ballymaloe Croissants

Who doesn't get an oops in their tummy when you take a tray of flaky, burnished croissants out of the oven? Start the dough one day and have them ready for breakfast the next morning.

MAKES 6 REGULAR-SIZED
CROISSANTS AND 2 SMALL
ONES
....

— 1 batch of laminated
  dough (page 186)
— egg wash (page 325)

Lightly flour the work surface. Roll the dough into a rectangle measuring approx. 20cm × 45cm. Brush away any excess flour. Measure and cut into triangles as shown in the diagram.

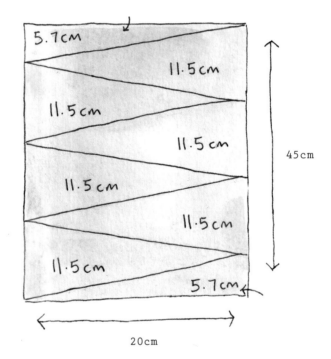

5.7cm

11.5cm

11.5cm

11.5cm

11.5cm

11.5cm

11.5cm

5.7cm

45cm

20cm

Line a baking tray with greaseproof paper. Stretch and roll each triangle tightly from the wide end to the narrow tip. Arrange on the baking tray with the tip tucked underneath. Brush with well-beaten egg wash. Allow to rise for 1 hour in a warm, draught-free place (above an oven is best).

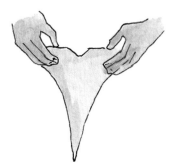

Cut a small notch in the short edge and stretch out the corners

Stretch and roll each triangle tightly from the wide end to the narrow tip

Tuck the tip underneath

Preheat the oven to 200°C/400°F/gas mark 6.

Brush carefully with egg wash once again. Bake in the preheated oven for 20–25 minutes, until well risen and a deep, burnished golden brown. Cool on a wire rack.

Pain au Chocolat

Use the best chocolate sticks – we buy ours from Valrhona.

MAKES 10

....

- 1 batch of laminated dough (page 186)
- 20 chocolate sticks
- egg wash (page 325)

Flour the worktop lightly. Roll the dough into a rectangle measuring approx. 20cm × 45cm. Brush away any excess flour. Cut the rectangle into 10 pieces measuring 9cm × 10cm, as shown in the diagram.

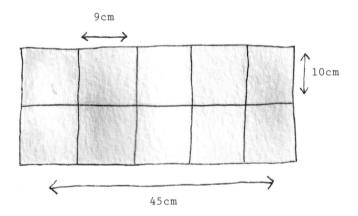

9cm

10cm

45cm

Place a chocolate stick at each end of the dough square. Roll each end into the centre and place each piece open side down on a baking tray lined with greaseproof paper Brush with well-beaten egg wash. Continue with the rest of the dough. Leave to rise for 1 hour near a warm, draught-free place (above a warm oven is best).

1 Place a chocolate
   stick at each end of
   the dough square

2 Roll each end into
   the centre

3 Place each piece open
   side down on a baking
   tray and brush with
   well-beaten egg wash

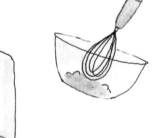

Preheat the oven to 200°C/400°F/gas mark 6.

Carefully and evenly brush with egg wash again. Bake
in the preheated oven for 10 minutes, then reduce the
temperature to 180°C/350°F/gas mark 4 and bake for a
further 10–15 minutes, until well risen and golden. Cool
on a wire rack.

Cinnamon Swirls

Who doesn't love a cinnamon swirl? But make sure to use pure cinnamon (*Cinnamomum verum*) from Sri Lanka or Mexico, not faux cinnamon or cassis (*Cinnamomum cassia*), which has a more acrid flavour. Powdered cinnamon is almost always adulterated, so for best results, grind and sieve your own.

- 1 batch of laminated dough (page 186)
- 75g butter, softened, plus extra melted butter for greasing
- 100g soft light brown sugar, plus extra for sprinkling
- 1 tablespoon ground cinnamon

Lightly flour the worktop. Roll the dough into a rectangle measuring approx. 20cm × 56cm. Brush away any excess flour.

Cream the butter, brown sugar and cinnamon together until soft, light and spreadable.

With a palette knife, spread the soft cinnamon butter evenly over the dough, all the way to the edges. Roll tightly from the wide end like a Swiss roll. Cut in half, then quarters. Cut each quarter into three even-sized swirls to get a total of 12 pieces.

Spread the butter evenly over the dough

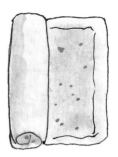

Roll tightly like a Swiss roll

Grease a muffin tray with melted butter. Put one piece of dough into each compartment. Sprinkle each with soft light brown sugar. Allow to rise for 30–60 minutes in a warm, draught-free place, until they are soft and puffy (above an oven is best).

Preheat the oven to 200°C/400°F/gas mark 6.

Bake in the preheated oven for 20–25 minutes, until the swirls are a rich golden colour. Remove from the tin immediately and serve bottoms up. These are best served freshly baked.

Cardamom Swirls	Substitute ½–1 tablespoon ground cardamom for the cinnamon in the butter and proceed as above.
Savoury Swirls	Substitute the cinnamon butter with a savoury filling. We love this combination but experiment with your own. Sprinkle 150g grated Gruyère cheese, 60g chorizo cut into 1cm cubes, 60g ripe tomatoes cut into 1cm pieces and 1–2 tablespoons of finely chopped fresh chives over the dough. Roll up tightly, cut into 12 pieces and leave to rise, as above. Bake in the preheated oven for 18–20 minutes.

Kouign-Amann

Kouign-amann, an unusual favourite, is a multi-layered Breton pastry made with laminated dough with lots of butter and sugar.

MAKES 12

....

- 1 batch of laminated dough (page 186)
- 200g caster sugar
- 50g butter, melted
- 75g granulated sugar

Roll the dough out until it's 0.5cm thick, 23cm wide and 30.5cm long. Sprinkle 100g of the caster sugar onto the dough, fold it into three and roll it out again into the same width and length as above. Use a ruler or a 7.5cm square cutter to cut out squares. You should get approx. 12 in total (three across and four down).

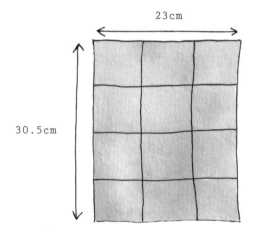

Brush the holes of a muffin tin with the melted butter and sprinkle with the granulated sugar.

Sprinkle the surface of the squares with 50g of the remaining caster sugar, fold the corners into the centre like a four-leaf clover and place into the prepared muffin tin. Sprinkle the pastries with the final 50g caster sugar and leave to rise at room temperature for 30–60 minutes, until puffy.

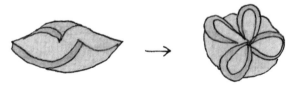

Fold the corners into the centre like a four-leaf clover

Preheat the oven to 200°C/400°F/gas mark 6.

Bake the kouign-amann in the preheated oven for 20–25 minutes, until golden brown and caramelised on the bottom.

Remove from the muffin tin and put on a wire rack but turn them upside down so they don't stick to the rack. Allow to cool slightly before eating (turn upright to serve). Kouign-amann is best eaten warm but it reheats well.

Cruffins

Another sinfully delicious version of laminated dough to enjoy with your morning coffee.

MAKES 5

....

- 1 batch of laminated dough (page 186)
- melted butter, for greasing
- caster sugar, to coat

Flour the worktop lightly. Roll the dough into a rectangle measuring approx. 45cm × 15cm. Brush away any excess flour. Cut the rectangle into 16 pieces, as shown in the diagram.

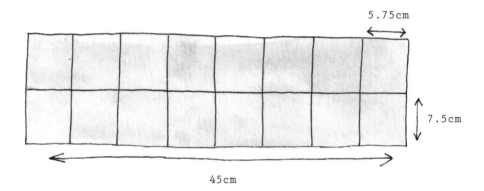

5.75cm

7.5cm

45cm

Overlap three pieces of dough per cruffin (you'll have one piece left over). Roll and pop into greased cruffin tins or dariole moulds. Leave to rise for 1 hour near a warm, draught-free place (above a warm oven is best).

Take three pieces of dough

Overlap slightly

Roll and pop into a tin

Preheat the oven to 200°C/400°F/gas mark 6.

Bake the cruffins in the preheated oven for 20–25 minutes, until golden and well risen. Allow to cool a little in the cruffin tin, then remove from the tin and toss in caster sugar to coat.

Filled Cruffins

You can eat these just as they are or you can put them back in the cruffin tin or dariole moulds and use a piping bag to fill with your desired filling. We like chocolate ganache (page 296) lemon curd (page 297), crème pâtissière (page 301) or chocolate and hazelnut spread (page 295).

Brioche

Brioche is the richest of all yeast doughs. It can often seem intimidating but this easy version works well – the dough can rise overnight in the fridge and be shaped and baked the following morning.

We serve individual brioches warm from the oven with butter and homemade strawberry jam (page 292), but you can use the dough to make loaves of brioche or add many delicious toppings – try the frangipane and almond (page 200) or butter and sugar (page 201) to start.

MAKES 15-20 INDIVIDUAL
BRIOCHES OR 2 LOAVES

....

- 25g fresh yeast
- 50g caster sugar
- 65ml tepid water
- 4 eggs
- 450g strong white flour
- large pinch of salt
- 225g butter, diced and softened, plus extra melted butter for greasing
- egg wash (page 325)

Sponge the yeast and sugar in the tepid water in the bowl of a stand mixer. Allow to stand for 4–5 minutes – it will have a creamy, slightly frothy appearance on top.

Add the eggs, flour and salt and mix to a stiff dough with the dough hook.

When the mixture is smooth, beat in the soft butter in small pieces. Don't add the next piece of butter until the previous piece has been completely absorbed. This kneading stage should be gradual and take about 30 minutes. The finished dough will have a silky appearance. It should come away from the sides of the bowl and when you touch the dough, it should be damp but not sticky.

Place in an oiled bowl, cover and rest it overnight in the fridge.

The following day, brush 15–20 individual brioche moulds or two 13cm × 20cm (450g) loaf tins with melted butter.

Working quickly, remove the chilled dough from the fridge and knock it back by folding it in on itself. It is crucial to work quickly, otherwise the butter will begin to melt and the dough will be too sticky to handle.

Weigh the dough into 50g pieces, roll into balls and drop one ball into each mould or the loaf tins. Or for a more classic brioche shape, with the side of your hand, roll each ball of dough into a teardrop shape – do this by rolling with the pressure slightly off centre. Put the dough heavy end first into the well-buttered brioche moulds. Push the 'little hat' towards the centre, leaving it just protruding above the body of the dough. Dip the thick end of a chopstick in a little flour and push it down through the dough almost to the bottom. This may sound strange, but we have found it is the best method to keep the 'little hat' in place.

With the side of your hand, roll each ball slightly off-centre to form a teardrop shape

Push the floured chopstick gently through the dough

Brush the top of each brioche gently and evenly with well-beaten egg wash. Allow the brioche to prove in a warm, draught-free place for 45–60 minutes, until doubled in size.

Preheat the oven to 180°C/350°F/gas mark 4.

Gently and evenly brush the brioche with egg wash once again. Bake in the preheated oven for 20–25 minutes for individual brioches, until they are deep golden and sound hollow when you tap the base. Large loaves will take 40–50 minutes to cook. A skewer inserted into the centre should come out clean.

Serve freshly baked with butter and homemade strawberry jam.

Frangipane and Almond Brioche

An irresistible riff on brioche.

MAKES 20-24

- melted butter, for greasing
- 1 batch of brioche dough (page 198)
- 150g flaked almonds
- icing sugar, for dusting
- warmed apricot jam, to glaze (optional)

FRANGIPANE:
- 300g ground almonds
- 200g butter, softened
- 150g caster sugar

Preheat the oven to 180°C/350°F/gas mark 4.

To make the frangipane, spread the ground almonds on a baking tray and toast in the preheated oven for 10–15 minutes, stirring frequently, until golden brown. Allow to cool. Cream the soft butter until it's soft and light, then add the caster sugar and the toasted ground almonds.

Brush two rectangular Swiss roll tins (33cm × 20.5cm × 5cm) with melted butter. Divide the brioche dough in half. Roll each half into a rectangle to fit the tins. Place in the tins and cover each with a layer of frangipane, then scatter over the flaked almonds. Allow to rise for approx. 1½ hours, until doubled in size.

Preheat the oven to 180°C/350°F/gas mark 4.

Bake the brioche in the preheated oven for 30–40 minutes, until risen and nicely golden. Sprinkle with icing sugar or brush with warmed apricot jam to glaze (optional). Cool on a wire rack, then cut into squares or rectangles. This is best eaten when freshly baked but it's also delicious the next day.

Butter and Sugar Brioche

Another irresistible variation.

MAKES 20-24
....

- 1 batch of brioche dough (page 198)
- egg wash (page 325)
- 110g butter, cut into 5mm dice, plus extra melted butter for greasing
- 110g granulated sugar

Brush two rectangular Swiss roll tins (33cm × 20.5cm × 5cm) with melted butter. Divide the brioche dough in half. Roll each into a rectangle to fit the tins. Place in the tins, brush with egg wash and allow to rise at room temperature for approx. 1½ hours, until doubled in size.

Preheat the oven to 180°C/350°F/gas mark 4.

When the dough has risen, dot the diced butter evenly over the top, then sprinkle with the granulated sugar. Bake in the preheated oven for 30–40 minutes, until risen and golden. Cool on a wire rack. This is best eaten when freshly baked but it's also delicious the next day.

Alex's Cinnamon Brioche

While still hot, dip each brioche in melted butter and toss in cinnamon sugar. Eat as soon as possible.

Blueberry Brioche

Roll 50g pieces of dough into rounds. Dot with finely diced butter, then gently press 6–8 blueberries onto each one. Sprinkle with a little sugar and bake in the oven for 15–20 minutes.

Rum Babas

Classic French Savarin and individual rum babas are having a moment again. If you make individual brioches, they can be easily converted into rum babas.

MAKES 8
....

- 8 freshly cooked
  individual brioches
  (page 198)
....

RUM SYRUP:
- 675ml water
- 250g granulated sugar
- 225ml Jamaican rum
....

TO DECORATE:
- whipped cream
- glacé cherries
- angelica
- toasted flaked almonds

To make the rum syrup, bring the water and sugar to the boil in a stainless steel saucepan. Stir until the sugar has dissolved, then allow to cool slightly and add the rum.

Put the freshly cooked individual brioches in a single layer in a deep container. Pour the hot rum syrup evenly over them. Allow the brioche to soak up all the syrup for 2½–3 hours, or better still, overnight.

To serve, put a rum baba on a plate. Decorate with whipped cream, glacé cherries, diamonds of angelica and some toasted flaked almonds.

Gingerbread

Elizabeth Mosse of Bennettsbridge, County Kilkenny, was the mother of the hugely talented Mosse family – potter, wood-turner, painter, sculptress, a gardener. Bennettsbridge House was always a warm, welcoming house and Elizabeth always had a cake and some biscuits in the tin. Once, when we arrived unexpectedly, we enjoyed this gingerbread, warm from the oven and slathered with butter, and of course she shared the recipe.

In Ireland, we bake gingerbread in a loaf tin and eat it thickly sliced and buttered. This one is particularly good when it's fresh, so eat it quickly! Alternatively, you could bake it in a 22cm square brownie tin for 40–45 minutes, then cut it into 12 squares and serve with a blob of cold apple purée and cream or with crystallised ginger cream on top. We love to make gingerbread and butter pudding with stale or leftover gingerbread (see the recipe on page 284).

MAKES 1 LOAF

- 225g plain flour
- ¾ teaspoon ground ginger
- 1 teaspoon baking powder
- ¼ teaspoon bicarbonate of soda
- ¼ teaspoon salt
- 110g soft dark brown sugar
- 175g treacle
- 75g butter, cut into cubes
- 150ml full-fat milk
- 1 very small egg, beaten
- 50g plump sultanas
- 25g chopped crystallised ginger (optional)

Preheat the oven to 180°C/350°F/gas mark 4. Line a 23cm × 12.5cm × 6.5cm loaf tin with parchment paper.

Sieve the flour, ground ginger, baking powder, bicarb and salt together in a large bowl.

Gently warm the brown sugar with the treacle and cubed butter, then add the milk. Allow to cool a little, then whisk into the dry ingredients, making sure there are no little lumps of flour left. Add the beaten egg along with the sultanas and the crystallised ginger (if using). Mix thoroughly, then transfer to the lined tin.

Bake in the preheated oven for approx. 1 hour. Cool in the tin. Serve thickly sliced with butter.

Pumpkin Spice Bread

This bread was inspired by a recipe by Sarit Packer and Itamar Srulovich from Honey & Co. that appeared in the *Weekend Financial Times*.

MAKES 1 LOAF OR
12 MUFFINS

- 190g spelt flour
- 190g soft dark brown sugar
- 100g dates, pitted and roughly chopped
- 50g crystallised ginger, chopped
- 50g hazelnuts, skinned and roughly chopped
- 50g rolled porridge oats
- 1 teaspoon ground ginger
- ¾ teaspoon bicarbonate of soda
- ½ teaspoon baking powder
- ½ teaspoon ground turmeric
- ½ teaspoon ground allspice
- ½ teaspoon freshly ground cardamom
- ¼ teaspoon salt
- 250g peeled and seeded pumpkin
- 200g butter, ghee or clarified butter (page 307), melted and cooled
- 2 large eggs, beaten

TOPPING:
- 25g hazelnuts, skinned and roughly chopped
- 15g Demerara sugar
- 10g rolled porridge oats

Preheat the oven to 180°C/350°F/gas mark 4. Line a 13cm × 20cm (450g) loaf tin with parchment paper (or grease a muffin tin).

Mix all the topping ingredients together.

Mix all the bread ingredients except the pumpkin, eggs and melted butter or ghee in a large bowl.

Grate the pumpkin using a coarse grater, then add it to the bowl along with the melted butter or ghee and the beaten eggs. Mix well to combine, then transfer to the lined loaf tin (or muffin tin). Make sure to leave some room for the bread to rise about 2–3cm below the top. Score the middle of the cake with a knife.

Sprinkle the topping all over the cake, then pop into the preheated oven to bake for approx. 1¼ hours, until springy to the touch (cover with parchment paper if the top is browning too quickly).

Allow to cool in the tin before removing. Serve thickly sliced and slathered with butter.

Banana Bread

I have always loved this moist, rich, tasty banana bread. It keeps for up to two weeks in a tin, but I doubt you will find this out as it will be gobbled up quickly. Serve it thickly sliced and spread with soft butter.

MAKES 1 LARGE LOAF

- 225g self-raising flour
- ½ level teaspoon salt
- 110g butter, diced
- 110g sultanas or seedless raisins
- 110g glacé cherries, washed and halved
- 30g chopped walnuts
- 450g very ripe bananas (weighed after peeling; see the note)
- 2 eggs

Preheat the oven to 180°C/350°F/gas mark 4. Line a 24cm × 13.5cm × 5cm loaf tin (or four small loaf tins, approx. 14.6cm × 7.6cm) with greaseproof or silicone paper.

Sieve the flour and salt into a large, wide mixing bowl, then rub in the butter. Stir in the sultanas or seedless raisins along with the glacé cherries and walnuts.

Put the bananas in a separate bowl and mash with a fork, then stir in the eggs. Stir this well into the other ingredients. The dough should have a nice soft consistency.

Pour the batter into the lined tin and spread it evenly. Place in the centre of the preheated oven and bake for 1½ hours. It is vital that the oven door is not opened during cooking or the banana bread will collapse. Cool before removing from the tin. It's even nicer served after a day or two.

NOTE: If the bananas are not very ripe, soft and squishy, you may need to add some caster sugar - maybe 110g.

Banana and Chocolate Bread

Add 60g chocolate drops (50%) to the dry mixture. Make and bake as above.

Rachel's Banana Muffins

Divide the batter between 12 regular muffin cases or 24 small muffin cases. Bake for 30 minutes in the preheated oven. Cool on a wire rack.

Cinnamon Swirl Bread

This wonderful sweet bread can be baked in a loaf or as cinnamon buns. When we make this bread, the scent of warm bread mixed with spice always entices people to the kitchen. It's a battle to keep the bread long enough to let it cool. We serve it sliced thickly. If by some miracle you have some left the next morning, it's great toasted.

MAKES 2 LOAVES OR
12-14 BUNS

....

- 25g fresh yeast
- 315ml tepid water
- 250ml tepid water
- 250ml tepid milk
- 110g granulated sugar, plus a pinch
- 70g unsalted butter, melted
- 2 eggs
- pinch of salt
- 1.2kg strong white flour

....

CINNAMON SUGAR:
- 115g light brown sugar
- 2 tablespoons ground cinnamon
- 25g unsalted butter, melted

In a small bowl, crumble the yeast into 65ml of the tepid water, sprinkle on a pinch of granulated sugar and leave to sponge for about 5 minutes. It will have a creamy, slightly frothy appearance on top.

In the bowl of a stand mixer, combine the remaining 250ml tepid water with the tepid milk, sugar, melted butter, salt, eggs and 285g flour. Beat together with the paddle attachment for 1 minute. It will be a very wet dough at this point.

Stir the sponged yeast into the ingredients in the mixer. Add the rest of the flour 1 tablespoon at a time. Switch to the dough hook attachment and mix for a few minutes, until a soft dough is formed. Rest for 5 minutes.

Knead in the bowl or turn out onto a lightly floured work surface and knead for about 5 minutes, until the dough is smooth and shiny.

Lightly oil a large, deep bowl. Put the dough in the bowl and turn it over so that it gets lightly coated with the oil. Cover and leave to rise in a warm, draught-free place for about 2 hours, until it has doubled in size.

Mix the light brown sugar and ground cinnamon in a small bowl. Set aside.

When the dough has risen fully, turn it out onto a floured surface and knock it back. Resist the temptation to work the dough any further – just divide it into two equal portions.

Roll each portion of the dough into a rectangle 23cm × 30.5cm. Brush each piece with melted butter and sprinkle evenly with the cinnamon sugar, leaving a 2.5cm border clear on all sides. Keep back 1–2 tablespoons of cinnamon sugar for dusting the top of the bread.

Begin at the narrowest edge of the dough and gently shape it into a roll.*

Pinch well along the edges and at both ends to seal in the sugar while it bakes. Put the dough into two lightly oiled loaf tins, seam side down. Brush the tops with melted butter and dust with the reserved cinnamon sugar. Cover loosely and leave to rise for 30–40 minutes, until the loaves have doubled in size.

Preheat the oven to 200°C/400°F/gas mark 6.

Bake in the centre of the preheated oven for 40 minutes. Remove from the tins and return to the oven for a further 10 minutes. Cool a little on a wire rack. This bread is excellent eaten slightly warm.

Cinnamon Buns

Follow the recipe up to the * at the end of page 206. Slice the cinnamon roll into 12–14 rounds, then arrange on one or two baking trays lined with parchment paper, allowing room for each to expand. Brush the tops with melted butter, dust with cinnamon sugar and leave to rise until doubled in size. Bake for 18–22 minutes, until puffy and golden. Cool on a wire rack.

Halloween Barmbrack

Halloween is a terrific time to have a party. In Ireland, a barmbrack is a must. The word *barm* comes from an Old English word, *beorma*, which means 'yeasted fermented liquor'. The word *brack* comes from the Irish word *breac*, meaning 'speckled' – which it is, with dried fruit and candied peel. Halloween has always been associated with fortune-telling and divination, so various objects were traditionally wrapped up and hidden in the cake mixture – a ring, a coin, a pea and a piece of cloth, which all symbolised something different. If making yeast barmbrack seems like hard work, try the tea brack on page 210.

MAKES 2 LOAVES

- 20g fresh yeast
- 75g caster sugar
- 300ml tepid milk
- 450g strong white flour
- ½ level teaspoon ground cinnamon
- ½ level teaspoon mixed spice
- ¼ teaspoon ground nutmeg
- pinch of salt
- 25g butter, diced
- 1 egg, beaten
- 225g sultanas
- 110g currants
- 50g chopped candied peel (page 298)

GLAZE:
- 1 tablespoon granulated sugar
- 2 tablespoons hot water or milk

FOR HALLOWEEN:
- a ring, a stick, a pea and a piece of cloth, all wrapped in greaseproof paper

It's a help if all your utensils are warm before you start to make barmbrack.

Mix the yeast with 1 teaspoon of the sugar and 1 teaspoon of the tepid milk in a jug. Leave for 4–5 minutes – it will have a creamy, slightly frothy appearance on top.

Sieve the flour, spices and salt into a large bowl, then rub in the butter. Add the rest of the sugar and mix well.

Pour the rest of the tepid milk and the beaten egg into the yeast mixture, then add this to the flour. Knead well, either by hand or in the warmed bowl of a stand mixer fitted with the dough hook at high speed for 5 minutes. The dough should be stiff but elastic. Beat in the dried fruit and chopped peel, cover with a cloth and leave in a warm, draught-free place for approx. 2 hours, until the dough has doubled in size.

Line two 18cm round tins or two 13cm × 20cm (450g) loaf tins with parchment paper.

Knock back the dough and knead again for 2–3 minutes. Divide the dough between the two lined tins. Add the ring, stick, pea and piece of cloth at this stage – tuck them in securely and make sure they are well hidden by the dough. Cover again and leave to rise for 45–60 minutes, until the dough has risen above the top of the tins.

Preheat the oven to 180°C/350°F/gas mark 4.

Bake in the preheated oven for about 1 hour, until golden and fully cooked. Cover with parchment paper for the final 15 minutes.

To make the glaze, mix the sugar with the boiling water or milk until it has dissolved. Brush the top of the loaves with this glaze, then put them back in the oven and bake for 2–3 minutes more to get a crystalline glaze. Remove from the tin and allow to cool on a wire rack. When cool, cut into slices and slather with butter.

Barmbrack keeps well, but if it gets a little stale, try it toasted. Or leftovers make a delicious barmbrack and butter pudding (page 284).

Ballymaloe Irish Tea Barmbrack

This is a more modern version of barmbrack, now commonly called a tea brack because the dried fruit is soaked in tea overnight to plump it up. You could add a drop of whiskey to the tea if you liked!

This little gem of a recipe is much easier to make at home than the Halloween barmbrack (page 208). Even though it is a very rich bread, in Ireland it is traditionally served sliced and buttered.

MAKES 1 LARGE LOAF OR
3 SMALL LOAVES

....

- 110g sultanas
- 110g raisins
- 110g currants
- 50g natural glacé cherries, halved or quartered
- 300ml hot strong tea or 225ml tea plus 50ml Irish whiskey
- 225g self-raising flour
- 175g soft brown sugar
- 50g homemade candied peel (page 298)
- 1 level teaspoon mixed spice
- 1 egg, whisked
- bun wash (page 216)

Put the dried fruit and cherries in a bowl. Cover with the hot strong tea (or the tea and whiskey) and leave to plump up overnight.

The next day, preheat the oven to 180°C/350°F/gas mark 4. Line a 13cm × 20cm (450g) loaf tin or three small loaf tins (14.6cm × 7.6cm) with parchment paper.

Add the flour, soft brown sugar, candied peel, mixed spice and whisked egg to the fruit and tea mixture. Stir well, then put the mixture into the lined loaf tin(s).

Bake in the preheated oven for about 1½ hours, until a skewer comes out clean. Brush with bun wash and cool on a wire rack. This keeps very well in an airtight tin.

Rachel's Zucchini and Walnut Bread

We've got several recipes for zucchini (courgette) bread, but this version, originally given to us by an American friend, is my favourite. It was first published in Rachel Allen's book, *Bake*.

MAKES 2 LOAVES

- 400g plain flour
- 1 teaspoon bicarbonate of soda
- ½ teaspoon baking powder
- 75g walnuts, chopped, plus extra for scattering on top of the bread
- ½ teaspoon salt, plus a pinch
- 1 teaspoon ground cinnamon
- ¼ teaspoon freshly grated nutmeg
- ¼ teaspoon ground cloves
- 300g caster sugar
- 100g Demerara sugar
- 3 eggs
- 200ml sunflower oil
- 2 teaspoons vanilla extract
- 380g courgette, grated (skin left on)

Preheat the oven to 150°C/300°F/gas mark 2. Line two 13cm × 20cm (450g) loaf tins with parchment paper.

Sieve the flour, bicarbonate of soda and baking powder into a large bowl, then mix in the chopped walnuts, salt and spices. Add the caster and Demerara sugar and stir well to mix.

In a separate bowl, beat the eggs with the oil and vanilla extract. Add the grated courgette and mix well until combined, then pour this into the dry ingredients and mix until just combined.

Divide the mixture between the two prepared loaf tins. Scatter more chopped walnuts over the top of each loaf.

Bake in the oven for 1–1¼ hours, until a skewer inserted into the middle comes out clean. Allow to cool in the tins for 5–10 minutes before turning out onto a wire rack. Cut into slices and serve on its own or toasted and buttered. Tightly wrapped in cling film, this bread keeps well for up to 10 days.

Mary Jo's Stollen

My lovely American friend and legendary baker, Mary Jo McMillin, shared this delicious stollen recipe with me. It's a three-day process, but really worth it.

Stollen is a fruit bread of nuts, spices and dried or candied fruit, coated with icing sugar and often containing marzipan. It's a traditional German Christmas bread. Apparently, it was baked for the first time at the Council of Trent in 1545.

MAKES 2 × 700G CAKES

BRANDIED FRUIT:
- 250g mixed fruit (sultanas, currants, candied peel (page 298) and/or diced glacé cherries)
- 2 tablespoons brandy

YEAST SPONGE STARTER:
- 15g fresh yeast (or 1 × 7g sachet of dried yeast)
- 115ml tepid milk
- 115g strong white flour

DOUGH:
- 55g caster sugar
- grated rind of ½ lemon
- 110g butter, softened
- 2 eggs
- 5g salt
- 250g strong white flour

TO FINISH:
- 175g marzipan (page 300)
- 2 tablespoons melted butter
- 3-4 tablespoons icing sugar

Day 1
Mix the dried fruit with the brandy in a bowl. Cover with cling film and allow the fruit to macerate overnight.

Day 2
To make the yeast sponge starter, crumble the fresh or dried yeast into the tepid milk in a medium bowl. Set aside in a warm, draught-free place. After about 5 minutes, it should be creamy and slightly frothy on top. Mix in the flour and beat well with a wooden spoon. Cover with cling film and allow to rest in a warm, draught-free place for 30–45 minutes, until light and well risen.

Meanwhile, put the caster sugar in the bowl of a stand mixer. Add the lemon rind and rub it into the sugar with your fingertips. Add the butter and beat with the paddle attachment until creamy. Add the eggs one at a time, beating well between each addition. Add the salt, scrape down the edges of the bowl with a spatula and continue to beat for 1–2 minutes, until soft.

Add the risen yeast sponge to the creamed mixture along with the 250g strong white flour. Switch to the dough hook attachment and knead on a medium speed for 10 minutes, until the dough is silky and soft. It should not stick to your fingers.

Cover the bowl and allow the dough to rise at room temperature for 2–2½ hours, until doubled in size.

Knock back the dough and scrape it out onto a clean flour-dusted surface. Flatten to 1cm and sprinkle the brandy-soaked fruit on top. Roll up like a Swiss roll and knead the fruit into the dough. The dough may grow sticky, but avoid adding more flour. Scrape the fruited dough into a bowl, cover and refrigerate overnight.

Day 3

Remove the dough from the fridge and scrape it out onto a lightly floured surface. Divide in half. Shape each half into an oval and roll to about 2cm thick. Make an indentation lengthways along the centre of the dough and lay a 75g long sausage-shaped piece of marzipan on it. Fold over and press to seal. Place each oval approx. 5cm apart on a parchment-lined baking tray. Cover with a clean tea towel and allow to rise in a warm, draught-free place for 4–5 hours, until doubled in size.

Preheat the oven to 180°C/350°F/gas mark 4.

Spray the loaves with a water mister. Bake in the preheated oven for 30–35 minutes, until deep golden and fully cooked. While still hot, brush with melted butter, then sieve some icing sugar thickly over the top.

Cool well on wire racks before slicing. The stollen will keep wrapped for four or five days and may be frozen.

SWEET BUNS

Some of you may fondly remember the sticky buns in the original Bewley's Oriental Café in Dublin. They were utterly delicious and made with the very finest ingredients. I don't believe Bewley's ever published recipes, but we've done our best to reproduce those delicious flavours that so many happy memories are made of – cherry buns, Chelsea buns, Bath buns, iced whirls, sticky pecan buns. Many sweet buns are based on one brilliant recipe: basic bun dough.

And then there's a super recipe for doughnuts. Who doesn't love doughnuts? Have a party and do lots of riffs on the original.

If you don't have any yeast in your pantry, you could still whip up a batch of balloons, a Ballymaloe House children's tea favourite. The batter cooks in random shapes, which delights and amuses the children. This is a simple little gem of a recipe that Myrtle Allen showed me how to make when I arrived in Ballymaloe in the late 1960s. It will probably become one of your family favourites too, so why not stick a list of the ingredients on the inside of one of your kitchen cupboard doors, just like I have, so you can make them in minutes and bring much fun and joy to all your family and friends?

Once again, don't skimp – use the finest ingredients for the most delicious, irresistible results. These buns are best eaten freshly baked on the day they are made but they can be gently reheated the next day and of course make a superb sweet bun and butter pudding even when stale (see page 284).

Basic Yeast Bun Dough

Many people in Ireland would originally have associated sticky buns with a small chain of Quaker cafés called Bewley's. Initially they were operated on an honour system – a plate of buns was put out on the table and people ate to their heart's content and then (hopefully) paid for everything they'd eaten. The recipe below makes a basic bun dough that can be used to make many variations: doughnuts, Bath buns, Chelsea buns, hot cross buns, and so on.

Baker's or strong white flour is higher in gluten than plain flour, so it is more suitable for yeast breads, puff and choux pastry.

MAKES 1.75KG DOUGH

- 50g fresh yeast
- 300-450ml tepid water
- 900g baker's or strong white flour (see the intro)
- 75g caster sugar
- 7g salt
- 175g butter, diced
- 2 eggs, whisked

Dissolve the yeast in a little of the tepid water and set aside. After 4–5 minutes, it will have a creamy, slightly frothy appearance on top.

Sieve the flour, sugar and salt into a large bowl. Rub in the butter, then add the whisked eggs. Add the yeast mixture and enough of the remaining water to make a fairly soft dough. Cover and leave to rest for 10 minutes.

Turn out onto a floured board. Knead well for 5–10 minutes, until the dough becomes firm and springy. It should bounce back when pressed with a finger.

Put the dough in a deep Pyrex bowl, cover with cling film and leave to rise in a warm, draught-free place for 2–2½ hours, until it has doubled in size.

Knock back the dough to knock out the air and redistribute the yeast back in contact with the dough. Knead well for 2–3 minutes. Leave to rest for a further 5 minutes, then use and shape as desired.

Bun Wash

Put 150ml water and 110g granulated sugar in a pan and boil for 5 minutes. Brush this over the buns as soon as they come out of the oven to give them a sweet, sticky glaze.

Doughnuts

Homemade doughnuts don't look quite as perfect as the ones you buy in the shops, but they are much more delicious. I can't say they're not detrimental to your waistline so you shouldn't live on them, but boy they are good from time to time.

Divide the basic yeast bun dough into 25g pieces. Shape each piece into a ball and poke a floured forefinger through the centre. Spin your finger around in a circle to widen the hole to about 2cm in diameter. Arrange the rings on a floured tea towel or tray, cover with oiled cling film and leave to rise for 40–45 minutes, until doubled in size.

Heat some good-quality sunflower oil in a deep-fryer to 160°C/320°F.

Mix 225g caster sugar and 3 teaspoons ground cinnamon in a wide, shallow bowl.

Gently slip a few risen doughnuts into the oil. Cook for about a minute on each side, turning them with a slotted spoon until they are evenly brown. Remove and drain on kitchen paper. Leave to cool slightly, then toss the doughnuts in the cinnamon sugar.

....

Berliner Doughnuts

Divide the basic yeast bun dough into 25g pieces. Shape each piece into a ball and flatten. Arrange on a floured tea towel or tray, cover and leave to rise for 40–45 minutes, until doubled in size.

Heat some good-quality sunflower oil in a deep-fryer to 160°C/320°F.

Gently slip a few risen Berliners into the oil. Cook for about a minute on each side, turning them with a slotted spoon until they are evenly brown. Remove and drain on kitchen paper. Leave to cool slightly. Toss in crunchy sugar and eat soon.

Alternatively, mix 110g caster sugar and 1 teaspoon ground cinnamon in a wide, shallow bowl. Toss the doughnuts in the cinnamon sugar or pipe crème pâtissière (page 301) or whatever you fancy into the centre through the side.

....

Jam Doughnuts

Roll the bun dough out until it's 5mm thick. This is far easier said than done – it will keep springing back! Cut with a cookie cutter into 7.5cm rounds and pop a blob of jam in the centre. Take another 7.5cm round and press the two rounds together, pinching the edges with your fingers so that the jam is trapped inside. Allow to rise for 30–45 minutes. Deep-fry as above and toss in caster sugar.

Doughnut Splits

Weigh the basic yeast bun dough into 25g pieces. Roll into an éclair shape and allow to rise. Deep-fry in hot oil and drain on kitchen paper, then cool on a wire rack and toss in caster sugar. Split lengthways and fill with whipped cream and homemade jam (pages 292–4) or chocolate and hazelnut spread (page 295) or dulce de leche and cream ... the possibilities are endless.

Iced Whirls

Divide 450g bun dough into 8 × 55g pieces. Form each piece into a roll, then pull until it's about 25cm long. Roll up from one end and seal with egg wash. Place on a greased baking tray, cut side up, and leave to rise again for 30–45 minutes, until doubled in size. Brush with egg wash and bake in an oven preheated to 220°C/430°F/gas mark 7 for about 15 minutes. Brush the tops with bun wash (page 216) and then ice with glacé icing (see below).

Glacé Iced Buns

Mix icing sugar with a little boiling water or freshly squeezed lemon juice to make a fairly thick icing that can be brushed onto the buns.

Bath Buns

Bath buns are probably the best known and best loved of all the sticky buns.

MAKES 12-16

- 110g sultanas
- 50g candied peel (page 298), chopped
- grated zest of 1 organic lemon
- 1.1kg basic yeast bun dough (page 216)
- egg wash (page 325)
- 50g sugar nibs or coarse sugar
- bun wash (page 216)

Knead the sultanas, candied peel and lemon zest evenly into the bun dough. Roll lengthways into a fairly tight cylinder, then divide into 12–16 pieces (as many as will fit into whatever size tin you have). Place them in a lightly greased 2.5cm deep tray, cut side down and fairly close together. Brush the tops with egg wash and leave to rise in a warm, draught-free place for 30–45 minutes, until doubled in size. All the buns will be touching each other.

Flatten slightly and brush the tops with egg wash again. Dip the tops in nibbed or coarse sugar and leave to prove for 30–45 minutes, until doubled in size.

Preheat the oven to 230°C/450°F/gas mark 8.

Bake the buns in the preheated oven for 10 minutes, until they are golden, fully cooked through. Remove from the oven and while still hot, brush with bun wash. Cool on a wire rack. Split and slather with butter for extra deliciousness.

Chelsea Buns

This is a basic recipe for rolled-up buns. Once you've mastered this technique, you can vary the fillings according to your fancy.

MAKES 12-16

- 1.1kg basic yeast bun dough (page 216)
- 50g butter, melted and cooled, plus extra for greasing
- 110g sultanas
- 110g candied peel (page 298)
- 50g Demerara sugar
- grated zest of 1 organic lemon
- 1 teaspoon mixed spice or ground cinnamon
- egg wash (page 325)
- bun wash (page 216)
- icing or caster sugar, for dusting

Roll the bun dough into a rectangle measuring about 25cm × 40cm. Brush with half of the cooled melted butter. Combine the sultanas, candied peel, Demerara sugar, lemon zest and mixed spice or cinnamon in a bowl.

Sprinkle the buttered dough evenly with the fruit mixture. Roll lengthways into a fairly tight cylinder, then brush with the remaining melted butter and divide into 12–16 pieces (as many as will fit into whatever size tin you have). Place them in a lightly greased 2.5cm deep tray, cut side down and fairly close together. Brush the tops with egg wash and leave to rise in a warm, draught-free place for 30–45 minutes, until doubled in size. All the buns will be touching each other.

Preheat the oven to 220°C/430°F/gas mark 7.

Bake the buns in the preheated oven for about 15 minutes, until golden on top and sounding hollow when tapped underneath. Reduce the temperature to 200°C/400°F/gas mark 6 after 10 minutes if the buns are colouring too much. Remove from the oven and while still hot, brush with bun wash and dust with icing or caster sugar.

Cherry Buns

These are also gorgeous made with sour cherries.

MAKES 16

- 110g washed and dried natural glacé cherries, halved or quartered (or more if liked), plus 16 whole cherries for the tops
- 1.1kg basic yeast bun dough (page 216)
- lemon or plain glacé icing (page 218)

Line a baking tray with a sheet of parchment paper.

Knead the cherries into the bun dough. Roll into a thick cylinder and break off into 16 equal pieces. Knead each piece into a round roll and place on the lined baking tray. Leave to prove for 30–45 minutes, until doubled in size.

Preheat the oven to 230°C/450°F/gas mark 8.

Flatten each roll slightly, then bake in the preheated oven for 10 minutes. Cool on a wire rack. When cool, ice with lemon glacé or plain glacé icing and put a cherry on top of each bun.

Sticky Pecan Buns

This recipe uses a similar technique to the Chelsea buns. It should have a government health warning on it – these are totally irresistible. Half the recipe will fill one tin. Walnuts are also delicious in this recipe.

MAKES 18

....

- 25g fresh yeast
- 500ml tepid water
- 800g strong white flour
- 10g salt
- 50g butter, softened

....

TOPPING:
- 125g butter
- 150g dark brown sugar
- 150g pecans or walnuts, roughly chopped
- 70g granulated sugar
- 1 teaspoon freshly ground cinnamon

Dissolve the yeast in 150ml of the tepid water and set aside. After 4–5 minutes, it will have a creamy, slightly frothy appearance on top.

Mix the flour and salt together in a large, wide bowl. Make a well in the centre and pour in the sponged yeast and the remaining water. Mix well to form a dough.

Turn out onto a lightly floured work surface and knead for about 5 minutes (or 2 minutes in a stand mixer fitted with the dough hook). The dough should be quite soft. Cover with a large mixing bowl and leave on the work surface for about 20 minutes to rest.

When rested, gently knead the dough for a couple of minutes, until it's smooth and shiny. Put the dough into a lightly oiled large mixing bowl, turning the dough over in the bowl to coat it with the oil. Cover and leave to rise for 1½–2 hours in a warm, draught-free place, until it has doubled in size.

Meanwhile, to make the topping, melt the 125g of butter over a low heat and add the brown sugar. Stir to mix, then take off the heat. Divide this between 2 × 23cm square cake tins. Tilt the tins a little so that the sugary mixture spreads evenly over the base. Sprinkle over the chopped pecans or walnuts and press them down slightly. Put the tins in a fridge to chill.

Mix the granulated sugar and cinnamon together in a bowl. Set aside.

When the dough has doubled in size, knock it back and divide in two. Roll each piece into a 33cm × 25cm rectangle. Divide the 50g of soft butter evenly between the two rectangles, spreading it all over but leaving the top 1cm of the dough unbuttered.

Sprinkle the cinnamon sugar evenly over the butter, again leaving the top 1cm bare. Starting at the bottom, roll up the dough like a Swiss roll. With a metal dough cutter or knife, divide each roll into nine equal-sized pieces.

Arrange them in each tin, cut edge down, allowing space between each one. Cover and leave to rise again for 1–1½ hours, until doubled in size.

Preheat the oven to 190°C/375°F/gas mark 5.

Bake in the preheated oven for 30–40 minutes, until the buns are golden brown and crusty. Leave to stand in the tins for 5 minutes, then turn out onto a large serving plate. The delicious sticky pecan caramel will spread down over the sides. Scrape out any of the precious remaining caramel from the tins and spoon it over the top.

Shanagarry Irresistibles

What can I say? These soft, pillowy sweet buns are totally irresistible. Embellished with softly whipped cream and homemade raspberry jam, they are sublime. We always make them for our students' farewell coffee.

MAKES 12

- 155g sourdough starter (page 82)
- 80g butter, melted
- 75g caster sugar, plus extra for sprinkling
- 54g tepid water
- 50g egg (1 medium egg)
- 26g fresh yeast
- 25g natural yogurt
- 25g cream
- 25g full-fat milk
- 330g strong white flour
- 2g salt
- bun wash (page 216)

TO SERVE:
- softly whipped cream
- raspberry jam (page 294) (optional)

Put the sourdough starter, melted butter, sugar, water, egg, fresh yeast, yogurt, cream and milk in the bowl of a stand mixer fitted with the paddle attachment. Mix gently to combine, then leave for 5 minutes to allow the yeast to activate.

In a separate bowl, mix together the strong white flour and salt. Add to the wet ingredients in the stand mixer. Mix with a dough hook on a slow setting for 12 minutes, then increase the speed of the mixer to its maximum speed and mix for a further 2 minutes.

Transfer the dough into a clean, dry bowl and cover. Leave to rise in the fridge for 2–3 hours, until doubled in size.

Knock the dough back, then cut it into 12 pieces, each weighing approx. 70g. Shape into smooth, tight, round balls. Put the dough balls on a baking tray lined with parchment paper and cover with a clean tea towel. Leave to rise in the fridge overnight.

The next day, preheat the oven to 220°C/430°F/gas mark 7.

Remove the baking tray from the fridge, transfer to the preheated oven and bake for 10 minutes. Reduce the oven temperature to 200°C/400°F/gas mark 6 and bake for a further 10–12 minutes, until golden brown. While the buns are still hot, glaze with bun wash and sprinkle with caster sugar. Cool on a wire rack.

Serve with softly whipped cream and raspberry jam. Or better still, when they are cold, cut them down the centre, almost all the way through, pipe in some whipped cream and put a blob of raspberry jam on top. Now you know why they are called irresistibles ...

London Buns

My father-in-law, Ivan Allen, always loved a London bun with a cup of coffee. Whenever I make this recipe, I think of him having a cup of coffee and a London bun in Thompson's Tivoli Café in Cork, now sadly long gone.

MAKES 18

TO ACTIVATE THE YEAST:
- 25g fresh yeast
- 1 tablespoon caster sugar
- 50ml tepid water

FOR THE DOUGH:
- 450g baker's or strong white flour
- pinch of salt
- 85g caster sugar
- 85g butter, diced
- 1 egg
- 225-300ml tepid water
- 110g sultanas
- 50g candied peel (page 298), chopped
- 50g granulated sugar, plus extra for sprinkling
- zest of 1 lemon
- egg wash (page 325)

Dissolve the yeast and the tablespoon of sugar in a measuring jug with the 50ml of tepid water and set aside. After 4–5 minutes, it will have a creamy, slightly frothy appearance on top.

Sieve the flour into a large, wide mixing bowl, then add the salt and the 85g caster sugar. Rub in the butter.

Whisk the egg in a separate large bowl. Add 225ml of the tepid water, then pour this into the measuring jug with the yeast mixture.

Make a well in the centre of the dry ingredients and pour in the liquid. Mix to a soft dough, adding more of the remaining tepid water if necessary. Leave to rest for 5–6 minutes.

Knead for approx. 5 minutes if using a stand mixer fitted with the dough hook, until the dough is smooth and shiny. Alternatively, turn the dough out onto a well-floured work surface and knead by hand for 8–10 minutes.

Transfer to an oiled bowl, cover the bowl and let the dough rise in a warm, draught-free place for approx. 2 hours, until doubled in size.

Knock back the dough in the bowl and leave to rest for a few minutes, then turn it out onto a well-floured work surface.

Knead the sultanas, candied peel, granulated sugar and lemon zest into the dough. Roll the dough into a thick cylinder. Divide into 18 equal pieces, approx. 50g each. Roll into buns and put them on a lightly floured baking sheet. Flatten the buns very slightly, brush them with egg wash and sprinkle with granulated sugar. Cover loosely and allow to rise for about 45 minutes, until the buns have doubled in size.

Preheat the oven to 220°C/430°F/gas mark 7.

Brush the buns with egg wash again, then bake in the preheated oven for 8–10 minutes, until golden. Cool on a wire rack. Split and slather with soft butter.

Easter Tea Ring

Use the Chelsea bun technique to make this irresistible Easter ring.

SERVES 8-10

....

- 1 batch of basic yeast bun dough (page 216)
- 50g butter
- 75g caster sugar
- 50g raisins
- 50g sultanas
- 50g candied peel (page 298)
- 1 teaspoon ground cinnamon (optional)

....

TO DECORATE:
- glacé icing (page 218)
- 25g toasted flaked almonds
- 50g glacé cherries
- 50g angelica, cut into diamonds

Make the bun dough and filling as outlined in the recipe for Chelsea buns and roll as directed in the recipe (page 220). But instead of cutting the buns, curl the dough around into a ring. Pinch the ends tightly together. Lift carefully onto a lined baking tray.

Cut two-thirds of the way through the ring at 2.5cm intervals with a scissors or knife. Twist each cut slightly to expose more filling. Cover with a clean tea towel and leave to prove for 15–20 minutes in a warm, draught-free place.

Cut through the ring at intervals

Twist each cut slightly

Preheat the oven to 200°C/400°F/gas mark 6.

Bake the tea ring in the preheated oven for 10 minutes, then reduce the temperature to 180°C/350°F/gas mark 4 and bake for 20–30 minutes more, until fully cooked and golden brown. Transfer to a wire rack.

Make a thickish glacé icing and spread it over the top of the Easter ring while it's still warm. Decorate with the toasted flaked almonds, glacé cherries and diamonds of angelica. Best served while still warm.

Ballymaloe Balloons (Cheat's Doughnuts)

My mother-in-law, Myrtle Allen, made these for her children, then passed on the recipe to her grandchildren and great-grandchildren. They've also been a favourite of guest children at the Children's Tea in Ballymaloe House for over 40 years. They cook into funny little shapes that are uneven in texture, which is a lot of fun – use your imagination to decide what they look like!

MAKES ABOUT 10

- 150g plain flour
- 2 teaspoons caster sugar
- 1 level teaspoon baking powder
- pinch of salt
- 200ml full-fat milk, plus more if needed
- light olive or vegetable oil, for deep-frying
- extra caster sugar or cinnamon sugar (granulated sugar mixed with a little ground cinnamon), to coat

TO SERVE:
- crème pâtissière (page 301)

Sieve the dry ingredients into a bowl. Mix to a thick batter (dropping consistency) with the milk.

Heat the oil in a deep-fryer to 190°C/375°F. If you don't have a deep-fryer, heat 4cm light olive or vegetable oil in a deep pan.

Take a heaped teaspoonful of the mixture and gently push it off with your finger so that it drops in a round ball into the fat. Fry until puffed and golden. Remove and drain on kitchen paper. Repeat the process until you have used up all the batter.

Roll the balloons in caster sugar or cinnamon sugar and serve at once. These are also delicious with sweet apple sauce flavoured with a little cinnamon and a bowl of crème pâtissière for dipping.

Hot Cross Buns

Hot cross buns were traditionally eaten in Ireland on Ash Wednesday and on Good Friday, but nowadays you can get them throughout Lent and over the Easter period.

MAKES 14

....

- 25g fresh yeast
- 110-125g caster sugar
- 225-300ml tepid milk
- 450g baker's or strong white flour
- 1 level teaspoon salt
- 3 teaspoons mixed spice
- ¼ teaspoon ground cinnamon
- ¼ teaspoon ground nutmeg
- 75g butter, diced
- 2 eggs
- 75g currants
- 50g sultanas
- 25g candied peel (page 298), chopped
- egg wash (page 325)
- bun wash (page 216)

....

LIQUID CROSS:
- 50g plain white flour
- 4-5 tablespoons cold water
- 1 tablespoon melted butter

Dissolve the yeast with 1 tablespoon of the sugar in a little tepid milk and set aside. After 4–5 minutes, it will have a creamy, slightly frothy appearance on top.

Put the flour in a large bowl with the salt, mixed spice, cinnamon, nutmeg and the rest of the sugar. Mix well, then rub in the butter.

Whisk the eggs and the remaining milk together. Make a well in the centre of the flour, then add the yeast and most of the egg and milk mixture and mix to a soft dough, adding a little more milk if necessary.

Cover and leave to rest for 2–3 minutes, then knead by hand or in a stand mixer fitted with a dough hook until smooth – it will be quite soft and sticky. Add the currants, sultanas and candied peel and continue to knead until the dough is shiny. Cover the bowl and let the dough rise in a warm, draught-free place for approx. 2 hours, until it has doubled in size.

Knock back the dough and knead for 3–4 minutes, then allow to rest for a few minutes. Divide the dough into 14 balls, each weighing approx. 50–60g. Knead each ball slightly and shape into buns. Place on a lightly floured tray, brush evenly with egg wash and leave to rise for 20–30 minutes, until doubled in size and puffy.

To make the liquid cross, mix the flour, water and melted butter together to form a thick liquid. Fill into a piping bag and pipe a cross on top of each bun.

Preheat the oven to 220°C/430°F/gas mark 7.

Bake in the preheated oven for 5 minutes, then reduce the temperature to 200°C/400°F/gas mark 6 and bake for a further 10 minutes, until golden. Brush each one with bun wash while still warm, then cool on a wire rack. Split in two and serve with butter.

| Hot Cross Bun Loaf | Brush the bottom and sides of a 13cm × 20cm (450g) loaf tin with oil. Make the dough as above and allow to rise. Knock back and roll into 8 × 50g balls of dough and arrange in the tin. Brush with egg wash, cover and allow to rise for 20 minutes, until the dough has almost reached the top of the tin. |

Preheat the oven to 220°C/430°F/gas mark 7. Just before baking, brush with egg wash and pipe a liquid cross on each bun.

Bake in the preheated oven for 10 minutes at 220°C/430°F/gas mark 7, then reduce the temperature to 190°C/375°F/gas mark 5 and bake for a further 10–15 minutes, until golden and sounding hollow when tapped on the base. Remove from the oven and brush with bun wash. Cool on a wire rack, then pull apart and eat slathered in butter.

| Hot Cross Tear and Share | Brush the base and sides of a 23cm round springform tin with oil. Arrange 12–14 × 50g balls of dough almost side by side in the tin. Brush with egg wash and allow to rise in a warm, draught-free place for 25–30 minutes, until doubled in size. Brush with egg wash again, then pipe a liquid cross on top of each bun. Bake in the preheated oven for 10 minutes, then reduce the temperature to 190°C/375°F/gas mark 5 and bake for a further 10–15 minutes, until golden and sounding hollow when tapped on the base. Remove from the oven and brush with bun wash while still warm. Cool on a wire rack. |

Cardamom Buns

We tested and retested this recipe until we were totally happy, and now these are totally irresistible. We freshly grind the whole green cardamom pods. Use the very best cardamom you can find. Put the whole green cardamom pods in a spice grinder and grind to a powder. No need to sieve out the husks, they are full of flavour.

MAKES 18

- 25g fresh yeast
- 400ml full-fat tepid milk (37°C/99°F)
- 650g strong white flour
- 75g butter, cut into cubes and softened
- 60g caster sugar
- ¾ tablespoon ground cardamom
- ½ teaspoon salt
- egg wash (page 325)

CARDAMOM BUTTER FILLING:
- 110g butter, softened
- 75g dark brown sugar
- 1 tablespoon ground cardamom

TOPPING:
- 50g pearl sugar or Demerara sugar

GLAZE:
- 100g granulated sugar
- 100ml water
- 3 teaspoons ground cardamom

Crumble the fresh yeast into the milk and set aside. After 4–5 minutes, it will have a creamy, slightly frothy appearance on top.

Put the flour, butter, sugar, ground cardamom and salt in the bowl of a stand mixer fitted with the dough hook. Add the sponged yeast and mix until combined, then cover with a clean tea towel and rest for 30 minutes. Mix again for 10 minutes on a low speed until it has come together into a smooth, elastic dough. Put in a large oiled bowl, cover and allow to rise again in a warm, draught-free place for 2–2½ hours, until doubled in size.

Meanwhile, to make the cardamom butter filling, cream the butter, brown sugar and ground cardamom until light and fluffy.

When the dough has doubled in size, knock it back and knead lightly. Allow to rest for 5 minutes.

Preheat the oven to 190°C/375°F/gas mark 5. Line two baking trays with parchment paper.

Roll the dough into a rectangle approx. 45.5cm long × 33cm wide. Spread the cardamom butter right to the edges. Working from the long side, fold the top one-third down and fold the bottom one-third up to cover the top fold. Square off the edges by pulling lightly on the dough to create a rectangle approx. 45.5cm × 11.5cm.

Press the layers gently together with the rolling pin, then cut the dough into 18 × 2.5cm pieces. Stretch out each strip, then twist both ends in opposite directions and tie in a loose knot. Alternatively, cut the strip in three pieces, top still attached, and plait, then tuck the ends underneath.

Stretch out
each strip

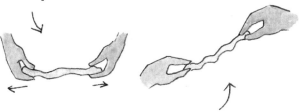

Twist both ends
in opposite
directions

Tie in a loose
knot

Put the shaped buns on parchment-lined baking trays spaced well apart, cover and allow to rise again for 20–30 minutes, until doubled in size.

Brush very gently with egg wash and sprinkle with the pearl or Demerara sugar. Bake in the preheated oven for 18–22 minutes, until nicely coloured.

While the buns are baking, make the glaze. Boil the sugar, water and cardamom together for 2 minutes. When the buns are baked, brush immediately with the hot glaze, then cool on a wire rack.

Cinnamon Buns

Substitute 1 teaspoon freshly ground cinnamon in the dough and in the cardamom butter. Form into a roll, cut into 5cm rounds and allow to rise. Brush with egg wash and cook side by side on a baking tray or in muffin tins.

Cardamom Wreath

You can also make a cardamom wreath with the dough by using two or three strands. Plait or twist and shape into a wreath, then press the edges together to seal.

Mary Jo's Cinnamon Raisin Rolls

We love to drizzle these cakey spirals with icing. Thank you, Mary Jo, for sharing your recipe.

MAKES 12

- 1 × 7g sachet of dried yeast
- 225ml tepid water
- 2 eggs, at room temperature
- 450g strong white flour
- 40g caster sugar
- 1 teaspoon salt
- pinch of ground ginger (optional)
- 50g butter, softened, plus extra for greasing

FILLING:
- 75g light or dark brown sugar
- 2-3 teaspoons ground cinnamon
- 25g butter, very soft
- 75g raisins

GLAZE:
- 75g icing sugar, sieved
- 1½ tablespoons milk

In the bowl of a stand mixer, dissolve the yeast in the tepid water and set aside. After 4–5 minutes, it will have a creamy, slightly frothy appearance on top.

Beat the eggs in a small bowl. Remove 2 tablespoons and set aside in a small cup for the egg wash.

When the yeast foams, add the beaten eggs and the flour, sugar, salt and ginger (if using) and stir to combine. Cover the bowl with a clean tea towel and allow the flour to thoroughly absorb the liquid for 10–15 minutes.

Using the dough hook attachment, knead the dough until it forms a neat ball, then add the soft butter a little at a time. Continue to knead for at least 10 minutes, until the dough is smooth and satiny. Resist adding any more flour than absolutely necessary – the dough must be soft for light rolls.

Cover the bowl with the tea towel again and allow the dough to rise in a warm, draught-free place for 1–2 hours, until doubled in volume.

Knock back, cover again and allow to rise for a further 30 minutes.

Grease a baking tray (24cm × 36cm × 7cm) or 2 × 20.5cm cake tins with butter.

To make the filling, thoroughly combine the brown sugar and cinnamon.

Roll the dough out on a lightly floured work surface to a 45cm × 23cm rectangle. Spread with the very soft butter, then dust evenly with the cinnamon sugar. Sprinkle the raisins over the sugar.

Roll up from the long side of the rectangle. Pinch the edges of the roll and gently rock it back and forth to even out. Use a 25cm piece of cotton string to 'tie cut' the log into 12 × 4cm 'snails'. Put the rolls in the prepared tins or on the baking tray. Cover with a clean tea towel and allow to rise in a warm, draught-free place for 30–40 minutes, until doubled in size and light.

Preheat the oven to 180°C/350°F/gas mark 4.

Before baking, brush the tops of the rolls lightly with the reserved egg wash. Bake in the preheated oven for 25 minutes, until golden brown.

While the rolls are baking, mix the sieved icing sugar with the milk to make a glaze. As soon as the rolls come out of the oven, use a pastry brush to ice and glaze the warm rolls or drizzle over the icing. Best served warm.

GLUTEN-FREE
BREAD

A BEGINNER'S GUIDE TO GLUTEN-FREE BAKING

....

All text and recipes in this chapter are by Debbie Shaw.

While baking gluten-free cakes and baked goods is a fairly straightforward affair, baking a truly satisfying loaf of gluten-free bread is the holy grail of gluten-free baking, especially if you are not coeliac but are avoiding gluten or are a newly diagnosed coeliac and have the taste of freshly baked traditional artisanal loaves etched in your sensory memory. Most people the world over eat some form of bread every day and being able to bake your own daily loaf is a life-enhancing joy. This chapter is a beginner's guide to gluten-free bread-making and explains the ingredients and methods required to produce your own nutritious and delicious daily gluten-free bread.

Ever practical, budget and time aware, in this chapter I endeavour to equip coeliacs and those avoiding wheat or gluten with a repertoire of nutritious, achievable, tasty recipes for everyday gluten-free sandwich loaves, bread rolls, scones and pizzas, for the most part using commercially available flour blends and a small range of additional, affordable gluten-free flours and ingredients.

The almond and sesame seed loaf (page 245), bastible Irish soda bread (page 252) and little oat loaves (page 256) are simple and quick to make and a perfect place for the novice to start. While the yeasted doughs have a particular method that should be adopted for best results, it is simply an approach that is easily mastered with practice. They all require only one rising, unlike many traditional yeasted breads that require two. I have included an express pizza (page 257) and griddle pan pizza recipe (page 247) that are cheaper and quicker to make than any take-away you could order (assuming they even have a gluten-free option) and can be enjoyed by everyone.

Many of the recipes perform double duty and expand your options and culinary prowess with little extra effort. For example, the flatbreads (page 246) can also be made into tempting griddle pan pizzas. The white sandwich loaf dough (page 248) can be turned into bread rolls and the bastible Irish soda bread dough (page 252) can be cooked flat in a tin and covered with all manner of delicious ingredients to make deep-pan-style soda bread pizza or soda bread focaccia. The drop scones (page 262) can be sweet or savoury and the rosemary and olive focaccia (page 255) is perfect for bruschetta.

Gluten-free bread-making has its challenges. Firstly, gluten-free flours contain no gluten – the protein in traditional wheat and rye that creates expansion, elasticity and structure in breads. This is where xanthan gum and psyllium husk come in as gluten replacements. Secondly, there is no one magic flour that is a direct substitute for or equivalent to white wheat flour or wholegrain wheat flour (i.e. white bread and brown bread/wholemeal bread).

As a gluten-free bread baker, you have two choices. You can either buy commercial gluten-free flour blends, such as Bob's Red Mill gluten-free all-purpose flour, Bob's Red Mill 1-to-1 baking flour, Doves Farm gluten-free plain flour, Doves Farm gluten-free self-raising flour and Doves Farm gluten-free bread flours, or you can create your own gluten-free flour blend by mixing different gluten-free flours together.

The first choice is convenient, as most supermarkets carry gluten-free plain (cream, all-purpose) and self-raising flours. This is also a more cost-effective approach, as buying individual gluten-free flours to make your own blend is expensive, not to mention the challenge of trying to find space for all those jars on your shelf and the short shelf life of some gluten-free flours. However, making a personalised flour blend gives you control over what you are eating and allows you to create nutritious and satisfying breads with different flavour profiles.

Of course, you can also buy commercially available gluten-free breads, but they are expensive, generally do not keep well and can be packed with excess sugar, salt and additives. As you have bought this book, I assume you want to start baking your own gluten-free breads or at least one good daily loaf.

As a naturopathic nutritionist and a chef, I believe there is a balance to be struck between nourishing yourself and eating pleasurable breads that keep well and are affordable. The gluten-free flours and ingredients I use most frequently for bread-making are ground almonds (almond meal), certified gluten-free oats, buckwheat flour and linseeds (flaxseeds), as they yield excellent results and are nutritionally dense, providing a great source of fuel for the rigours of everyday life. I also have gluten-free self-raising flour in my pantry for drop scones, sweet and savoury scones and the odd pizza.

The good news when making gluten-free breads is that there is a world beyond gluten and a vast array of flours that are naturally gluten-free, nutritious and completely delicious. For the inquisitive baker they provide a wonderful canvas for experimentation. My purpose in this chapter is to help you start your journey to allow you to confidently bake delicious, nutritious, child-friendly gluten-free breads for everyday living and eating.

GLUTEN-FREE FLOURS

Gluten-Free Flour Blends

The gluten-free flour blends that I use for the bread recipes in this chapter are Doves Farm gluten-free plain flour, self-raising flour, white bread flour and brown bread flour, and Bob's Red Mill gluten-free all-purpose flour (or plain flour) and 1-to-1 baking flour. It is important to understand that not all brands of gluten-free plain (all-purpose) flour have the same ingredients. For example, Doves Farm gluten-free plain flour contains rice flour, potato starch, tapioca starch, maize flour and buckwheat, while Bob's Red Mill gluten-free all-purpose (plain) flour contains garbanzo bean (chickpea) flour, potato starch, tapioca starch, wholegrain sorghum flour and fava bean (dried broad beans) flour.

Both brands are good, but they are poles apart in terms of ingredients. Bob's Red Mill gluten-free all-purpose flour is one of my favourite flour blends. It costs a little more and can be hard to source, although it is available online. It is high in wholegrain fibre and bean protein, which also helps slow down the sugar release from the starches (tapioca, potato, etc.) in the flour.

Below is an outline of the main flours used in gluten-free bread-making, their nutritional profile and what influence they have on the texture and flavour of breads. These flours can be bought from supermarkets, your local health food store and online.

Almond Flour

Ground almonds give lightness, longevity, open texture, delicious nutty flavour and much-needed moisture to gluten-free bakes and breads. Almonds are very high in vitamin E, are a good source of healthy fats and fibre and are protein-rich, all of which elevates the nutritional value of gluten-free bakes. They are also low in carbohydrates and very rich and filling.

In Ireland I buy what we call ground almonds and use them a great deal in my gluten-free baking. Here the ground almonds are skinned, then ground into a fine-ish almond meal that is white in colour. In the US and perhaps elsewhere, almond meal (coarsely ground almonds with their brown skin left on) and almond flour (a white flour made from skinned, finely ground almonds) are available. Almond flour in the US is the equivalent to what I buy in Ireland as ground almonds.

Other nut flours can also be successfully used in gluten-free baking, including hazelnuts, pecans and Brazil nuts, but ground almonds are the most economical. These flours are clearly not suitable for anyone with a nut allergy.

Buckwheat Flour

Buckwheat, despite its name, is not related to wheat. It is a flowering shrub with seeds (or buckwheat groats) that can be cooked and used like a grain in risottos, salads and to make porridge. The hulled seeds, or buckwheat groats, are ground to make buckwheat flour (called sarrasin in France), which lends a pleasing nutty taste and chewy texture to gluten-free breads. Its high fibre content and protein value make it very filling, energising and a great blood-sugar balancer. It is also very absorbent and gives volume to gluten-free breads. It boasts a high antioxidant and anti-inflammatory profile, which promotes heart health and can help lower cholesterol. I appreciate that it can be expensive, but as a nutritionist, this complex-flavoured, nutritionally dense flour is one of my essential store cupboard ingredients for gluten-free breads.

Chickpea Flour

As with all pulse and bean flours, chickpea flour (called gram flour in India or besan flour in France) is a good source of protein and fibre, in particular for vegetarians and vegans. It can lend a beany taste to breads that some people find unpalatable, but which I enjoy. Bob's Red Mill gluten-free all-purpose flour has both chickpea flour and fava bean flour. When used to make soda breads, it produces a wholesome, nutritious, well-risen loaf.

Beans flours can also be made from adzuki beans, fava beans, green peas, mung beans, peanuts, red lentils, soya beans and yellow peas.

| Flaxseeds (Linseeds) | Ground flaxseeds impart a nutty, light and springy texture to gluten-free breads. They can also be used as an egg replacer for vegans or those with an egg allergy or intolerance using the following standard formula: |

```
1 tablespoon ground flaxseeds
+ 3 tablespoons water
= 1 egg
```

Flaxseeds are a good source of dietary fibre and omega-3 fats, in particular for vegetarians and vegans. They also contain phytoestrogens called lignans, which are similar to the hormone oestrogen. In addition, these seeds have a high vitamin and mineral content, promote digestive health and boost heart health by reducing bad cholesterol (LDL). Chia seeds, which have an even higher nutritional profile, can also be used as an egg replacer and in breads but are considerably more expensive.

To grind your own flaxseeds, simply buy an inexpensive electric coffee grinder (I've had mine for 25 years) and grind the whole seeds yourself or buy ground flaxseeds.

Oats

Oats are a nutrient-dense, wholegrain superfood, packed with vitamins and minerals. They are also a great source of fibre and slow-release energy. Although naturally gluten-free, oats can be cross-contaminated during the growing or manufacturing process, so always look for the circular crossed grain symbol to ensure that you are buying certified gluten-free oats (I use the Irish organic certified gluten-free oats from the Merry Mill and Rebelicious Oats).

Potato Starch

As the name suggests, this is starch extracted from potatoes, which in gluten-free breads helps absorb excess moisture and bind flours together. It is used to thicken and improve the texture of gluten-free breads, making for a light, less crumbly bake. Potato starch is washed out of crushed potatoes, then dried to a fine, bright-white powder. It is not to be confused with potato flour, which uses the whole potato. Similar to tapioca starch, potato starch should be used sparingly in gluten-free bread-making in combination with more nutritious wholegrain flours as it has a high glycaemic index and can cause imbalances in blood sugar on its own.

Rice Flours

The rice flours used most frequently in gluten-free breads are white rice flour and brown rice flour due to their affordability and neutral taste. White rice flour has a high carbohydrate value, which impacts blood sugar balancing. Thus, my preference is generally for the coarser, more nutritious wholegrain brown rice flour with the bran intact, containing the fibre and B vitamins important for energy production and nervous system balance.

Whether you are using white or brown rice flour in gluten-free bread-making, these flours are best blended with other, more absorbent gluten-free flours and starches that help offset their sandy texture and keep breads moist. Although mild flavoured and light coloured, rice flours tend to give a sandy texture to baked goods.

Bob's Red Mill 1-to-1 gluten-free baking flour, which I use in my focaccia recipe (page 255), also contains sweet rice flour made from starchy glutinous rice, which, unlike other rice flours, has a superfine texture and binds very well.

Sorghum

Sorghum is an ancient wholegrain cereal originating from Africa (called Guinea corn) and is cultivated widely in India (called jowar, cholam or jonna) and in the 'sorghum belt' in the US. It has a similar taste and texture to wheat and a similar nutritional profile in terms of protein content but without the gluten. It is richer in essential micronutrients, such as iron, magnesium and B-vitamins, than wheat and has a high antioxidant value. Sorghum has a slightly sweet, malty flavour and makes light, tasty bread. If you are experimenting with your own flour blends, this is a good flour to include. Bob's Red Mill produces a certified gluten-free sorghum flour.

Tapioca Starch

Extracted from dried cassava (manioc) root, tapioca starch helps to bind and lighten gluten-free bakes. The name may also evoke good or bad memories of school dinners with tapioca pudding made from tapioca pearls. As it is almost 100% pure carbohydrate and has a low nutritional value, it is best used in smaller quantities and paired with more nutritious, protein-rich, wholegrain flours such as buckwheat, quinoa or nut flours (almond, hazelnut, etc.). Its presence in a flour blend is important, however, as it has a stretchy quality, great binding capacity and brings a lightness to breads.

Other Gluten-Free Flours	Amaranth flour, chestnut flour, coconut flour, hemp flour, millet flour, quinoa flour and a wide variety of bean and lentil flours are also available.

GLUTEN-FREE RAISING AGENTS

Gluten-Free Baking Powder	Baking powder, which helps breads rise, is generally a combination of an acid (cream of tartar), bicarbonate of soda (baking soda) and a starch to absorb moisture and prevent clumping. While in the past wheat starch (as opposed to wheat protein or gluten) was sometimes used, these days it is usually potato starch, cornflour or rice flour, all of which are naturally gluten-free. However, if it is produced in a factory where wheat-based products are processed, there could be cross-contamination. Doves Farm does a certified gluten-free baking powder suitable for coeliacs. If you are simply avoiding gluten, you could buy a supermarket brand of baking powder – just check the label first to ensure it does not contain wheat.
Gluten-Free Bicarbonate of Soda	Bicarbonate of soda (also called baking soda, bread soda and sodium bicarbonate) is an alkalising agent that generally reacts with an acid to help breads rise (for example, bread soda with buttermilk in soda breads). If it is produced in a factory where wheat-based products are processed, there could be cross-contamination. Doves Farm does a certified gluten-free bicarbonate of soda suitable for coeliacs. If you are simply avoiding gluten, you could buy any supermarket brand of bicarbonate of soda.

| Xanthan Gum | Not a name that rolls off the tongue easily, xanthan gum is a fermented sugar made from bacteria that is used as a binding, thickening and gelling agent in gluten-free baking. It is effectively a gluten replacement, providing gluten-free bakes with a degree of elasticity and spring. However, it is possible to make gluten-free breads without it – for example, see the recipes for the almond and sesame seed loaf (page 245) and the buckwheat and flaxseed bread (page 258). I tend to use it sparingly as it can give gluten-free bakes a sticky, gummy texture. In addition, some people may be sensitive to it. |

OTHER KEY GLUTEN-FREE INGREDIENTS

| Psyllium Husk | Psyllium husk is the outer coating, or husk, of the psyllium seeds from the *Plantago ovata* plant, a herb grown primarily in India. It is a rich source of soluble fibre and is often used as a dietary supplement to improve gut health. It is an essential and, dare I say, magical ingredient in gluten-free bread-baking. It improves the structure, elasticity and texture of breads; keeps them moist and less crumbly; and prolongs their shelf life. Above all, it creates a structure for yeast to put air into your bread for a lighter bake. |

The hydrocolloidal ability of psyllium husk to bind water helps to form a sticky, elastic gel that transforms gluten-free bread from a loose, batter-like consistency into a springy dough that you can rise, shape and handle, similar to traditional yeasted bread doughs. While psyllium husk is the best gluten replacement for breads, xanthan gum is a more successful gluten replacement for cakes, muffins, cookies, pastries, etc. I buy packets of whole psyllium husks from my local health food store and use my electric spice grinder to make psyllium husk powder.

| Dairy Substitutes | Many of the recipes in this chapter use butter, natural yogurt, milk and buttermilk made from cow's milk as they impart a pleasing texture to gluten-free breads and keep them moist. If you are dairy-free or lactose |

	intolerant, I suggest replacing these ingredients with your favourite (preferably unsweetened) plant-based dairy-free substitutes.
Sugars	I tend to use natural sugars such as honey, maple syrup and blackstrap molasses or treacle to feed the yeast in my gluten-free yeasted breads, as they are a more natural product than sugar. However, sugar is fine as a direct 1:1 substitute.

AVOIDING CROSS-CONTAMINATION FOR COELIACS

Coeliac disease is an autoimmune disease. There is a particularly high prevalence of the disease in Ireland (one in every 100). Coeliac disease is serious as it inhibits the absorption of nutrients in the small intestine, including key minerals and vitamins. It causes the erosion of the villi – small hair-like protrusions lining the wall of the small intestine that facilitate the absorption of essential nutrients from carbohydrates, fats and proteins for transportation throughout the body – leading to nutrient deficiencies and malnourishment.

It is important to ensure that all the bread-making ingredients you are buying are certified for use by coeliacs and have not been cross-contaminated during the growing or manufacturing process. Look for the circular crossed grain symbol on gluten-free products, which certifies that they are gluten-free. If in doubt, email the manufacturer.

Whether cooking in a domestic environment or professionally for coeliacs, it is vital to ensure the following to avoid cross-contamination, which can make coeliacs very sick:

+ Have separate cooking utensils and equipment, even separate tea towels, for coeliac cooking and thoroughly wash equipment before use for coeliac cooking.
+ Have a dedicated section of the kitchen or time of the day for coeliac cooking, ensuring all surfaces are thoroughly cleaned beforehand.
+ Store gluten-free ingredients separately in well-labelled airtight containers.
+ Have a dedicated deep-fryer with fresh oil for coeliacs (in restaurants/cafés).
+ Have a separate toaster for coeliacs.
+ Educate family members or staff about coeliac disease, the importance of avoiding cross-contamination of coeliac food and how to prepare and serve coeliac food safely.

In terms of baking your own breads, the following flours should be permanently avoided by coeliacs: wheat varieties (spelt, einkorn, khorasan/kamut, farro, durum/semolina), barley, rye and all their derivatives.

Gluten-Free Almond and Sesame Seed Loaf

This quick, dairy-free, moist sandwich loaf keeps and freezes very well. It's a rich source of vitamin E and good fats from the almonds. It's a super-nutritious, protein-rich and filling bread, especially for sporty folk.

MAKES 1 LOAF

....

- 230g ground almonds
- 60g tapioca flour
- 30g ground golden linseeds (flaxseeds) - I like the colour of the golden flaxseeds in this bread, but ground brown linseeds can also be used
- 1 heaped tablespoon sesame seeds, plus extra for sprinkling on top
- 1 rounded teaspoon gluten-free baking powder
- 1 teaspoon sea salt
- ½ teaspoon gluten-free bicarbonate of soda
- 3 large eggs
- 2 egg whites (60g)
- 50ml unsweetened almond milk
- 50ml fruity extra virgin olive oil

Preheat the oven to 180°C/350°F/gas mark 4. Line a 13cm × 20cm (450g) loaf tin with non-stick parchment paper.

Combine all the dry ingredients in a large, wide bowl and whisk together.

Combine all the wet ingredients in a separate bowl and whisk together vigorously to aerate the mixture. Add the wet ingredients to the dry ingredients and stir to incorporate without over-mixing. Pour into the lined tin, smooth the top of the batter with a wet spatula and sprinkle a few extra sesame seeds on top.

Bake in the preheated oven for 40–45 minutes, until a skewer inserted into the bread comes out clean. Allow to cool completely in the tin before cutting.

This bread keeps moist for days and freezes well. I usually slice the whole loaf and freeze it in two-slice packs for convenience.

Gluten-Free Griddle Pan Flatbreads

This simple, speedy flatbread lends itself well to a myriad of different flavour additions. It's great with Middle Eastern dips and with curries.

MAKES 4

- 250g thick natural yogurt (or see the note)
- 240g gluten-free self-raising flour
- 1 teaspoon extra virgin olive oil
- ¼ teaspoon xanthan gum
- generous pinch of sea salt

Mix all the ingredients together with your hand in a wide bowl to from a soft dough, then knead lightly in the bowl until smooth. Add a little more flour if the dough is too wet or a little more yogurt if it's too dry. Cover the bowl and rest for 30 minutes at room temperature.

Meanwhile, cut out four strips of non-stick parchment paper, each measuring 15cm × 21cm.

Put a ridged grill pan or an ordinary cast iron pan over a high heat for 5–8 minutes. It is important that the pan is hot to form a crust immediately on the first side of the flatbreads. For best results, ensure your dough is nice and thin and your pan is hot.

Tip the rested dough out onto a dry, well-floured surface and divide into four balls. Roll each ball lightly in flour. Place a ball of dough on a floured parchment strip and press it into an oval shape approximately 3mm thick using a floured hand. You can use a floured rolling pin to get a nice even, flat surface. Repeat with the other three pieces of dough.

Use the parchment paper to flip the bread carefully onto the dry preheated pan. Remember, the pan will be very hot, so don't let your hand touch the pan. You can also put a wide metal slice under the paper to flip the flatbreads onto the pan. Peel back the paper immediately. Cook on one side for 2–3 minutes, until light golden brown, then flip over and cook on the other side for a further 2–3 minutes. The flatbreads should be soft and pliable.

NOTE: If you don't have thick natural yogurt, you can put your thinner yogurt into a piece of muslin and hang it over a bowl for a couple of hours to extract the whey, leaving you with a thicker yogurt.

These flatbreads freeze well once cooled and can be revived from frozen in a moderate oven for 6-7 minutes or thawed out and warmed in the microwave for 20 seconds.

Suggested Flavourings	You can use any number of savoury herbs and spices to flavour these simple flatbreads. I sometimes put a level teaspoon of ground turmeric, 1 tablespoon of finely chopped fresh coriander and 1 teaspoon of freshly ground coriander seeds into the dough along with all the dry ingredients.
Gluten-Free Griddle Pan Pizzas	These are so delicious and quick to make and you can top them with anything you fancy. First prepare your favourite pizza sauce and toppings. Preheat your ridged grill pan or regular cast iron frying pan as above and preheat your grill to 230°C/450°F/gas mark 8. Ensure that whatever pan you are using is suitable for putting under a hot grill – plastic handles do not fare well!
	Make and shape the dough as described above so that you have four flatbread doughs on parchment strips. Put two strips of dough at a time in the preheated pan, immediately remove the parchment paper strips and cook for 2–3 minutes. Flip the flatbreads and cook on the other side for 2 minutes. Now remove the pan from the heat and quickly add a smear of pizza sauce (thick, not watery) and your favourite toppings, finishing with cheese. Put the pan under the preheated grill and cook until the cheese is melted. Serve immediately with a handful of rocket on top and a splash of good balsamic vinegar.

Gluten-Free White Sandwich Loaf or Rolls

I adapted the following recipe from Becky Excell's recipe for a crusty white sandwich loaf in her book *How to Make Anything Gluten Free*. This child-friendly, deliciously crusty and light white yeast bread is ideal for sandwiches and packed lunches, as it stays fresh for days. This dough can also be made into rolls for burgers or anything you like. In the interest of energy savings (yours and the oven's), I recommend making a double batch of this dough to bake into loaves or rolls or a combination thereof.

MAKES 1 LOAF OR 6 ROLLS

- 2 teaspoons honey
- 470ml warm water
- 20g fresh yeast or 10g Doves Farm gluten-free quick yeast
- 185g Doves Farm gluten-free white bread flour
- 175g white rice flour
- 25g psyllium husk powder
- 1 teaspoon xanthan gum
- 1 teaspoon salt
- 3 egg whites (75g)
- 2 teaspoons cider vinegar

In a jug, dissolve the honey in the warm water, then crumble the fresh yeast on top or stir in the dried yeast. Allow to stand somewhere warm for 10 minutes, until it froths up.

Put the gluten-free white bread flour, white rice flour, psyllium husk powder, xanthan gum and salt in the bowl of a stand mixer. Mix the dry ingredients together with the paddle attachment until well combined. Add the egg whites, vinegar and the frothy yeast mixture. Mix on high speed for 5 minutes, until well combined and there are no lumps. (Alternatively, put all the ingredients in a wide bowl and use an electric hand mixer.) Cover the bowl and let the dough rest for 10 minutes to absorb some of the liquid. This is an important step in the recipe.

For a loaf of bread, put the rested dough into a 13cm × 20cm (450g) lined loaf tin, allowing the edges of the non-stick parchment to come 5cm above the tin all the way around. Secure the short end of the paper with toothpicks (make sure the paper does not touch the top of your oven, as it can catch light). This is important as it creates a stable structure for the bread to rise above the tin. Smooth the top of the dough with a spatula, cover with muslin and allow it to rise in a warm, draught-free place for 35–45 minutes, until it is approx. 2.5cm above the top of the tin.

For bread rolls, turn the rested dough out onto a well-floured surface. With floured hands, roll gently into a wide sausage shape. Divide the dough into six even pieces and shape lightly into rounds, tucking the edges under. Place on a tray lined with non-stick greaseproof paper, dust with gluten-free flour (using a sieve) and cover lightly with a piece of muslin. I like the rolls to join together during the rising to give greater stability, so they do not need to be spaced apart. Allow to rise in a warm, draught-free place for 30–40 minutes.

After the first 25 minutes of rising for either the loaf or the rolls, preheat the oven fully to its maximum temperature or at least 250°C/480°F/gas mark 9. Put a metal roasting tray on the bottom shelf of the oven and put the kettle on, as you will need boiling water when the bread is ready to cook.

When the loaf has risen sufficiently, dust the top with a little flour, place in the preheated oven and carefully add a mug of boiling water to the roasting tray to create steam, which will help the bread to rise and create a crust. Bake for 20 minutes, then turn the oven down to 220°C/430°F/gas mark 7 and bake for an additional 40–50 minutes, until golden brown. Remove from the oven, take it out of the tin and tap the base – it should sound hollow if it's cooked. Cool completely on a wire rack before slicing.

The bread rolls can rise more quickly than the loaf, so check them after 30 minutes. If they have more or less doubled in size, dust them with gluten-free flour and bake them as for the loaf, not forgetting the mug of boiling water. When the oven temperature is reduced to the lower heat, check them after 20 minutes – if they feel light and crusty, they are ready. Cool completely on a wire rack before cutting or freezing.

Gluten-Free Brown Sandwich Loaf

This deliciously nutty, light brown yeast bread is ideal for sandwiches and toasting. It has a higher nutritional profile than the white sandwich loaf on page 248 and great flavour. It keeps and freezes well.

- 1 heaped teaspoon black treacle
- 470ml warm water
- 20g fresh yeast or 10g Doves Farm gluten-free quick yeast
- 185g Doves Farm gluten-free brown bread flour
- 175g buckwheat flour
- 25g psyllium husk powder
- 1 teaspoon xanthan gum
- 1 teaspoon salt
- 3 egg whites (75g)
- 2 teaspoons cider vinegar
- pinch of sesame seeds for the top (optional)

In a jug, dissolve the black treacle in the warm water, crumble the fresh yeast on top or stir in the dried yeast and allow to stand somewhere warm for 10 minutes, until it froths up.

Put the gluten-free brown bread flour, buckwheat flour, psyllium husk powder, xanthan gum and salt in the bowl of a stand mixer. Mix the dry ingredients together until well combined, then add the egg whites, vinegar and the frothy yeast mixture. Mix on high speed with the paddle attachment of your stand mixer for 5 minutes, until well combined and there are no lumps. (Alternatively, put all the ingredients in a wide bowl and use an electric hand mixer.) Cover the bowl and let the dough rest for 10 minutes to absorb some of the liquid. This is an important step in the recipe.

Put the rested dough in a lined 13cm × 20cm (450g) loaf tin, allowing the edges of the non-stick parchment to come 5cm above the tin all the way around. Secure the short end of the paper with toothpicks (make sure the paper does not touch the top of your oven, as it can catch light). This is important, as it creates a stable structure for the bread to rise above the tin. Smooth the top of the dough with a spatula and allow it to rise in a warm, draught-free place for 35–45 minutes, until it is approx. 2.5cm above the top of the tin.

After the first 25 minutes of rising, preheat the oven fully to its maximum temperature or at least 250°C/480°F/ gas mark 9. Put a metal roasting tray on the bottom shelf of the oven and put the kettle on, as you will need boiling water when the bread is ready to cook.

When risen, dust the top of the loaf with a little buckwheat flour, place in the preheated oven and carefully add a mug of boiling water to the roasting tray to create steam, which will help the bread to rise and create a crust. Bake for 20 minutes, then turn the oven down to 220°C/430°F/gas mark 7 and bake for an additional 40–50 minutes, until golden brown. Remove from the oven, take it out of the tin and tap the base – it should sound hollow if it's cooked. Cool completely on a wire rack before slicing.

Gluten-Free Bastible Irish White Soda Bread

A bastible is a flat-bottomed, cast iron pot used for baking and cooking meals in 19th- and early 20th-century Ireland. It sat on or was suspended over an open fire and was the primary source of cooking in most Irish country cottages of old. The joy of cooking Irish soda bread in this traditional way is not only keeping our culinary heritage alive, but also the resulting loaf has a pleasing crust and remains moist and fluffy inside. This quick dough can also be used to make Irish soda bread focaccia (page 254) and Irish soda bread pizza (see the next page).

MAKES 1 LOAF

....

- 225g Bob's Red Mill gluten-free all-purpose flour
- 225g gluten-free plain white flour
- 1¼ teaspoons gluten-free baking powder
- 1 level teaspoon gluten-free bicarbonate of soda, finely sieved
- 1 teaspoon salt
- scant ¾ teaspoon xanthan gum
- 1 egg, whisked
- 1 tablespoon olive oil (or rub 25g butter into the dry mixture)
- 400ml buttermilk

Trace around the base of your cast iron pot or a casserole/Dutch oven on a piece of non-stick parchment paper and cut it out (I use an oval 21cm Le Creuset cast iron casserole). Cover the pot with its lid, put it in the oven and preheat it to 230°C/450°F/gas mark 8 for 15 minutes.

Meanwhile, sieve the dry ingredients together in a large, wide bowl and whisk to ensure all the raising agents, salt and xanthan gum are well dispersed through the flours. Make a well in the centre, add the whisked egg and olive oil and pour in most of the buttermilk (about 90%). Using one hand, with the fingers open and rigid, mix in a full circle, drawing in the flour from the sides of the bowl, adding more milk if necessary. The dough should be very soft but holding a shape – no kneading is required. It is very important not to overmix a soda bread as it makes for a heavy loaf.

When the dough comes together, which should take no more than a minute, tip it out onto a dry, well-floured surface. Shake more flour on top and shape it gently with dry, well-floured hands into the approximate shape for your bastible (oval, round, etc.), tucking the edges under.

Carefully remove the preheated bastible from the oven with a dry cloth or oven gloves. Line it with your cut-out parchment paper and drop the shaped dough into it. Press the top down slightly. With a floured knife, cut a deep cross into the dough. Put the lid on – remember, it's very hot! – and bake in the preheated oven for 30–35 minutes. Remove the lid and bake for a final 10 minutes with the lid off, until golden brown. The bread should sound hollow like a drum or bodhran when tapped if properly cooked. Allow to cool on a wire rack completely before cutting.

This bread is best eaten on the day it is made and does not keep or freeze well. However, it does make great breadcrumbs for stuffing if there is any left (see page 266 on how to make breadcrumbs).

Irish Soda
Bread Pizza

Roll out the dough on a well-floured surface into 2 × 22cm round pizza bases 1cm thick. Simply put the pizza bases on a floured baking tray, spread with pizza sauce and the toppings of your choice. Bake in an oven preheated to 230°C/450°F/gas mark 8 for 10 minutes, then reduce the temperature to 200°C/400°F/gas mark 6 and bake for a further 20–25 minutes, until the bottom of the pizza is golden brown and crusty. Serve immediately.

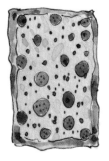

Gluten-Free Irish Soda Bread Focaccia with Roasted Pumpkin and Rosemary

This delicious recipe was inspired by Rory O'Connell, who puts sprigs of rosemary on the bottom of the tray and places the dough on top so that the rosemary gets crisp and cooks into the dough, then studs the top with roasted pumpkin.

MAKES 1

....

- 1 batch of gluten-free bastible Irish white soda bread dough (page 252)
- 2 tablespoons good olive oil
- 10 small sprigs of fresh rosemary

....

FOR THE TOPPING:
- 450g butternut squash or pumpkin (peeled weight), peeled and cut into 2cm cubes
- 1 tablespoon good olive oil
- 2 teaspoons fennel seeds, toasted and coarsely ground
- pinch of chilli flakes
- sea salt and freshly ground black pepper
- 1 tablespoon chopped fresh rosemary
- 50g Ardsallagh goat's cheese
- 110g Irish Cheddar cheese, grated

Preheat the oven to 230°C/450°F/gas mark 8.

Put the squash or pumpkin in a bowl and toss with the olive oil, ground fennel seeds and chilli flakes. Season with sea salt and freshly ground black pepper and toss again to coat. Tip out onto a baking tray in a single layer and bake in the preheated oven for 15–20 minutes, until tender and golden. Allow to cool slightly.

While the squash or pumpkin is cooking, make the dough as in the recipe for the gluten-free bastible Irish white soda bread.

Liberally oil a 23cm × 33cm Swiss roll tin with the 2 tablespoons of olive oil and scatter the rosemary sprigs evenly over the tin. Put your dough on a dry, well-floured surface and roll evenly to the approximate size of the tin. Put the dough in the tin, dot with the roasted squash or pumpkin, sprinkle with the chopped rosemary and dot with teaspoons of the creamy goat's cheese. Finally, scatter the grated Cheddar on top.

Bake in the preheated oven for 10 minutes, then reduce the temperature to 200°C/400°F/gas mark 6 and bake for a further 20–25 minutes, until the bottom of the focaccia is golden brown and crusty. Loosen the bread from the edges of the tin and slide it onto a cooling rack before slicing it into generous square chunks. Deliciously filling with a nice bowl of soup.

Gluten-Free Focaccia with Rosemary, Olives and Sea Salt

This is a light, tasty, single-rise bread. It's best eaten on the day it's made, but if it's gone stale, slice and use for bruschetta.

- extra virgin olive oil
- 20g fresh yeast or 10g Doves Farm gluten-free quick yeast
- 2 teaspoons honey
- 2 tablespoons warm water
- 550g Bob's Red Mill gluten-free all-purpose flour (or see the note)
- 1½ teaspoons xanthan gum
- 1 teaspoon salt
- 2 eggs, well beaten
- 300ml tepid milk
- 3 tablespoons natural yogurt
- 1 teaspoon white wine vinegar
- 12 black olives, stones removed
- 1½ tablespoons chopped fresh rosemary
- pinch of flaky sea salt

Line a 25cm square brownie tin with parchment paper and oil it with good olive oil.

Put the yeast, honey and warm water in a small bowl in a warm place for 10–15 minutes, until it froths up.

Sift the flour and xanthan gum into a large, wide bowl. Add the salt, eggs, warm milk, yogurt, vinegar and the yeast mixture, mixing well. Put the dough into the lined tin. Wet your fingers with cold water and make a few deep dimples in the dough. Put a damp cloth or piece of muslin over the tin and put it in a warm place to rise for 1–1½ hours, until doubled in size.

Preheat the oven to 190°C/375°F/gas mark 5.

Gently dot the top of the dough with the stoned olives, then sprinkle on the chopped rosemary and sea salt. Bake in the preheated oven for 50 minutes, until it sounds hollow and light when you tap the base. Drizzle with a little more good olive oil and allow to cool completely on a wire rack before cutting.

NOTE: I use Bob's Red Mill all-purpose flour for its nutritional value in this recipe and because it bakes well. However, it has a beany taste that not everyone enjoys. For a less dense, more neutral-tasting loaf, I find that using 275g Bob's Red Mill 1-to-1 baking flour and 275g Doves Farm gluten-free plain flour produces a light loaf with a lovely texture. I have also successfully made this recipe with 550g Doves Farm gluten-free plain white flour.

Gluten-Free Little Oat Loaves

This bread keeps well and is speedy to make, with just two core ingredients: certified gluten-free oats and natural yogurt. I have given a standard recipe here, but you can add honey, seeds or chopped nuts to make it even more nutritious and tasty. I have also made this bread successfully without the egg, which is a useful option for anyone with an egg allergy or intolerance.

MAKES 2 MINI LOAVES OR
1 LARGE LOAF

....

- 450-500ml natural yogurt
- 1 heaped teaspoon blackstrap molasses or treacle
- 1 egg, beaten
- 425g certified gluten-free whole oats, not jumbo (make sure they have the crossed-grain symbol)
- scant 1½ teaspoons gluten-free bicarbonate of soda, finely sieved
- ¾ teaspoon salt
- ½ teaspoon gluten-free baking powder, finely sieved
- 2 tablespoons poppy seeds
- 2 tablespoons sesame seeds

Preheat the oven to 200°C/400°F/gas mark 6. Line 2 × 225g loaf tins or one 13cm × 20cm (450g) loaf tin with parchment paper.

Put the yogurt, molasses or treacle and the egg in a bowl and whisk together to combine.

Put the whole oats, sieved bicarbonate of soda, salt and baking powder in a large, wide bowl. Mix well, then add the yogurt mixture. Use your hand to bring the dough together lightly, but do not overwork. The dough will be soft but not wet.

Divide the dough between the two lined mini tins or place in one large tin, then sprinkle the seeds on top. Bake in the preheated oven for 50–55 minutes for the minis and up to 1 hour 10 minutes for the large loaf. Remove the loaves from their tins and put them back on the rack of the oven and bake for a further 5 minutes to form a crust. Cool completely on a wire rack before cutting. These loaves keep and freeze well.

Gluten-Free Express Pizza

This simple recipe offers hungry, budget-conscious folks a speedy homemade pizza in a jiffy that everyone will enjoy, gluten-free or not.

MAKES 1 × 30CM BASE

- 140g Doves Farm gluten-free self-raising flour
- ¼ teaspoon gluten-free bicarbonate of soda, finely sieved
- ¼ teaspoon salt
- 200ml natural yogurt
- pizza sauce and toppings of your choice (see below)

You need to have your pizza sauce made and your toppings prepped before you start making this dough.

Put a large, flat baking tray that can accommodate a 30cm pizza in the oven while it preheats to 230°C/450°F/gas mark 8. It's important that the oven and tray are hot.

Draw a 30cm circle using a large dinner plate or the metal base from a 30cm tart tin on a piece of non-stick parchment paper.

Put the flour, bicarbonate of soda and salt in a medium-sized bowl, then make a well in the centre and add the natural yogurt. Mix with a fork to remove any lumps. The dough will be disconcertingly soft.

Put blobs of the dough onto the circle on the parchment paper and use a palette knife or the back of a large spoon to spread the dough evenly but gently, creating a ridge on the edge of the circle. Time is of the essence here, as the lactic acid in the yogurt is already reacting with the alkalising bicarbonate of soda and bubbling up, so it needs to be put into the oven quickly.

Carefully drag the whole sheet of parchment with the spread-out dough onto the preheated baking tray. Bake in the preheated oven for 8 minutes, until it has a pale golden crust. Take it out of the oven and spread a little thick (not watery) pizza sauce on the precooked base and top with ingredients of your choice, finishing with cheese. Resist the temptation to overload the pizza or it will be soggy! Return to the oven and cook for 10–15 minutes, until crisp.

Here are some of my favourite toppings:

+ Crozier Blue cheese, caramelised onions
+ Thin courgette ribbons, Ardsallagh goat's cheese, marjoram oil
+ Roast peppers, grilled aubergines, feta cheese, black olives
+ Roast pumpkin, goat's cheese, crispy sage, chilli oil (page 322)
+ Wild mushrooms, thyme, Cashel Blue cheese

Gluten-Free Buckwheat and Flaxseed Bread

I love this nutty and nutritious wholegrain loaf. It's ideal for sandwiches and great for toasting. It's a light yeasted dough that doesn't require any xanthan gum or psyllium husk, which is a bonus if you have run out! I make it frequently.

MAKES 1 LOAF

....

- 1 teaspoon black treacle or honey
- 120ml tepid milk
- 15-18g fresh yeast or 10g Doves Farm gluten-free quick yeast
- 1 large egg
- 2 egg whites (50g)
- 50g freshly ground brown flaxseeds
- 100g buckwheat flour, sieved
- 30g brown rice flour, sieved
- ½ teaspoon salt
- 110g tapioca starch, sieved - measure into a separate bowl
- olive oil, for greasing
- sesame seeds

Add the treacle or honey to the tepid milk, stirring to dissolve it, then sprinkle the fresh or dried yeast on top. Allow to stand somewhere warm for 10 minutes to froth up.

Whisk together the large egg and the egg whites in a large bowl. Stir the milk and yeast mixture into the whisked eggs, then mix in the ground flaxseeds. Set aside to allow the flaxseeds to absorb the liquid for 10–15 minutes. The resting time is important, as it helps the mixture to thicken.

Stir in the sieved buckwheat and brown rice flours and the salt and allow to absorb for a further 5 minutes. Add the sieved tapioca starch to the rested dough.

Preheat the oven to 230°C/450°F/gas mark 8. Oil a 13cm × 20cm (450g) loaf tin very well.

Transfer the dough to the well-oiled loaf tin, cover with a clean tea towel, put it in a warm spot and allow it to rise for 50–60 minutes, until it reaches 1cm below the top of the tin. Bake in the preheated oven for 10 minutes, then reduce the temperature to 200°C/400°F/gas mark 6 and bake for a further 30–35 minutes, until the bread sounds hollow when you tap the bottom and the loaf feels light. Remove the loaf from the tin and put it back on the rack of the oven to form a crust for a further 5 minutes. Cool completely on a wire rack before cutting. This bread keeps well.

Gluten-Free Skillet Cornbread

I like to bake this sweet and spicy cornbread in a 26.6cm cast iron skillet in the traditional Southern USA way. However, it also works well in a 20cm square tin, lined with parchment paper. It is at its most delicious straight out of the oven, smeared generously with butter, or it's great served warm fresh from the oven with a big bowl of veggie chilli or chilli con carne with all the fixings.

MAKES 1 LARGE SKILLET OR TIN

- 260g coarsely ground yellow polenta or cornmeal
- 2 rounded teaspoons gluten-free baking powder, sieved
- 1 level teaspoon gluten-free bicarbonate of soda, finely sieved
- 1 teaspoon salt
- 2 medium eggs or 1 very large egg
- 350ml natural yogurt, at room temperature
- 50g butter, melted
- 60ml maple syrup
- 1-2 green jalapeño chillies, seeds removed and very finely chopped
- oil or butter, for greasing

TO SERVE:
- soft butter (mixed with a splash or two or hot sauce if you like it extra hot!)

Preheat the oven to 200°C/400°F/gas mark 6.

You will need two large, wide bowls: one for the dry ingredients and one for the wet ingredients. Put the polenta or cornmeal, baking powder, bicarbonate of soda and salt in one bowl and use a whisk to mix them together to ensure the raising agents and salt are evenly dispersed throughout the polenta.

Put the eggs in a second bowl and whisk well, then add the yogurt, melted butter, maple syrup and chopped jalapeño and whisk everything together thoroughly.

Using a spatula, gently fold the wet ingredients into the dry ingredients, ensuring they are well mixed without overworking the batter, which leads to a heavy bake. Transfer the batter into a 26.6cm greased cast iron skillet or a 20cm square tin lined with parchment paper.

Bake in the preheated oven for 20–25 minutes, until golden brown and springy to the touch. Serve immediately smeared with soft butter or the hot sauce butter. This bread is best eaten on the day it's baked.

Gluten-Free Sweet Raisin Scones

Freshly baked scones are a national institution in Ireland and are eaten at any time of the day. This is my deliciously light gluten-free version.

MAKES 10

- 225g gluten-free self-raising flour, sieved
- 85g ground almonds
- 3 tablespoons caster sugar
- 1 rounded teaspoon gluten-free baking powder, sieved
- 1 scant teaspoon xanthan gum, sieved
- pinch of salt
- 100g butter, cut into cubes and chilled
- 75g raisins (optional)
- 1 large egg
- 1 egg white (30g)
- 100-110ml natural yogurt
- egg wash (page 325)
- 3 tablespoons Demerara sugar (optional)

Preheat the oven to 250°C/480°F/gas mark 9. Do not use a fan oven as it's a drying heat. If you only have a fan oven, though, reduce the temperature by 20°C (70°F).

Thoroughly mix the flour, ground almonds, sugar, baking powder, xanthan gum and a pinch of salt in a large bowl. Lightly rub the cold, cubed butter into the dry mixture using your fingers. Add the raisins (if using).

Whisk the egg, egg white and yogurt together. Make a well in the centre of the dry ingredients and add the egg and yogurt mixture. Gently mix to a form a soft dough that holds a shape, adding a little more yogurt if it's too dry and a little more flour if it's too wet to handle.

Turn the dough out onto a floured surface and knead lightly, just enough to shape into a round. Roll out to about 2.5cm thick and stamp into scones using a 6.5cm fluted cutter. Brush each scone with a little egg wash and dip in the Demerara sugar (if using). Place on a lightly floured baking tray, leaving a 2.5cm gap between them.

Bake on the centre shelf of the preheated oven for 8–10 minutes, until they are golden brown on top and feel hollow and light. Cool on a wire rack.

These scones are best eaten on the day they are made but are also acceptable frozen and revived in the microwave for 20 seconds or in a moderate oven for 8–10 minutes.

Variations

Very finely chopped sour cherries, dried figs, dates or apricots are a delicious addition. Lemon or orange zest, cinnamon or other sweet spices are also yum (cardamom and orange is a wonderful combination). Kids (and a few adults I know) also love them with dark chocolate chips. These ingredients should be added at the dry stage after the butter has been rubbed in and before the wet ingredients are added.

Gluten-Free Savoury Gubbeen Chorizo and Cheese Scones

The Gubbeen chorizo, which is naturally gluten-free, and Gubbeen cheese make these delicious scones a bit special. Perfect with a hearty soup.

MAKES 10

....

- 225g gluten free self-raising flour, sieved
- 85g ground almonds
- 1 rounded teaspoon gluten-free baking powder, sieved
- 1 scant teaspoon xanthan gum, sieved
- pinch of salt
- 100g butter, cut into cubes and chilled
- 75g Gubbeen chorizo, cut into 1cm dice (or ensure the chorizo sausage you are using is gluten-free)
- 1 large egg
- 1 egg white (30g)
- 100-110ml natural yogurt
- egg wash (page 325)
- 110g grated Gubbeen cheese or Irish Cheddar

Preheat the oven to 230°C/450°F/gas mark 8.

Thoroughly mix the flour, ground almonds, baking powder, xanthan gum and a pinch of salt in a large bowl. Lightly rub the cold, cubed butter into the dry mixture using your fingers. Add the very finely diced chorizo sausage.

Whisk the egg, egg white and yogurt together. Make a well in the centre of the dry ingredients and add the egg and yogurt mixture. Gently mix to a form a soft dough that holds a shape, adding a little more yogurt if it's too dry and a little more flour if it's too wet to handle.

Turn the dough out onto a floured surface and knead lightly, just enough to shape into a rectangle. Roll out to about 2.5cm thick and cut into 10 equal-sized squares using a floured dough cutter or long knife.

Sprinkle the Cheddar cheese onto a plate. Brush each scone with egg wash and dip them into the grated cheese. Place on a lightly floured baking tray, leaving a 2.5cm gap between them.

Bake on the centre shelf of the preheated oven for 8–10 minutes, until the cheese is golden brown and the scones feel hollow and light. Cool on a wire rack.

These scones are best eaten on the day they are made but are also acceptable frozen and revived in the microwave for 20 seconds or in a moderate oven for 8–10 minutes.

For inspiration for more savoury scone options, see page 263. As this is a small batch, you may need to adjust the quantities of add-ins accordingly.

Gluten-Free Drop Scones

One of the many joys of this speedy recipe, apart from its adaptability for sweet or savoury dishes, is that you don't need a weighing scales to make it. I use the same wide-brimmed pottery cup to mix this light drop scone batter. I cook it for everyone and do not announce its gluten-free status unless I'm making it for a coeliac or gluten-/wheat-intolerant guest and it is always very well received.

....

- 4 rounded tablespoons gluten free self-raising flour (or 3 rounded tablespoons gluten-free self-raising flour and 1 rounded tablespoon buckwheat flour for added nutrition)
- generous pinch of gluten-free bicarbonate of soda, finely sieved
- 1 large egg
- 1 generous tablespoon natural yogurt
- 1 tablespoon olive oil
- 1 teaspoon butter (optional)

Heat a cast iron or non-stick frying pan over a medium heat.

While the pan is heating up, put the flour and bicarbonate of soda in a large wide-brimmed cup or small bowl. Add the egg and yogurt and mix vigorously with a fork until any lumps are removed. This batter can be used immediately and does not need to stand.

Put the olive oil and butter (if using) in the preheated pan and swirl to coat it. Drop dessertspoonfuls of the batter into the pan without overcrowding it – I fit five at a time in my 23cm cast iron frying pan. Cook for 1 minute, then turn the heat down to low. As soon as you see bubbles appearing on the surface of the drop scones, flip them over gently and cook for 2–3 minutes more.

Serve immediately with your favourite toppings. This batter is best used immediately, not kept for the next day.

Sweet Suggestions

+ Smear butter (or dairy-free spread) and homemade jam on the hot drop scones.
+ Serve with fresh berries in summer and apple sauce with cinnamon in winter. Drizzle with maple syrup and spoon on natural yogurt, natural kefir yogurt or coconut yogurt for a dairy-free option.
+ Before you flip the drop scones over and when you see the bubbles appearing on the surface, dot each drop scone with a few chocolate chips, pushing them lightly under the batter, then flip to cook the other side for a minute or two. I serve these chocolate chip drop scones with sliced bananas fried in a little olive oil, a

generous knob of butter, 1 teaspoon dark soft brown sugar, a splash of maple syrup and the juice of ½ orange. A big hit with smallies!

Savoury Suggestions + Add a tablespoon of chopped fresh chives to the batter. When cooked, serve with smoked salmon, crème fraîche and a grating of lemon zest.
+ Serve the hot drop scones with crisp bacon and maple syrup.

LEFTOVER BREAD

Bread is sacred in so many cultures around the world. Consequently, it's considered to be unlucky or even sinful to waste a single morsel. Every cuisine has its favourite ways to use up stale bread. Here are a few suggestions. Bread also freezes well. It's worth keeping a few slices in the freezer, well wrapped, as a standby to make toast.

How to Refresh a Loaf of Stale Bread	If a loaf is just slightly stale, simply pop it back into a hot oven at 200°C/400°F/gas mark 6 for about 5 minutes or until it gets crusty. If it is several days old, however, dip it in or brush it quickly with cold water, shake and then bake for 8–10 minutes, until the bread is crusty and delicious – it will resemble a freshly baked loaf. Eat immediately. To refresh just a slice, moisten the surface of the slice of stale bread lightly on both sides, then toast. The steam generated will soften the crumb. Enjoy immediately.
Fried Bread	We ate fried bread a lot when we were children, usually Mummy's brown soda bread, fried in bacon fat. We'd have that with a rasher, an egg and a fried tomato.
A Bread Tureen	Slice a lid off a stale-ish round loaf of sourdough or yeast bread (preferably one or two days old). Scoop out all the soft crumbs (save for breadcrumbs – see page 266). Brush the inside with extra virgin olive oil and season with a little sea salt. Dip your hand in cold water and rub it all over the outside and the lid. Pop into a hot oven preheated to 220°C/430°F/gas mark 7 for 5–8 minutes to crisp up. Fill with stew or thick, nourishing soup and serve immediately. The crust will be delicious too.
Stale Cake	There are plenty of traditions for using up bits of stale cake. We make a summer pudding that uses cake instead of stale sliced bread and call it Marie Antoinette summer pudding, which references her famous 'let them eat cake' remark during the French Revolution. Some cakes would have included cake crumbs in the mixture. Or you can make a chocolate biscuit cake out of leftover biscuits and melted chocolate (or dried fruit, perhaps), mixed together, poured into a cake tin and cooled.

Breadcrumbs

Any time you have a slice or two of bread or a heel left over, make breadcrumbs. I've seen breadcrumbs for sale for more than the price of a loaf of bread for a 250g bag, so let me share the secret of how simple it is to make your own.

You can make breadcrumbs by grating squares of stale bread on the coarsest part of a box grater. The breadcrumbs won't be as uniform as those made in a food processor, but that's fine. This doesn't work with modern sliced bread, which tends to be more rubbery. Breadcrumbs are normally made with white yeast bread, but soda breadcrumbs are also delicious.

Any time you have stale bread, get into the habit of whizzing it in the food processor, putting the breadcrumbs in a bag and popping it into the freezer. They don't freeze solid, so you can get to them at any time. There's something psychological about having them at the ready, which will make you more inclined to use them in stuffings, for coating fish, in plum puddings, croquettes, fish cakes and bread sauce, or as buttered crumbs or pangrattato.

Soft White Breadcrumbs	Cut off the crusts and tear each slice into three or four pieces. Drop them into a blender or food processor, whizz for 30–60 seconds and hey presto: breadcrumbs. Use immediately or freeze in conveniently sized bags for another time.
Brown Breadcrumbs	Do as above for soft white breadcrumbs but include the crusts. They will be flecked with lots of crust but are good to use for stuffings, for example, or any other dish where all the crumbs don't need to be white.
Dried Breadcrumbs	Cut the crusts off the bread slices, then spread out the crusts on a baking tray (use the rest of the slice for soft white breadcrumbs). Bake in an oven preheated to 100°C/210°F/gas mark ¼ for 2–3 hours. Leave to cool, then whizz the dry crusts a few at a time into fine breadcrumbs. Sieve and store in a screw-top jar or plastic

box until needed. They will keep for months. Use for coating cheese or fish croquettes.

Buttered Crumbs

We keep a box of buttered crumbs in the fridge to sprinkle over creamy gratins. They are even better when mixed with grated Cheddar cheese. Melt 50g butter in a pan and stir in 110g soft white breadcrumbs. Remove the pan from the heat and leave to cool. These will keep in the fridge for up to a week in a covered box or tray for an instant sprinkle.

Pangrattato

Pangrattato, the Italian name for buttered crumbs, uses extra virgin olive oil instead of butter and sprinkles in a handful of chopped fresh herbs as well. This Italian version of buttered crumbs is delicious sprinkled over all sorts of things, from pasta to roast chicken.

Chorizo Crumbs

Chorizo crumbs are delicious used in so many ways. We like to scatter them over potato, celeriac, Jerusalem artichoke or watercress soup. They are particularly good sprinkled over cauliflower or macaroni cheese. Put 4 tablespoons oil in a cool pan and add 125g peeled and diced chorizo (cut into 5mm dice). Toss on a low heat until the oil starts to run and the chorizo begins to crisp. Be careful – it's easy to burn the chorizo. Drain through a metal sieve, save the oil and return it to the pan. Increase the heat, add 100g coarse breadcrumbs and toss in the chorizo oil until crisp and golden. Drain and add to the chorizo. Keep in an airtight box in the fridge for several weeks to use when you fancy.

Ballymaloe
Breadcrumb and
Fresh Herb Stuffing

Our favourite for roast chicken, turkey, pheasant or guinea fowl. Melt 45g butter in a saucepan over a gentle heat. Add 75g chopped onions, cover the pan and sweat for approx. 10 minutes, until soft. Stir in 75–100g soft white breadcrumbs, 2 tablespoons of freshly chopped herbs (e.g. parsley, thyme, chives and/or annual marjoram), a little salt and pepper to taste. Allow it to get quite cold unless you are going to stuff a chicken with it and cook it immediately.

French Toast

French toast is fantastic, economical and, best of all, uses bread that you'd otherwise throw out – hence the French name, pain perdu, or 'lost bread'. French toast, poor knights of Windsor and eggy bread are all pretty much the same thing. It's not only a delicious sweet or savoury way to use up leftover bread, but a crafty way to get eggs into reluctant toddlers.

The Spanish have another version, torrijas, where they dip the bread in a mixture of egg yolks and sweet sherry, fry it in hot oil and serve it dusted with icing sugar and cinnamon. I love it piled high with berries or slathered with butter, marmalade and a blob of vanilla ice cream or crème fraîche. Panettone is also delicious cooked this way. It would hardly be a sacrifice to eat stale bread prepared like this!

SERVES 4

- 3 eggs
- 2 tablespoons full-cream milk or light cream
- pinch of salt
- 4 slices of good bread or brioche (page 198)
- 50g clarified butter (page 307)
- icing sugar, for dusting

Whisk the eggs, milk and salt together until well blended. Strain the mixture through a sieve into a shallow bowl in which you can easily dip a slice of bread. Dip both sides of each slice of bread in the mixture.

Melt 2 tablespoons of the clarified butter in a frying pan big enough to hold two slices at once. Fry the bread over a medium heat until pale golden, turning once. Keep warm in the oven while frying the other pieces in the remaining butter.

Serve warm, sprinkled with icing sugar.

Melba Toast

Melba toast is so retro now, reminiscent of grand hotels. Simply delicious to nibble on.

MAKES 16 TRIANGLES
....

— 4 slices of good white bread, cut into slices 5mm thick

Preheat the grill to its maximum heat.

Slide an oven rack under the grill as close to the element as possible. Put the bread on the oven rack and toast it on both sides.

Working quickly while the toast is still hot, cut off the crusts and split the bread in half horizontally. Scrape off any excess dough with a serrated knife or a teaspoon, then cut each slice into two or four triangles.

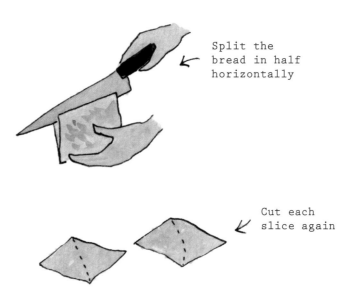

Split the bread in half horizontally

Cut each slice again

Lower the oven rack so it is about 12.5cm from the element, giving the toast room to curl up. Put the toast back under the grill on the oven rack. It will probably curl up within seconds but be careful not to let it burn. Alternatively, this second stage may also be done in an oven preheated to 150°C/300°F/gas mark 2.

Melba toast will keep in an airtight tin for a day or two but is best served immediately.

Parmesan Toasts

In many upmarket delis, day-old bread is sliced thinly, sprinkled with finely grated Parmesan cheese, baked and sold for four times the original price of the bread. Yet who could complain? It's delicious!

- day-old yeast or sourdough bread or good-quality baguette, cut into slices 3mm thick (if using a baguette, cut it at a long angle)
- extra virgin olive oil
- finely grated Parmesan cheese

Preheat the oven to 150°C/300°F/gas mark 2.

Brush one side of the thinly sliced bread with extra virgin olive oil and sprinkle with the freshly grated Parmesan cheese. Arrange in a single layer on a baking tray and bake in the preheated oven for about 30 minutes, until golden brown and crisp. Serve warm.

Bruschetta

Originally this recipe was just a way of using up day-old sourdough bread. Nowadays, people pile all kinds of things on top of it, sometimes to delicious effect, but if you've got good bread and beautiful new season extra virgin olive oil, it's perfect in and of itself. When I first ate it at a Tuscan family lunch, where we had the original, it was divine.

You can top bruschetta with rocket, tapenade (page 315), tomatoes and basil; roasted peppers, rocket and shavings of Parmesan; blue cheese and honey; or any number of other good things. Or in Catalonia, they rub a halved very ripe tomato on the surface of the bread and call it pan con tomate.

- 4 slices of crusty country white bread, cut into slices 1cm thick
- 1 garlic clove, cut in half
- extra virgin olive oil
- flaky sea salt

Toast or chargrill the bread on both sides, then rub it immediately with the cut clove of garlic. Drizzle with extra virgin olive oil and sprinkle with flaky sea salt.

Croutons

Croutons can be made several hours or even a day ahead with extra virgin olive oil flavoured with sprigs of rosemary, thyme or onion. Cut into cubes or stamp out into various shapes – hearts, stars, clubs, diamonds or whatever else takes your fancy – and sprinkle over salads or serve with soups.

- 2 slices of slightly stale white bread
- sunflower or olive oil

First cut the crusts off the bread, then cut the bread into strips 5mm thick and finally into cubes.

Heat some oil in a frying pan. It should be at least 2cm deep and almost smoking. Put a stainless steel sieve over a Pyrex or stainless steel bowl.

Add the bread cubes to the hot oil. Stir once or twice – they will colour almost immediately. When the croutons are golden brown, pour the oil and croutons into the stainless steel sieve, then drain the croutons on kitchen paper. Reheat the oil to cook another batch or save it for another purpose.

French Toast Breakfast Pudding

Another irresistible way to use up leftover challah, brioche or panettone. Be careful not to pack the dish too tightly or it will be heavy rather than deliciously light and fluffy.

SERVES 8-10

- butter, for greasing
- 300g approx. challah (page 164), brioche (page 198) or panettone
- 8 eggs
- 4 tablespoons honey or soft dark brown sugar
- 1 teaspoon pure ground cinnamon
- 1 teaspoon vanilla extract
- good pinch of salt
- 300ml cream
- 300ml milk

TO SERVE:
- icing sugar
- 20g pistachios or praline, coarsely chopped
- maple syrup

Grease a 23cm × 33cm × 5cm baking dish with butter. Fill the buttered dish loosely with slices and/or small chunks of challah, brioche or panettone.

Whisk the eggs in a large bowl. Add the honey or brown sugar, cinnamon, vanilla and a good pinch of salt, then whisk in the cream and milk. Pour this over the bread in the dish, cover and refrigerate for a couple of hours, or better still, overnight.

Preheat the oven to 180°C/350°F/gas mark 4.

To make a bain-marie, put the dish in a roasting tin and pour just-boiled water from the kettle into the tin until it comes halfway up the sides of the dish. Bake for 45 minutes, until the top is nicely golden and the custard is just set. Dust with a little icing sugar and a sprinkling of coarsely chopped pistachio or praline. Alternatively, cut into squares and drizzle with maple syrup.

Breakfast Bread Pudding

An even more economical version of the French toast breakfast pudding on page 273 but still delicious. I love this with a couple of slices of crisp streaky bacon.

SERVES 6-8

....

- butter, for greasing
- 210g leftover bread, cut into 2-2.5cm dice
- 3 eggs
- 75g caster sugar
- 250ml full-fat milk
- 1 teaspoon pure ground cinnamon
- 1 teaspoon vanilla extract
- pinch of salt

Grease a 20.5cm × 20.5cm square baking dish with butter. Scatter the bread cubes in the dish in a single layer.

In a separate bowl, whisk the eggs with 50g of the sugar and the milk, cinnamon and vanilla and a generous pinch of salt. Pour this over the bread cubes in the dish. Sprinkle the remaining sugar over the top and allow to sit for 20–30 minutes to absorb the custard.

Preheat the oven to 190°C/375°F/gas mark 5.

Put the dish in a roasting tin and pour just-boiled water from the kettle into the tin until it comes halfway up the sides of the dish. Put in the preheated oven and bake for 30 minutes, until just set.

Variation

Double the recipe for a 23cm × 33cm baking dish and increase the baking time by approx. 10 minutes.

Cheesy Bread Pudding

A yummy supper or light lunch made from leftover bread and a feisty cheese.

- 2 tablespoons very soft butter, plus extra for greasing
- 4-6 slices of white bread, cut into slices 2-3cm thick and crusts removed - about 150g prepared weight
- 100g mature Cheddar cheese, coarsely grated, plus extra for sprinkling
- 2 medium eggs
- 300ml milk
- 1 teaspoon fresh thyme leaves, chopped
- pinch of ground mace or nutmeg
- pinch of Dijon mustard
- flaky sea salt and freshly ground black pepper

Grease a 1-litre ovenproof soufflé dish with soft butter.

Butter the bread slices, then cut into cubes roughly 3cm × 3cm. There should be enough to fill the soufflé dish three-quarters full. Put the bread cubes in the dish, then add the grated cheese. Mix well so the cheese is evenly distributed.

Whisk the eggs in a separate bowl, then add the milk, thyme, mace or nutmeg and Dijon mustard. Whisk for 1–2 minutes. Season well with flaky sea salt and freshly ground black pepper. Slowly pour this over the bread and cheese mixture. Cover and pop in the refrigerator for at least 1 hour if you're in a hurry or overnight.

Preheat the oven to 200°C/400°F/gas mark 6.

Sprinkle some more cheese on top, then bake in the preheated oven for 40 minutes, until golden and puffed up deliciously.

Soda Bread and Butter Pudding with Cheese and Herbs

A delicious way to use up a few slices of stale soda bread. Vary the fresh herbs as you please.

SERVES 4-6

- 50g butter, softened, plus extra for greasing
- 12 slices of wheaten bread (brown soda bread; page 34) - 330g approx.
- 2 teaspoons chopped fresh thyme
- 2 teaspoons chopped fresh rosemary
- 2 teaspoons chopped fresh chives
- 100g mature Cheddar cheese, grated
- 8 eggs
- 100ml milk
- sea salt and freshly ground black pepper

Butter the slices of soda bread. Arrange half the bread side by side in a generously buttered 1.2-litre baking dish, butter side up, allowing a little space between each slice. Sprinkle with half of the chopped herbs and half of the grated cheese.

Whisk the eggs with the milk. Season well with sea salt and freshly ground black pepper. Carefully pour half the egg mixture into the dish, making sure the slices are evenly covered. Arrange the rest of the soda bread on top. Pour the rest of the egg mixture over the surface, then scatter with the remaining herbs and cheese. Leave to soak for 30 minutes or more if time allows.

Preheat the oven to 170°C/325°F/gas mark 3.

Pop the dish into the preheated oven and bake for 25 minutes, until the custard has puffed and the bread is golden brown at the edges. Cover loosely with parchment paper if it's getting too dark on top. Check that the custard is set in the middle – a skewer should come out clean when inserted into the centre, but be careful not to overcook.

Serve with a salad of organic leaves.

Aged Cheddar Cheese and Ham Strata

Strata is a savoury bread and butter pudding. This one is super tasty even just with cheese and spring onions, but if you have a little leftover cooked ham or bacon, it's even better. A few morsels of cooked turkey wouldn't go astray either or a little diced chorizo, which everyone seems to have in their fridge these days – but be careful not to add too much, it can be overpowering.

SERVES 6

- 50g very soft butter
- 6 slices of good white bread, cut into slices 1-2cm thick and crusts removed - about 100g prepared weight
- 175-225g cooked ham or bacon, diced into 7mm cubes
- 110g mature Cheddar cheese (or a mixture of Cheddar, Gruyère and Parmesan), coarsely grated, plus extra for sprinkling
- 3 medium eggs
- 450ml milk (or 225ml milk and 225ml cream)
- 3-4 teaspoons fresh thyme leaves, chopped
- 1½ teaspoons Dijon mustard
- a generous pinch of ground mace or nutmeg
- sea salt and freshly ground black pepper

Grease a 1-litre ovenproof soufflé dish with some of the soft butter.

Spread the slices of bread with the rest of the soft butter, then cut into roughly 2.5cm squares. Put the bread in the dish, add the ham or bacon and the grated cheese and toss to combine.

Whisk the eggs in a separate bowl, then add the milk, thyme leaves, Dijon mustard and mace or nutmeg. Continue to whisk for a minute or two, then season well with salt and freshly ground black pepper. Pour this over the bread, cheese and ham mixture. Cover and pop in the refrigerator for a couple of hours or overnight.

Preheat the oven to 180°C/350°F/gas mark 4.

Sprinkle a little grated cheese over the top and bake the strata in the preheated oven for 40 minutes, until puffed up and golden like a soufflé. Serve with a salad of organic leaves.

Variation

We also love an asparagus and fontina strata.

Cheat's Tarts with Various Fillings

I'm frightfully snooty about sliced bread but this a brilliant trick shown to us by one of my favourite cookery writers, Eric Treuille, when he came to teach at the school a few years ago.

I've suggested several fillings you could use. Look in your fridge, experiment and use fresh herbs and herb flowers.

– sliced white or brown bread (best sliced pan)

Preheat the oven 200°C/400°F/gas mark 6.

Cut the crusts off the bread. Roll the bread very thinly with a rolling pin – it should be completely flat. Stamp out rounds with a 4.5cm cutter. Fit into a mini muffin tin. Bake in the preheated oven for 5–7 minutes. Cool on a wire rack. Unfilled cheat's tarts will keep in an airtight tin for several days.

Suggested Fillings

+ Wild salmon pâté with cucumber pickle and dill flowers
+ Chicken liver pâté with sun-blush tomatoes and chervil
+ Goat's cheese with kumquat compote and arugula
+ Goat's cheese with basil pesto (page 312) and cherry tomatoes
+ Goat's cheese with piquillo pepper and basil leaves
+ Prawns or shrimp with guacamole and fresh coriander
+ Crab mayonnaise with grape tomatoes
+ Smoked mussels with mayo

Panzanella (Tuscan Bread Salad)

Every country has recipes for using up leftover bread: panzanella in Italy, fattoush in the Middle East, shahi tukra in India. This Tuscan bread salad is a delicious way to use up slightly stale sourdough bread and enjoy lots of herbs and greens. We love to add little sprigs of purslane to add extra juiciness to both panzanella and fattoush.

SERVES 8

- 2-3 garlic cloves, thinly sliced
- 3-4 tablespoons extra virgin olive oil
- 110g crusty sourdough bread, cut or torn into 1cm cubes
- 1 red onion, roughly chopped and rinsed under cold water
- 75g black olives
- lots of fresh basil leaves, torn into pieces (include some purple, opal and lemon basil if available)
- a couple handfuls of purslane
- 8 ripe medium tomatoes, cut into quarters
- 125ml extra virgin olive oil
- 2 tablespoons balsamic vinegar
- 1 tablespoon white wine vinegar
- sea salt and freshly ground black pepper

Preheat the oven to 180°C/350°F/gas mark 4.

Put the garlic and extra virgin olive oil in a large bowl. Add the bread cubes and toss to coat evenly. Spread them out on a baking sheet and bake in the preheated oven for 4–5 minutes, just long enough to barely toast – they shouldn't be hard.

Return the croutons to the bowl along with the rinsed onion, olives, basil, purslane and tomatoes.

Whisk the oil, vinegars and some salt and pepper together, then drizzle this dressing over the salad and toss gently. Season to taste. Serve soon.

NOTE: Though not traditional, a few pomegranate seeds make this salad extra delicious.

Fattoush

There have always been delicious ways of using up bread, particularly in Asian, South American, Mediterranean and Middle Eastern countries. Sumac gives this Syrian bread salad a characteristic slightly sour taste. Sumac is a wine-coloured spice with a tart lemony flavour that's beloved in the Middle East. It comes from the dried seeds of the *Rhus staghorn* tree. You can find it in the spice aisle of most supermarkets these days, but if you can't get it, the salad will still taste delicious if not as authentic.

SERVES 6

- 2 stale pitta (page 124) or 2-3 thick slices of stale sourdough or good country bread
- a little bunch of rocket or purslane, coarsely chopped
- 4 vine-ripened tomatoes, cut into quarters and then into half crosswise
- 3 spring onions, sliced at an angle
- 1 mild sweet red pepper, cut into rounds or diced (optional)
- ½ cucumber, coarsely chopped
- 2-3 tablespoons chopped fresh parsley
- 2-3 tablespoons fresh mint
- 2 tablespoons fresh coriander leaves
- sea salt and freshly ground black pepper
- 2-3 teaspoons sumac (if available)

DRESSING:
- 6 tablespoons extra virgin olive oil
- 3 tablespoons freshly squeezed lemon juice
- 2 garlic cloves, crushed
- pinch of caster sugar (optional)
- dash of balsamic vinegar (optional)

If the bread isn't stale, toast it until it's crisp.

Put the rocket or purslane in a salad bowl with the tomatoes, spring onions, red pepper (if using), cucumber, herbs and bread. Season with salt, freshly ground pepper and some sumac (if using).

Whisk all the dressing ingredients together and season to taste. Spoon it over the salad, toss gently and taste to correct the seasoning.

Allow the salad to sit for at least 30 minutes, or better still, an hour before serving, so the bread soaks up lots of yummy dressing and juice. Sprinkle with any remaining sumac.

Smashed Croissants with Burrata, Charcuterie and Rocket

A versatile and totally delicious way to use up leftover stale croissants and any number of other toppings.

SERVES 2

....

- 2 stale croissants
- 30g butter
- 2 scant tablespoons runny honey
- 3-4 tablespoons stracciatella, buffalo burrata (roughly chopped) or cream cheese
- 2 tablespoons roughly chopped pistachio nuts
- freshly cracked black pepper
- a couple slices of mortadella or fennel salami
- a handful of rocket leaves

Flatten the croissants with a rolling pin.

Melt the butter in a wide frying pan on a medium heat. When it foams, add the croissants and cook until crisp on both sides. Drizzle each side with honey, then reduce the heat to medium-low, put a piece of parchment paper on top and weigh it down with a heavy saucepan. Continue to cook for about 5 minutes more, until golden, sticky and lightly caramelised on both sides.

To finish, top with stracciatella, burrata or cream cheese and a sprinkling of chopped pistachios. Add a generous grind of freshly cracked pepper. Top with a couple of ruffles of mortadella or fennel salami and a few rocket leaves.

Peanut Butter and Bananas

Also delicious with peanut butter, sliced bananas and a few flakes of sea salt.

Almond Croissants

Another tasty way to use up stale croissants.

- croissants, 1-2 days old
- crème d'amande (page 302)
- flaked almonds

Preheat the oven to 200°C/400°F/gas mark 6.

Split the croissant in half lengthways. Spread a generous tablespoon of crème d'amande onto one half. Close up like a sandwich, then spread some more crème d'amande evenly over the top with a palette knife. Dip into or sprinkle with flaked almonds, then place on a baking tray.

Bake in the preheated oven for 10–12 minutes, until the flaked almonds are golden and the croissant is warmed through. Cool on a wire rack.

Florence Bowe's Queen of Puddings

Another pud that conjures up childhood memories. Interestingly, everybody seems to have a different opinion about what Queen of Puddings should both look and taste like. This recipe is a combination of several people's firmly held views. It's delicious but, as I've discovered, it's hard to please everyone! My aunt, Florence Bowe, who was very fussy as far as Queen of Puddings was concerned, gave this version her seal of approval.

SERVES 6

....

- 600ml milk
- 50g butter, plus extra for greasing
- 1 teaspoon pure vanilla extract
- 150g soft white breadcrumbs (page 266)
- 135g caster sugar, plus 2 teaspoons for sprinkling
- grated zest of 1 lemon
- 3 eggs, separated
- 3 tablespoons raspberry jam (page 294)

....

TO SERVE:
- pouring cream

Preheat the oven to 180°C/350°F/gas mark 4. Grease a 1.2-litre pie dish.

Put the milk and butter in a saucepan and bring almost to the boiling point, then add the vanilla extract.

Mix the breadcrumbs with 25g of the sugar and the lemon zest in a large bowl. Stir in the hot milk and leave for about 10 minutes, then whisk in the egg yolks one by one. Pour this into the buttered pie dish and bake for about 25 minutes, until just set. Remove from the oven.

Meanwhile, whisk the egg whites in a spotlessly clean, grease-free bowl. When they are just starting to become fluffy, add half of the remaining 110g of sugar. Continue to whisk until the mixture holds a stiffish peak. Fold in the rest of the sugar.

Warm the jam slightly and spread it gently over the surface of the custard in the pie dish. Pile the meringue on top in soft folds. Sprinkle the remaining 2 teaspoons of sugar over the top. Return to the oven and bake for 15 minutes, until the meringue is pale gold, crisp on top and soft in the centre. Serve with pouring cream.

Best Ever Bread and Butter Pudding

One of the most delectable ways to use up bread. There's nothing frugal about this recipe – it's got lots of fruit in it and a generous proportion of cream to milk. When people taste it, they just go 'Wow!' I know it has a lot of cream in it, but don't skimp – just don't eat it every day! We play around with this formula and continue to come up with more delicious combinations, depending on what's in season and what we have around (see the next page for some of them). Substitute freshly ground cardamom for the nutmeg, cinnamon or mixed spice for an Indian flavour.

SERVES 6-8

- 50g butter, preferably unsalted, plus extra for greasing
- 12 slices of good-quality white bread, crusts removed
- 200g plump raisins or sultanas or a mixture
- ½ teaspoon ground nutmeg, cinnamon or mixed spice
- 450ml cream
- 225ml milk
- 4 large eggs, lightly beaten
- 1 teaspoon pure vanilla extract
- 110g caster sugar, plus 1 tablespoon for sprinkling
- pinch of salt

TO SERVE:
- softly whipped cream

Grease a 20.5cm square pottery or ovenproof baking dish with butter.

Butter the bread and arrange four slices, buttered side down, in one layer in the buttered dish. Try to leave about 1cm of space between the slices to allow for expansion. Sprinkle the bread with half the raisins or sultanas and half the spice, then arrange another layer of bread, buttered side down, over the raisins. Sprinkle the remaining raisins and spice on top. Cover the raisins with the remaining bread, again buttered side down.

In a bowl, whisk together the cream, milk, eggs, vanilla, 110g sugar and a good pinch of salt. Pour the mixture through a fine sieve over the bread. Sprinkle a tablespoon of sugar over the top and let the mixture stand, loosely covered, at room temperature for at least 1 hour, or better still, overnight.

Preheat the oven to 180°C/350°F/gas mark 4.

Put the pudding in a roasting tin and pour in enough boiling water to come halfway up the sides of the baking dish to create a bain-marie. Bake the pudding in the middle of the preheated oven for about 1 hour, until the top is crisp and golden.

Serve the pudding warm with lots of softly whipped cream. Believe it or not, this bread and butter pudding reheats really well.

Bread and Butter Pudding with Cardamom and Pistachios	Substitute ½–1 teaspoon freshly ground cardamom instead of the nutmeg, cinnamon or mixed spice. Proceed as in the master recipe. Sprinkle 50g coarsely chopped pistachios on top before serving. You could sprinkle a few extra pistachios over the raisins or sultanas while assembling if desired.
Other Delicious Bread and Butter Puddings	Try using one of these as the base: + Barmbrack (page 208) – add mixed spice or cinnamon. + Panettone – proceed as in the master recipe. + Brioche (page 198) – proceed as in the master recipe or use apricot jam laced with apricot brandy. + Challah (see 164) – proceed as in the master recipe. + Hot cross buns (page 228) – proceed as in the master recipe. + Scones (page 177) – proceed as in the master recipe. + Gingerbread (page 203) – proceed as in the master recipe. + Sweet buns (page 216) – proceed as in the master recipe.

Apple Charlotte

This is the scrummiest, most wickedly rich apple pudding ever. A friend, Peter Lamb, makes it as a special treat for me every now and then. It's also a brilliant and delicious way to use up bread and apples. I make my apple charlotte from old varieties of eating apples – my favourites are Egremont Russet, Charles Ross, Cox's Orange Pippin or Pitmaston Pineapple. It's sinfully rich but gorgeous.

SERVES 4-6

- 1 batch of clarified butter (page 307)
- 1kg dessert apples (see the intro), peeled, cored and cut into cubes
- 175g caster sugar, plus extra to dust
- 2-3 tablespoons water
- 2 egg yolks
- 4-6 slices of white yeast bread (page 52)

TO SERVE:
- softly whipped cream

Preheat the oven to 200°C/400°F/gas mark 6.

Melt a little of the clarified butter in a stainless steel saucepan, then add the apples, sugar and water. Cover and cook over a gentle heat until the apples break down into a thick pulp. Beat in the egg yolks one by one – this helps to enrich and thicken the apple purée. Taste and add a little more sugar if necessary.

Melt the remaining clarified butter and use a little of this to brush the inside of a 13cm × 20cm (450g) loaf tin, then dust it with caster sugar.

Cut the crusts off the bread, then cut the bread into strips about 4cm wide and 13cm high and quickly brush them with the clarified butter. Line the sides of the tin with the butter-soaked bread. Cut another strip to fit tightly into the base of the tin. Brush it on both sides with butter and tuck it in tightly. Fill the centre with the apple purée. Cut another strip or strips of bread to fit the top. Brush with melted butter on both sides and fit it neatly to cover the purée.

Bake in the preheated oven for 20 minutes, then reduce the heat to 180°C/350°F/gas mark 4 and bake for a further 15 minutes, until the bread is crisp and a rich golden colour.

To serve, run a knife around the edges in case the bread has stuck to the tin. Invert the apple charlotte onto a warm oval serving plate. It won't look like a thing of beauty and it may even collapse a bit, but it will taste wonderful. Serve with lots of softly whipped cream.

Chester Cake

This recipe is from a newspaper cutting of Mary Frances Keating's recipes from the early 1950s. It tastes good despite the quantity of bread. This is the Cork version of gur cake. Scotland has black bun. Canny bakers everywhere probably have their own recipe for using up stale bread and cake.

MAKES 9-12 SQUARES

PASTRY:
- 450g plain flour
- small pinch of salt
- 275g butter, diced
- 8 tablespoons very cold water

FILLING:
- 600ml measure of stale bread, cut up small
- 75g plain flour
- 1 teaspoon mixed spice
- 1 teaspoon baking powder
- 75g butter, diced
- 225g brown sugar
- 225g currants
- 225g raisins
- 1 egg
- 150ml milk
- grated rind of 1 lemon
- caster sugar, for sprinkling

Preheat the oven to 180°C/350°F/gas mark 4.

To make the pastry, sieve the flour and salt into a large bowl. Add the butter and cut it through the flour until it resembles coarse breadcrumbs. Add the cold water, mixing it in with a knife to a fairly stiff dough. Gather and knead gently for a few seconds. Divide in two.

Soak the bread in cold water, then squeeze it as dry as possible. Sieve the flour, mixed spice and baking powder into a large bowl. Add the butter and rub it in, then add the brown sugar and fruit. Mix well.

Beat the egg in the milk, then add this to the flour mixture along with the lemon rind and the squeezed bread. The mixture should be soft but not sloppy.

Roll out the pastry into two sheets. Use one sheet to line a 25cm square baking tin. Put the filling on top of the pastry in the tin. Put the other sheet of pastry on top and prick the top of pastry. Bake in the preheated oven for 1½ hours. Cut into squares. Dust well with caster sugar.

Brown Bread Ice Cream

Really good cream makes really good ice cream. The basis of this recipe for Ballymaloe vanilla ice cream is made with an egg mousse base with softly whipped cream. It produces a deliciously rich ice cream with a smooth texture that does not need further whisking during the freezing period or an ice cream machine to make. This ice cream should not be served frozen hard – remove it from the freezer at least 10 minutes before serving. You can add other flavourings to the basic recipe. Liquid ingredients such as melted chocolate or coffee should be folded into the mousse before adding the cream. For chunkier ingredients such as chocolate chips or muscatel raisins soaked in rum, finish the ice cream, semi-freeze it and then stir them through, otherwise they will sink to the bottom.

Brown bread ice cream is also known as poor man's praline ice cream because it gives a similar texture but uses cheaper ingredients. This is a particularly delicious way to use up brown soda or wholemeal yeast breadcrumbs that would otherwise be wasted.

SERVES 12-16

- 4 egg yolks
- 100g granulated sugar
- 200ml water
- 1 teaspoon pure vanilla extract or the seeds from 1/3 vanilla pod
- 1.2 litres softly whipped cream (measured after it is whipped for accuracy)
- 350g chunky brown soda or wholemeal yeast breadcrumbs (see page 266)
- 150g vanilla sugar (page 303)
- 150g soft dark brown sugar

Put the egg yolks in a bowl and whisk until light and fluffy (keep the whites for meringues).

Combine the sugar and water in a small heavy-based saucepan. Stir over a medium heat until the sugar has completely dissolved, then remove the spoon and boil the syrup until it reaches the thread stage (106°C–113°C (223°F–235°F) on a candy thermometer). It will look thick and syrupy, and when a metal spoon is dipped in, the last drops of syrup to drip off the spoon will form thin threads. Pour this boiling syrup in a steady stream onto the egg yolks, whisking all the time by hand. (If you are whisking the mousse in a stand mixer, remove the bowl and whisk the boiling syrup in by hand, otherwise it will solidify on the sides of the bowl.)

Add the vanilla extract or seeds and continue to whisk until the mixture becomes a thick, creamy white mousse. (This is the stage at which, if you're deviating from this recipe, you can add liquid flavourings such as coffee.)

Fold the softly whipped cream into the mousse, pour into a bowl, cover and freeze just until semi-frozen.

Meanwhile, preheat the oven to 230°C/450°F/gas mark 8.

Spread the chunky breadcrumbs on a baking tray. Sprinkle with the vanilla sugar and the dark brown sugar and toast in the preheated oven for 10–15 minutes, stirring every 4–5 minutes, until the sugar caramelises and coats the breadcrumbs. Turn out onto a piece of parchment paper (or a silicone baking mat if you have one) and leave to cool, then pulse the caramelised breadcrumbs into small, chunky bits in a food processor.

When the ice cream is semi-frozen, fold in the breadcrumbs, then freeze until fully frozen. Serve in chilled bowls.

ESSENTIAL
EXTRAS

This chapter has a variety of recipes for essential extras. Of course, there are a couple of favourite jam recipes to slather on your freshly made breads that take the mystery out of jam-making. If you've never made jam before, try this made-in-minutes raspberry jam – it's a revelation.

Here at the cookery school, when we are teaching scones we often pop a batch of scones into the oven, then while they're baking, we make a few pots of raspberry jam. The jam is ready as the scones are cooling on a wire rack. Magic!

Other recipes like roasted tomato sauce are an integral part of a pizza recipe. Some, like guacamole, tapenade or anchoïade, are accompaniments, and others are spreads, drizzles or dips. I hope I haven't forgotten something essential!

Strawberry Jam

Particularly delicious with brioche (page 198), homemade strawberry jam can be sensational but only if the fruit is a good variety. It's one of the most difficult jams to make because strawberries are low in pectin (see page 327), so don't attempt it if your fruit is not perfect. Redcurrants are well worth searching out for this jam. They are very high in pectin and their bittersweet taste greatly enhances the flavour. Frozen redcurrants may be used also. If you don't have redcurrant juice, add the zest and juice of 2 lemons instead.

MAKES 8 × 290ML JARS

....

- 450g fresh or frozen redcurrants (or see the intro)
- 175ml water
- 1.3kg granulated sugar (not caster sugar) or half jam sugar and half granulated sugar
- 1.8kg unblemished strawberries (see the intro)

Put the redcurrants and water in a stainless steel saucepan. Bring to the boil, then reduce the heat and simmer for about 20 minutes. Strain through a fine sieve to obtain 150ml juice. This juice can be frozen for use another time if necessary.

Meanwhile, wash, dry and sterilise your jars in an oven preheated to 100°C/210°F/gas mark ¼ for 15 minutes.

Take the jars out of the oven and increase the temperature to 180°C/350°F/gas mark 4. Pour the sugar into a Pyrex or stainless steel bowl and heat in the oven for 5–10 minutes, until it feels hot to the touch.

Put the strawberries in a wide stainless steel saucepan with the redcurrant juice (or the lemon zest and juice if not using the redcurrant juice). Use a potato masher to crush the berries, but leave a few intact. Bring to the boil and cook the crushed strawberries in the juice for 2–3 minutes.

Add the warm sugar to the fruit, stirring over a gentle heat until the sugar is dissolved. Increase the heat and boil for 10–15 minutes. This jam sticks and burns very easily, so make sure to stir the base of the pot regularly using a wooden spatula. Test for a set by putting a teaspoon of jam on a cold plate and leaving it in a cold place for a few minutes. It should wrinkle when pressed with a finger. If the jam overcooks it will be too thick, but if that happens just add a little boiling water to loosen.

Skim meticulously and pot into sterilised jars, cover immediately and store in a cool dry cupboard.

Mummy's Strawberry Jam	Put the strawberries and lemon juice in a stainless steel saucepan (omit the redcurrant juice in this version). Cover with sugar and leave overnight. The next day, use a potato masher to crush the berries, leaving a few intact. Bring to the boil, stirring until the sugar is dissolved. Continue to boil until it reaches a set. Pour into sterilised jars, cover immediately and store in a cool, dry, dark cupboard.
Strawberry and Redcurrant Jam	Add 225g redcurrants to the strawberries and proceed as above (leftover redcurrant pulp from redcurrant jelly may also be used).

Raspberry Jam

Raspberry jam is the easiest and quickest of all jams to make, and one of the most delicious. Loganberries, boysenberries or tayberries may also be used in this recipe.

Jams are more fresh tasting and delicious when made in small batches.

MAKES 3 × 450G JARS

- 790g granulated sugar
- 900g fresh raspberries

Wash, dry and sterilise 3 × 450g jars in an oven preheated to 100°C/210°F/gas mark ¼ for 15 minutes.

Take the jars out of the oven and increase the temperature to 180°C/350°F/gas mark 4. Pour the sugar into a Pyrex or stainless steel bowl and heat in the oven for 5–10 minutes, until it feels hot to the touch.

Put the raspberries in a wide stainless steel saucepan over a medium heat and cook for 3–4 minutes, until the juice begins to run. Add the hot sugar and stir until fully dissolved. Increase the heat and boil steadily for about 5 minutes, stirring frequently. Remove the pan from the heat.

Test for a set by putting a teaspoon of jam on a cold plate and leaving it in a cold place for a few minutes. It should wrinkle when pressed with a finger. If the jam overcooks, it will be too thick. If that happens, just add a little boiling water to loosen.

When the jam passes this wrinkle test, remove the pan from the heat. Skim and pour into the sterilised jam jars. Cover immediately.

Store the jam in a cool place or else put on a shelf in your kitchen so you can feel great every time you look at it. Anyway, it will be so delicious it won't last long!

Raspberry and Cassis Preserve

Add 4 tablespoons cassis to the jam just before potting.

Chocolate and Hazelnut Spread

You'll never go back to the well-known brand. Taste the hazelnuts first, though, to make sure they are fresh-tasting and haven't gone rancid.

MAKES 2 × 200ML JARS

- 250g hazelnuts
- 150g icing sugar
- 45g cocoa powder
  (we use Valrhona)
- 4 tablespoons hazelnut oil
- 1 teaspoon vanilla extract
- ⅛-¼ teaspoon salt

Preheat the oven to 190°C/375°F/gas mark 5.

Spread the hazelnuts out in a single layer on a baking sheet. Roast in the preheated oven for 12–15 minutes, until the skins start to loosen and the nuts are golden and evenly roasted. Tip the nuts into a clean tea towel, rub the skins off the hazelnuts and discard.

Cool and transfer to a food processor. Whizz the hazelnuts for 2–5 minutes, until the oil begins to separate from the soft paste, scraping down the sides of the bowl occasionally. Add the icing sugar, cocoa powder, hazelnut oil, vanilla extract and salt to taste. Keep whizzing until the spread is loose, glossy and a spreadable texture. Taste – it may need another pinch of salt or another tablespoon of hazelnut oil.

Spoon into little jars, cover and use within a month – but usually it doesn't last that long!

Chocolate Ganache

A brilliant multipurpose recipe. Use this as a sauce over ice cream, to ice a chocolate cake or allow it to cool and whisk it into a mousse for feather-light chocolate truffles.

- 225g plain chocolate, chopped - we use 52% (Valrhona or Callebaut), but you could use up leftover chocolate
- 175ml cream
- 1-2 teaspoons rum or orange liqueur (optional)

Put the chocolate in a large heatproof bowl. Bring the cream to the boil, then pour it over the chocolate. Add the liqueur (if using) and stir to melt the chocolate. Leave for 8–10 minutes, until cool and thickened slightly.

Lemon Curd

Tangy, delicious lemon curd can be made in the twinkling of an eye. Use the best eggs you can find and fresh, zesty, organic lemons. Smear it on a sponge, fresh bread or scones or drizzle it over meringues.

MAKES 2 × 200ML JARS
....

- 50g butter
- 100g caster sugar
- grated zest and juice of 2 organic lemons
- 2 organic eggs and 1 organic egg yolk, whisked

Melt the butter in a saucepan on a very low heat. Add the sugar and the lemon zest and juice, then add the whisked eggs. Stir carefully over a gentle heat with a straight-ended wooden spatula until the mixture coats the back of it. Remove the pan from the heat and pour the curd into a bowl or sterilised jars (it will thicken further as it cools).

Cover when cold and refrigerate. This is best eaten within a fortnight.

Candied Peel

Of course you can use shop-bought candied peel, but homemade candied peel uses up leftover citrus and is incomparably more delicious.

Fruit should be organic if possible, otherwise scrub the peel well. Grapefruit and other citrus may also be candied. Or all of one fruit (i.e. oranges only or lemons only) can be used.

MAKES 1 × 1.5-LITRE
KILNER JAR OR
5 × 450G JARS

- 5 organic unwaxed
  oranges
- 5 organic unwaxed
  lemons
- 1 teaspoon salt
- 1.1kg granulated sugar

Cut the fruit in half and squeeze out the juice. Reserve the juice for another use (perhaps homemade lemonade). Put the squeezed-out halves in a large bowl (not aluminium), add the salt and cover with cold water. Leave to soak for 24 hours.

The next day, throw away the soaking water. Put the peel in a saucepan and cover with fresh cold water. Bring to the boil, then cover and simmer very gently for approx. 3 hours, until the peel is soft.

Remove the peel and discard the water. Scrape out any remaining flesh and membranes from inside the cut fruit, leaving the white pith and rind intact. (You could do the next step the next day if that is more convenient.)

Cut each half in half or slice the peel into nice long strips.

Pour the sugar and **750ml water** into a large, deep saucepan. Bring to the boil, stirring to dissolve the sugar. Add the peel and simmer gently for 30–60 minutes, until it looks translucent and the syrup forms a thread when the last drop falls off a metal spoon.

Meanwhile, wash, dry and sterilise the jars in an oven preheated to 100°C/210°F/gas mark ¼ for 15 minutes.

Remove the peel with a slotted spoon, put the candied peel into the sterilised glass jars and pour the syrup over. Cover and store in a cold place or in a fridge. It should keep for 6–8 weeks or longer under refrigeration.

Alternatively, spread the candied peel out on a baking tray or trays and allow to sit for 30–60 minutes to cool. Toss in caster sugar and store in covered glass jars until needed.

Candied Peel for
Petit Fours

Cut the freshly made candied peel into slices 5mm–
1cm thin. Roll in caster sugar and serve with coffee.
Alternatively, dip one end or all of the candied orange
peel in melted dark chocolate, allow to set and serve.

Marzipan

So versatile and delicious. Use marzipan to stuff croissants, brioche or pastries.

MAKES 300G
....

- 110g granulated sugar
- 62ml water
- 175g ground almonds
- 1 small egg white
- natural almond
  extract, to taste
  (do not use more than
  4 drops)

Put the sugar and water in a deep saucepan over a medium heat, stirring to dissolve the sugar. Bring to the boil, then cover the pan for 2 minutes to steam any sugar from the saucepan sides. Remove the cover and boil rapidly just to the thread stage (106°C–113°C (223°F–235°F) on a candy thermometer).

Remove the pan from the heat. Stir the syrup for a second or two, until cloudy. Stir in the ground almonds. Set aside to cool briefly.

Lightly whisk the egg white, then add the almond extract and stir this into the almond mixture. Transfer the paste from the saucepan to a bowl. Cool.

Knead the cool marzipan – it should feel like moulding clay. Put in a bowl or jar, cover and use as required. This will keep for months stored in a covered box in the fridge.

Crème Pâtissière (Pastry Cream)

Crème pâtissière is an essential ingredient in the pastry chef's pantry. All these crèmes can be flavoured with chocolate, coffee, hazelnut or pistachio, cream, liqueurs, etc.

MAKES 460G

- 5 egg yolks
- 75g caster sugar
- 40g plain flour
- 450ml full-fat milk
- pinch of salt
- ½ vanilla pod, split in half lengthways

Whisk the egg yolks with the caster sugar in a heatproof bowl until thick and light. Gently stir in the flour – do not beat!

Scald the milk by bringing it just to the boil with the salt and vanilla pod. Cover the pan with a lid, take the pan off the heat and leave to infuse for 10–15 minutes.

Remove the vanilla pod (save it to make the vanilla sugar on page 303) and reheat the milk to boiling point again. Whisk the boiling milk into the egg mixture, then return this to the pan and whisk until smooth over a gentle heat, until boiling. Be sure the pastry cream is smooth before letting it boil. If lumps form as it thickens, take the pan from the heat and beat until smooth.

Cook the cream gently, whisking constantly, for 2 minutes, until the cream thickens slightly, which means the flour is completely cooked. Take the pan from the heat, then transfer the pastry cream to a bowl. Rub a piece of butter over the surface to prevent the formation of a skin, cover and allow to cool. Store in the fridge for up to two days.

Diplomat Cream

Soak two leaves of gelatine in cold water for a few minutes, until soft. Strain and stir into the crème pâtissière when it thickens. Allow to get cold, then fold in 400g stiffly whipped cream.

Crème Saint Honoré

Fold one stiffly whipped egg white into the diplomat cream.

Crème d'Amande

This is a super-versatile almond mixture. Use it to fill the irresistible almond croissants on page 282 or other pastries or tarts.

MAKES APPROX. 450G
....

- 130g ground almonds
- 125g butter, softened
- 125g caster sugar
- 30g plain flour
- 2 eggs
- 2 tablespoons Jamaican rum

Whizz all the ingredients in a food processor until just combined. Store in an airtight container in the fridge for up to seven days.

Crème de Noisette

Substitute hazelnuts for almonds in the recipe above. Pistachios or walnuts may also be used.

Vanilla Sugar

Get double value from vanilla pods by storing them in caster sugar. You can even reuse a vanilla pod after it's been used to infuse milk or cream, but it will have less flavour after each use, especially if the seeds have been scraped out.

- caster sugar
- dry vanilla pods

Fill a large-mouthed jar with caster sugar. Bury dry vanilla pods in the sugar to store – the more vanilla pods you use, the stronger the flavour. Use for biscuits, cakes, custard, ice creams, etc.

Homemade Pure Vanilla Extract

Pure vanilla extract is gorgeous but enormously expensive. You can make your own superb extract quite easily. The flavour of the vanilla is extracted by the alcohol, which in turn becomes more mellow. The vanilla pods can later be used to flavour custards, creams and mousses.

- 3-4 vanilla pods, split in half lengthways
- 600ml vodka or brandy

Put the split vanilla pods in a 600ml bottle of vodka or brandy, seal tightly and leave to infuse for at least three days, but better still, for up to six weeks before using. Shake occasionally. Before use, strain the liquid through a fine nylon sieve. Store in small airtight bottles. It keeps almost indefinitely.

Isaac's Roasted Tomato Sauce for Pizza

Roasting the tomatoes in a wood-fired oven adds an extra *je ne sais quoi*. A blazing hot conventional oven also works well. Choose very ripe tomatoes.

A mouli legume is the preferred utensil here. You can use a plastic sieve if you don't have one, but it's pretty laboursome. A mouli legume is not expensive. Like an oyster knife, it may sit in your cupboard unused for months on end but when you need it, you really need it.

MAKES 300ML

- 450g very ripe tomatoes, halved
- 6 garlic cloves, unpeeled
- 2 tablespoons extra virgin olive oil
- 1 tablespoon basic balsamic vinegar
- flaky sea salt and freshly ground black pepper
- pinch of caster sugar

Preheat the oven to 250°C/480°F/gas mark 9.

Arrange the halved ripe tomatoes in a single layer, cut side up, in a small square roasting tin, approx. 20.5cm × 20.5cm, to retain maximum liquid. Add the whole garlic cloves, oil and vinegar, tossing to coat. Season well with flaky sea salt, pepper and a little sugar.

Roast in the preheated oven for 15–20 minutes, until the tomatoes are completely soft. Push through a mouli legume (food mill) until only the skins and seeds remain. Taste and correct the seasoning – it may need more sugar if the tomatoes are a little under-ripe.

Refrigerate or freeze until needed. This sauce keeps for four or five days in the fridge and freezes well too but use it sooner rather than later.

Peperonata

This is one of the indispensable trio of vegetable stews that we always have to hand. We use it not only as a vegetable, but also as a topping for pizzas, as a sauce for pasta, grilled fish or meat, and as a filling for omelettes and pancakes. Use organic ingredients when possible.

SERVES 8-10

- 2 tablespoons olive oil
- 225g onion, sliced
- 1 garlic clove, crushed
- 2 red peppers
- 2 green peppers
- 6 large, dark red and very ripe tomatoes (or 1 × 400g tin of chopped tomatoes if fresh are out of season)
- sea salt and freshly ground black pepper
- pinch of caster sugar
- a few leaves of fresh basil

Heat the olive oil in a casserole/Dutch oven over a gentle heat. Add the onion and garlic, toss to coat in the oil, cover the casserole/Dutch oven and allow to soften while you prepare the peppers.

Halve the peppers and remove and discard the seeds. Cut into quarters, then cut the pepper flesh into 2–2.5cm squares or slices. Add to the onion and garlic and toss in the oil. Replace the lid and continue to cook.

Meanwhile, to peel the tomatoes, prick each one with the tip of a knife or cut a cross in the bottom of each tomato before scalding them in boiling water for 10 seconds. Pour off the water and peel immediately. Slice the tomatoes and add to the casserole/Dutch oven. Season with salt, freshly ground black pepper, sugar and a few leaves of fresh basil, if available. Cook for approx. 30 minutes, until the vegetables are just soft and the peperonata is reduced somewhat.

Spicy Peperonata

Add 1 teaspoon smoked paprika and a pinch of chilli flakes to the onions and garlic. The quantity will depend on the aroma and pungency of your spices – add more to taste if you like it a little spicier.

Tomato Fondue

Tomato fondue is one of our great convertibles. Super-versatile, we serve it as a vegetable or as a sauce for pasta, a filling for omelettes, a topping for pizza or a base for vegetable stews.

SERVES APPROX. 6

- 2 tablespoons extra virgin olive oil
- 110g sliced onions
- 1 garlic clove, crushed
- 900g very ripe tomatoes in summer but peel before using, or 2 × 400g tins of tomatoes in winter)
- salt and freshly ground black pepper
- pinch of caster sugar
- 1 tablespoon freshly chopped mint, thyme, parsley, lemon balm, marjoram or torn basil
- balsamic vinegar (optional)

Heat the oil in a stainless steel sauté pan or casserole/Dutch oven. Add the sliced onions and garlic, toss until coated in the oil, cover and sweat on a gentle heat for approx. 10 minutes, until soft but not coloured. It is vital for the success of this dish that the onions are completely soft before the tomatoes are added.

Meanwhile, to peel the tomatoes, prick each one with the tip of a knife or cut a cross in the bottom of each tomato before scalding them in boiling water for 10 seconds. Pour off the water and peel immediately.

Slice the peeled fresh tomatoes and add them with all their juices (or the tinned tomatoes) to the onions. Season with salt, freshly ground black pepper and sugar – tinned tomatoes need lots of sugar because of their high acidity. Add a generous sprinkling of chopped fresh herbs. Cover and cook for just 10–20 minutes more, until the tomatoes soften.

Uncover and continue to cook to reduce a little. Cook fresh tomatoes for a shorter time to preserve their lively fresh flavour. Tinned tomatoes need to be cooked for longer depending on whether you want to use the fondue as a vegetable, sauce or filling.

A few drops of balsamic vinegar at the end of the cooking time greatly enhances the flavour but is optional.

Store the tomato fondue in the fridge for up to 10 days or it can be frozen for up to three months.

Tomato Fondue with Chilli

Add 1–2 chopped fresh chillies to the onions when sweating.

Tomato Fondue with Cabanossi, Chorizo or Merguez

Add 1–2 sliced cabanossi, chorizo or merguez sausages to the tomato fondue 5 minutes before the end of the cooking time. Great with pasta. 'Nduja is also a delicious addition.

Clarified Butter

Clarified butter is excellent for cooking because it can withstand a higher temperature when the salt and milk particles are removed. You still have all the delicious buttery flavour without the risk of burning.

– 225g butter

Melt the butter gently in a saucepan or in the oven. Allow it to stand for a few minutes, then spoon the crusty white layer of salt particles off the top of the melted butter. Underneath this crust there is clear liquid butter, which is the clarified butter. The milky liquid at the bottom can be discarded or used in a white sauce. Clarified butter will keep covered in the fridge for several weeks.

Flavoured Butters

Flavoured butters are one of the best flavour bombs in the cook's armoury. They can be whizzed up in a flash and are delicious slathered on a slice of bread, toast or crostini or melting on a piece of grilled meat, fish or roast vegetables. Form into a log for ease of slicing. They also freeze well but use within a week or two.

It's so easy to make your own garlic butter, one of a myriad of flavoured butters in our repertoire. Or add chopped olives, crispy chicken skin, chilli, 'nduja, tapenade, chopped fresh herbs, caramelised onion, miso, bone marrow, harissa ...

— 110g butter, softened

For all the flavoured butter variations below, start by creaming the softened butter. Once you've added your chosen flavourings, roll into butter pats or form into a roll and wrap in greaseproof paper or tin foil, twisting each end so that it looks like a Christmas cracker. Refrigerate to harden.

Maître d'Hôtel Butter

Sounds fancy, but it's basically just parsley butter. It's really good served with a piece of pan-grilled fish or steak. Add 2 tablespoons finely chopped fresh parsley and a few drops of freshly squeezed lemon juice to the softened butter.

Anchovy Butter

Add six anchovy fillets to the soft butter, mashing them in. Serve with pan-grilled fish or fresh radishes.

Blue Cheese Butter

Add 50g Cashel Blue, Crozier Blue or Young Buck blue cheese, 1 tablespoon finely chopped fresh parsley and 1 teaspoon freshly ground black pepper to the soft butter. Mix all the ingredients together in a bowl, or better still, whizz in a food processor.

Bottarga Butter

Add 60g grated bottarga (dried mullet roe), 1 tablespoon finely chopped fresh flat-leaf parsley (optional), flaky sea salt and freshly ground black pepper to the soft butter.

Brandy or Rum Butter	If you have a food processor, use it for this recipe and you will get a wonderfully light and fluffy butter. Cream 75g unsalted butter until it's very light. Add 75g icing sugar and beat again, then beat in 2 tablespoons of brandy or Jamaican rum, drop by drop. Serve with plum pudding or mince pies.
Chilli and Coriander Butter	Add one finely chopped fresh chilli, 1 tablespoon chopped fresh coriander or marjoram, freshly ground black pepper and a few drops of lime or lemon juice to the soft butter.
Dill or Fennel Butter	Substitute fresh dill or fennel fronds for parsley in the maître d'hôtel butter recipe. Serve with fish.
Dijon Mustard Butter	Add 1 tablespoon Dijon mustard to the maître d'hôtel butter recipe. Serve with herrings.
Fresh Herb Butter	Substitute a mixture of chopped fresh herbs (chives, thyme, fennel, lemon balm ...) for parsley in the maître d'hôtel butter recipe. Serve with pan-grilled fish.
Garlic Butter	Add 3–5 cloves of crushed garlic to the maître d'hôtel butter recipe. Slather over bruschetta or toast. Also great with pan-grilled fish, meat or vegetables.
Grainy Mustard Butter	Add 1 tablespoon Dijon mustard and 2 teaspoons grainy mustard to the creamed butter. Particularly good with mackerel or herring.
Mint or Rosemary Butter	Substitute 2 tablespoons finely chopped mint or 1–2 tablespoons finely chopped fresh rosemary for the parsley in the maître d'hôtel butter recipe. Serve with pan-grilled lamb chops.
Miso Butter	Mix 50g soft butter with 2 tablespoons miso and some freshly cracked black pepper. Delicious on pan-grilled fish, steaks, roast carrots, asparagus, Romanesco or broccoli.

Nasturtium Butter	Substitute 3 tablespoons chopped nasturtium flowers (red, yellow and orange) for the parsley in the mâitre d'hôtel butter recipe. Serve with pan-grilled fish.
'Nduja Butter	Add 1 tablespoon 'nduja to the soft butter.
Olive and Anchovy Butter	Add 2–3 anchovies and 4 stoned black olives to the mâitre d'hôtel butter recipe.
Tapenade Butter	Add 1 tablespoon tapenade (page 315) to the soft butter.
Wasabi Butter	Add 1–1½ tablespoons of wasabi to the mâitre d'hôtel butter recipe.
Watercress Butter	Substitute fresh watercress leaves for parsley in the mâitre d'hôtel butter recipe. Serve with pan-grilled fish.
Wild Garlic Butter	Substitute wild garlic leaves for parsley in the mâitre d'hôtel butter recipe. Serve with pan-grilled fish or meat.

Spiced Aubergines

A brilliant topping for pizzas or flatbread. Scatter with fresh coriander leaves when cooked.

SERVES 6

- 250ml extra virgin olive oil, plus 6 tablespoons
- 500g aubergines, cut into slices 2cm thick
- 2.5cm cube of fresh ginger, peeled and coarsely chopped
- 6 large garlic cloves, coarsely crushed
- 50ml water
- 2 teaspoons cumin seeds
- 1 teaspoon fennel seeds
- 350g very ripe tomatoes, peeled and finely chopped, or 1 × 400g tin of chopped tomatoes plus 1 teaspoon caster sugar
- 1 tablespoon ground coriander seeds
- ¼ teaspoon ground turmeric
- ¼ teaspoon cayenne pepper (more if you like)
- pinch of salt
- 25-50g raisins

Heat 175ml of the oil in a deep (25–30cm) frying pan. When it's almost smoking, add a few aubergine slices and cook until golden and tender on both sides. Remove and drain on a wire rack set over a baking sheet. Repeat with the rest of the aubergines, adding more oil if necessary. Alternatively, brush the aubergines slices generously with extra virgin olive oil and cook on a hot griddle pan.

Meanwhile, put the ginger, garlic and water in a blender. Blend until fairly smooth and set aside.

Heat the 6 tablespoons of extra virgin olive oil in a separate large pan over a medium heat. Add the cumin and fennel seeds. Stir for just a few seconds, being careful not to let them burn, then add the chopped tomatoes, ginger-garlic mixture, coriander seeds, turmeric, cayenne and a pinch of salt. Simmer, stirring occasionally, for 5–6 minutes, until the spice mixture thickens slightly.

Add the fried aubergine slices and raisins and coat gently with the spicy sauce. Cover the pan, turn the heat to very low and cook for another 3–4 minutes. Serve warm. Alternatively, the spiced aubergines are also good served cold or at room temperature as an accompaniment to hot or cold lamb or pork.

Spiced Aubergines and Cauliflower

Add the florets of one cooked cauliflower to the above cooked mixture for a delicious spiced cauliflower dish.

Basil Pesto

Pesto, the famous Ligurian basil sauce, is best made with summer basil and Italian pine nuts. The price of pine nuts has skyrocketed in recent years, so we now use cashews instead, which work brilliantly. Home-peeled almonds are also a good alternative. Homemade pesto takes minutes to make and tastes a million times better than most of the ones you can buy.

To avoid mould growing, clean the top of the jar every time you take some out and cover the surface of the pesto with a layer of olive oil to exclude the air. That way you should be able to use every scrap. We make a wide variety of pestos throughout the year, depending on the season – enjoy experimenting with the variations listed.

MAKES APPROX. 2 × 200ML
JARS
....

- 110g fresh basil
  leaves
- 175-225ml extra virgin
  olive oil
- 25g cashews or fresh
  pine nuts (taste when
  you buy to make sure
  they are not rancid),
  chopped
- 2 large organic garlic
  cloves, crushed
- 50g finely grated
  Parmesan cheese
  (Parmigiano Reggiano
  is best)
- sea salt, to taste

Whizz the basil with the olive oil, chopped cashews or pine nuts and garlic in a food processor or pound in a pestle and mortar. Remove to a bowl and fold in the Parmesan cheese. Season to taste.

Pesto keeps for months, covered with a layer of olive oil in a jar in the fridge. It also freezes well, but for best results don't add the grated Parmesan until it has defrosted. Freeze in small jars or containers for convenience.

Kale Pesto

Strip 450g curly kale from the stalks and clean well. If you prefer a mellower flavour, blanch the kale in boiling salted water for 3–4 minutes, drain and refresh under cold running water, then drain well again. Put in a food processor with one garlic clove, 2 teaspoons sea salt, 50g freshly grated Parmesan cheese and 325–350ml extra virgin olive oil and whizz to a thick paste. Taste – it may need a little honey. Store in a covered jar in the fridge for several days. Serve on crostini or drizzle over soups and stews. This makes 4 × 150ml jars.

Parsley Pesto	Finely chop 35g cashews. Put in a food processor with 50g flat-leaf parsley leaves and two garlic cloves and whizz for a second or two. Gradually add 200ml extra virgin olive oil. Add 50g freshly grated Parmesan cheese and whizz for another couple of seconds. Season to taste. This makes 2 × 150ml jars.
Watercress Pesto	Substitute watercress sprigs for basil in the basic recipe.
Wild Garlic Pesto	Wash 110g wild garlic leaves (no stalks). Whizz in a food processor with 50g chopped cashews, two garlic cloves, ¼ teaspoon salt and 350–450ml olive oil. Remove to a bowl and fold in 75g freshly grated Parmesan cheese. Season to taste with sugar or honey if necessary. Makes 3 × 200ml jars.

Pistou

Pistou is a Provençal sauce, like a cousin of Italian pesto.
It can be used in a similar way to pesto but is nut free.

MAKES 200ML

- 5 large garlic cloves
- 1 large bunch of fresh
  basil leaves (approx.
  30 large leaves)
- 50g freshly grated
  Parmesan cheese
- 6 tablespoons extra
  virgin olive oil

Peel and crush the garlic well or pound it in a mortar,
then add the basil and continue to pound to a paste. Stir
in the grated Parmesan, mixing well, then add the oil little
by little. (Use a food processor if you prefer.) Pour into
small sterilised jars, cover and store in a cold, dark place.

Tapenade

The strong, gutsy flavour of tapenade can be an acquired taste. However, it becomes addictive and has become a new basic. Use it as a brilliant dip, pizza topping or drizzle.

It may be tempting to buy stoned olives but try to resist the temptation. Whole olives have an infinitely better flavour. It takes a little more effort to remove the stones, but it's *so* worth it.

MAKES 180G

....

— 50g best-quality
  anchovy fillets
  (see the note)
— 100g stoned black
  olives (ideally
  Kalamata or Niçoise)
— 1 tablespoon capers
— 1 teaspoon Dijon
  mustard
— 1 teaspoon freshly
  squeezed lemon juice
— freshly ground black
  pepper
— 2-3 tablespoons olive
  oil

Whizz the anchovy fillets in a food processor with the stoned black olives, capers, mustard, lemon juice and pepper. Alternatively, use a pestle and mortar. Add the olive oil as you process or pound to a coarse or smooth purée, as you prefer. Store in a covered glass jar. This keeps for months in a fridge with a layer of extra virgin olive oil on top.

NOTE: Buy the best anchovies you can find for this. Poor-quality ones are horrible.

Green Tapenade

Substitute green for black olives in the recipe.

Anchoïade

A traditional Provençal anchovy sauce made with the addition of mustard, fresh herbs and extra virgin olive oil. It makes a delicious, addictive spread to serve with crudités or just slathered on toast, fougasse (page 144) or warm pitta (page 124).

(page 144) or warm pitta (page 124).

MAKES APPROX. 450ML

....

- 110g best-quality tinned anchovy fillets (weight out of the tin; see the note)
- 2 garlic cloves, chopped
- 1 tablespoon chopped fresh basil
- 1 tablespoon red wine vinegar
- ½-1 tablespoon best-quality Dijon mustard
- ½ teaspoon fresh thyme leaves
- lots of freshly ground black pepper
- 300ml extra virgin olive oil

Whizz all the ingredients except the oil in a food processor. With the motor running, add the oil gradually, blending until smooth. Taste, adding a little more oil if necessary. Store in a covered jar in the fridge for a month or more.

NOTE: Buy the best anchovies you can find for this. Poor-quality ones are horrible.

A Simpler Version

A simpler version is made with 8 plump anchovies; 2 garlic cloves, peeled and crushed; 2 teaspoons red wine vinegar; 225ml extra virgin olive oil; and plenty of freshly ground black pepper. Make, use and store as above.

Hummus Bi Tahina

Hummus bi tahina, with its rich, earthy taste, soon becomes addictive. It makes an excellent starter served as a dip with pitta and it's also delicious as a base for kebabs and meatballs and as part of a mezze platter.

SERVES 4-8

- 170g dried chickpeas
- ½ teaspoon bicarbonate of soda (optional)
- freshly squeezed juice of 2-3 lemons, or to taste
- 2 large or 3 small garlic cloves, crushed
- 150ml Lebanese tahini (we use the Al Nakhil brand)
- 1 teaspoon dry roasted and freshly ground cumin seeds
- pinch of salt
- 60ml iced water

TO SERVE:
- pitta (page 124) or any crusty white bread

Soak the chickpeas in 1.2 litres of cold water overnight. Drain and discard the water.

Put the chickpeas in a medium saucepan on a high heat. Sprinkle with the bicarbonate of soda (if using) and stir for 2–3 minutes. Add at least 1 litre of water and bring to the boil. Cook for about 30 minutes, but the timing can vary from 20 to 50 minutes depending on the freshness of the chickpeas. Skim off any foam and loose skins that rise to the top and discard. The chickpeas are cooked when they collapse easily when pressed between your thumb and finger. They should be soft but not mushy. Drain the chickpeas and reserve the cooking water.

Put the cooked chickpeas in a food processor with the freshly squeezed lemon juice. Add the crushed garlic, tahini, cumin and salt to taste and whizz to combine. Add the iced water and blend to a soft, creamy paste. Taste and continue to add lemon juice and salt until you are happy with the flavour. It should be soft and silky. Enjoy straight away or keep covered and refrigerated and use within three days.

Baba Ganoush

The success of this much-loved dish depends not just on the quality of the aubergines, but the charring of the skin, which imbues the flesh with an irresistible smoky flavour. It makes a delicious dip or flatbread topping. The quality of tahini also varies, so choose carefully. We use the Al Nakhil brand.

SERVES 6

- 6 medium purple aubergines
- 3 garlic cloves, crushed
- 8 tablespoons tahini (we use the Al Nakhil brand)
- 1 dessertspoon or more of cumin, roasted and freshly ground
- 1-2 tablespoons freshly squeezed lemon juice
- sea salt

First roast the aubergines. If you have a gas burner just rest the aubergines on a wire rack over the direct flame. If not, roast them in a hot oven preheated to 230°C/450°F/gas mark 8 for about 30 minutes or until the skin is well blackened and the flesh is really soft. Allow the cooked aubergines to cool a little, then peel off the charred skin and leave the flesh to drain in a colander for 30 minutes.

Transfer the aubergine flesh to a food processor or blender (in batches). Add the garlic and whizz to a smooth or chunky paste. Stir in the tahini and cumin, then add the freshly squeezed lemon juice and salt. Taste and adjust the proportions of cumin, garlic, tahini and lemon juice to your taste.

Serve with warm pitta or flatbread.

Guacamole

For the best flavour, try to find organic Mexican or Californian avocados. They must be really ripe for guacamole. Look out for the Hass variety, with its slightly knobbly skin.

SERVES 4-6
....

- 2 or more ripe avocados, preferably organic
- 2 tablespoons chopped fresh coriander
- 2 tablespoons freshly squeezed lime juice
- 2 tablespoons extra virgin olive oil
- sea salt and freshly ground black pepper

Cut the avocados in half, scoop out the flesh into a bowl and mash it with a fork. Add the coriander, lime juice, olive oil and salt and pepper to taste. Serve immediately or cover the surface to exclude the air, keeping cool until needed.

Tomato and Coriander Salsa

Salsa is ever present on Mexican tables to serve with all manner of dishes. Salsas of all kinds, both fresh and cooked, are a favourite accompaniment to everything from pan-grilled meat to a piece of sizzling fish and of course they make an excellent dip.

SERVES 4-6

- 4 very ripe tomatoes, chopped
- 1 garlic clove, crushed
- ½-1 fresh jalapeño or serrano chilli, deseeded and finely chopped
- 1-2 tablespoons chopped fresh coriander
- 1 tablespoon finely chopped red or white onion
- squeeze of fresh lime juice
- sea salt and freshly ground black pepper
- pinch of caster sugar

Mix all the ingredients together. Season with salt, freshly ground black pepper and sugar. Taste and adjust the seasoning if necessary.

Chilli Honey

This sweet, perky chilli honey is a delicious condiment to drizzle over pizza, bread, toast ...

MAKES 1 × 360G JAR

....

- 360g runny honey
- 2-3 tablespoons chilli flakes, depending how hot you like it
- pinch of salt
- 1 tablespoon apple cider vinegar

Pour the honey into a small saucepan. Add the chilli flakes and a generous pinch of salt. Warm gently on a medium heat. As soon as it begins to simmer, turn off the heat and stir in the cider vinegar. Pour into sterilised jars. Stored in a cool, dark place, this will keep for months – no need to refrigerate.

Olio Piccante (Chilli Oil)

Drizzle these perky flavoured oils over pizzas or use as a dip.

- 1 bottle of extra virgin olive oil
- 1-6 fresh whole chillies

Pour a little oil out of the bottle, then drop 1–6 fresh whole chillies into the bottle. Top up with oil and leave to infuse for a few days before using. Dried chillies may also be used, though the flavour will be more pungent.

Chilli Oil in a Hurry

Put 25g chilli flakes in a saucepan with 450ml olive oil. Gradually heat them together until hot but certainly not at smoking point, then turn off the heat immediately and leave to cool and decant into sterilised bottles. This chilli oil has instant zing and lasts almost indefinitely.

Chilli, Herb and Pepper Oil

One of my favourite combinations is one or two chillies, a sprig or two of rosemary or annual marjoram and a teaspoon of black peppercorns. This is particularly good for brushing over steaks, lamb chops or chicken breasts for a barbecue.

How to Make Lard

Lard is made from pig fat rendered slowly in the oven. Don't bother making lard unless the pig is at least free range, and better still, organic. The best lard is made from the back fat and also the flare fat from around the kidneys.

To render fat into lard, chop up the pig fat and put it in an ovenproof dish or roasting tin. Roast in a low oven at 110°C/230°F/gas mark ¼. The liquid fat will render out slowly. The length of time depends on the quantity you are rendering, but this should take 30–60 minutes – don't hurry it.

Store in a fridge or larder in jars or in a covered stainless steel bowl until needed. The lard will keep for three or four months. Use for frying, roasting or for pastry. When we were children, chips were always cooked in lard. You could buy big blocks of lard, render it down and put it in the chip pan. It had a particular flavour that I loved.

Tuscan Butter

Add chopped fresh rosemary, dried chilli flakes, flaky sea salt and freshly ground black pepper to taste.

GLOSSARY

....

AUTOLYSE METHOD

Gently mix a portion (or all) of the water and flour together, cover and leave for 20 minutes or up to several hours before adding salt and the other ingredients. This process allows the flour to fully hydrate. Consequently, the kneading time is reduced.

BANNETON

A French word that means 'bread basket'. It's a round or oblong basket for proving bread, usually made from rattan, cane or wood pulp. They can be floured or lined with a linen or cotton cloth. An inexpensive bread basket lined with a cotton tea towel may be used instead.

BENCH REST

A period of rest that allows the dough to relax and fully absorb the water, which in turn makes it easier to knead. Turn the dough out onto the worktop, cover and allow it to rest for 15–25 minutes.

BIGA

A liquid starter or pre-ferment used to make many Italian breads including ciabatta, pizza, etc.

CLARIFIED BUTTER

Butter that has had the salt and milk particles removed. It is excellent for cooking because it can withstand a higher temperature, giving you all the delicious buttery flavour without the risk of burning. It's easy to make it yourself at home – see the recipe on page 307.

COUCHE

Heavy unbleached or natural canvas or linen flax cloth that's easy to pleat. It's used to support artisan baguettes while proving before being gently flipped onto a baking tray into the oven. The dough doesn't stick to the couche because of its rougher texture. Brush and dry the couche after use. Available from bakers' suppliers or specialist kitchen shops.

DAIRY SALT

Dairy salt is widely available. It is sold in plastic bags as dairy salt or cooking salt or it's sometimes referred to as vacuum salt. It is less refined than table salt and doesn't usually contain emulsifying agents.

DARIOLE MOULDS	Little moulds of varying sizes for mousses or puddings, often made of aluminium.
EGG WASH	Whisk 1 egg thoroughly with about 1 dessertspoon of milk or cream. This is brushed over breads, scones, etc. to help them brown in the oven.
FERMENTATION TIME	Fermentation time allows the bread to develop more flavour and become more stretchy and easier to shape. The resulting loaf is lighter, with a more open crumb, and cuts that open more fully, giving you bread that has a better keeping quality.
FLATBREAD	As the name suggests, these are flat breads and they are made all over the world. Many are unleavened but some, like pizza and pitta, are leavened with yeast.
GHEE	A type of clarified butter originating in India. Ghee is used for cooking and finishing dishes and as a medicine in some Hindu religious ceremonies. It's easy to make at home – see the recipe for clarified butter on page 307.
GLASS CLOTH	A light cotton or linen tea towel that is often used for polishing glasses or to cover yeast bread as it proves.
GRANARY FLOUR	A mixture of malted wheat and rye, with a proportion of whole wheat kernels.
HEAPED SPOONFUL	A *heaped* teaspoon has as much of the ingredient as the spoon will hold.
JAM SUGAR	Sugar with added pectin – a blend of sugar, apple pectin and citric acids. Overall, I'm not a fan. It seems to result in a 'commercial' type of jam but it can certainly be useful to help set jams made from fruits that are low in pectin, such as blackberries, commercial strawberries, blueberries, cherries, peaches, etc.
KNOCK BACK	A term used to describe the process used after the first rising of yeast bread to redistribute the yeast back in contact with the dough so that when it rises for a second

time, the dough is more even in texture. To knock back dough, just punch the puffy, risen dough to deflate it, knead for 2–3 minutes, shape and allow to rise again.

LAME	A slightly curved, doubled-sided blade in a holder used to score or slash the top of a loaf of bread just before it goes into the oven. A very sharp serrated knife works just as well. Scoring allows moisture and some of the carbon dioxide gas to escape, allows the baker to control where the crust will open and enhances the appearance of the bread. The pattern cut into the top of the loaf with the lame can be simple or fancy.
LAMINATED DOUGH	A light, flaky, buttery dough made up of multiple layers produced by repeated rolling and folding. During baking the butter between each layer melts and the water vaporises, which results in a light, flaky pastry used for croissants, kouign-amann, Danish pastries, puff pastry and many variations on the theme.
LEVAIN OR LEAVEN	A sourdough starter made with naturally occurring yeast from the atmosphere.
LEVEL SPOONFUL	A *level* teaspoon is just that and is the equivalent of a half-rounded heaped teaspoon.
'NDUJA	An Italian spreadable, spicy fermented sausage from Calabria, similar in flavour to chorizo and sobrassada from the Balearic Islands in Spain.
OVEN SPRING	When a fully risen loaf of bread is initially put into the preheated oven to bake, it will expand further – up to 30% of its original size. The gas created during proving expands the pockets of gluten in the dough, making the bread rise rapidly during the first 10–15 minutes before the crust hardens.
PÂTE FERMENTÉE (OLD DOUGH)	A piece of dough that is held back and added to the next batch of bread.

PEARL SUGAR	Also called nib or hail sugar. It's made from compressed sugar crystals that form larger particles that stay crunchy and don't melt easily.
PECTIN	The natural gelling agent in fruits. Some fruits, such as apples, redcurrants, plums, damsons and blackcurrants, are high in pectin. Others, such as blackberries, blueberries, peaches, cherries, mulberries and strawberries, are low in pectin so you will need to add pectin or lemon juice to the fruit to facilitate setting. You may also want to combine low- and high-pectin fruits, e.g. blackberry and apple, strawberry and redcurrants. Under-ripe fruit tends to have more pectin.
POOLISH	Poolish 'sponge' is a type of pre-ferment, frequently used in French bread-making.
ROUNDED SPOONFUL	A *rounded* spoonful has exactly the same amount on top as underneath.
SELF-RAISING FLOUR	Contains a raising agent, so no additional leavening is needed. (To make your own, use 2 teaspoons baking powder to 450g plain flour. Store in a sealed container and use as soon as possible.)
SOURDOUGH	The term 'sourdough' refers to breads leavened with a wild yeast starter rather than commercial baker's yeast.
SPONGE	A term used to describe the process of mixing yeast with water and sometimes sugar, honey or treacle to activate it before mixing into the other ingredients for bread-making.

ACKNOWLEDGEMENTS

This revised edition of *The Ballymaloe Bread Book* has been the passion of so many people who all love baking bread and who love to share.

The basis of this new revised hardback edition is the much-loved original published in 2001 and written by my husband, Tim. This updated tome now includes over 180 master recipes and nearly 200 variations.

Special thanks go to Jen Allen in the Ballymaloe Bread Shed and to the many teachers at the Ballymaloe Cookery School who tested and retested recipes and made suggestions and tweaks until everyone was happy: Pat Browne, Gary Masterson, Richard Healy, Maggie Draddy, Pamela Black and Florrie Cullinane.

Very special thanks also to Debbie Shaw, who contributed all the recipes for the gluten-free chapter of this revised edition. Debbie was originally a student and is now a senior tutor and in-house nutritionist here at the Ballymaloe Cookery School. She has diligently perfected her gluten-free and free-from recipes throughout the years. Thank you, Debbie, for sharing and enhancing the lives of so many.

Sharon Hogan typed most of the manuscript from my challenging handwritten version, a labour of love for which I am deeply grateful.

Susan McKeown also helped with the page proofs and Rosalie Dunne contributed greatly at an earlier stage.

As ever, huge thanks to Nicky Howard and Aoibheann Molumby of Gill Books, to my patient and meticulous editor, Kristin Jensen, and to designer Luke Doyle and to Graham Thew for the front cover.

The beautiful illustrations that have brought my words to life are the work of our daughter, Lydia Hugh Jones. Thank you, Lydia. I not only love them, but I'm super proud that this is a family collaboration.

A special word of thanks also to my friend and agent of many years, Heather Holden-Brown.

A very special thank you to Haulie Walsh, manager of our organic farm here in Shanagarry who grows wheat for us to mill into flour and to the other farmers who grow nutrient-dense heirloom grains. It's such an exciting time in bread-making as so many artisan bakers spring up in towns and villages all over the country.

Finally, a shout out to Real Bread Ireland, whose members are so generous in sharing their knowledge and expertise for the greater good.

INDEX

old dough (pâte fermentée), 326
olio piccante (chilli oils), 322
olive and anchovy butter, 310
olive soda scones, 29
omega-3 fats, 239
One Pot Feeds All, 32
orange blossom swirls, 183
Oriel Sea Salt, 19
oven spring, 15, 326
oven temperatures, 19, 21
oven thermometers, 4, 21

P
....
Packer, Sarit, 125, 204
pain au chocolat, 190–1
pan con tomate, 271
panettone, 268, 273
pangrattato, 267
panzanella (Tuscan bread salad), 279
paratha, 136–7
parma sticks, 56
parmesan toasts, 270
parsley pesto, 313
pastry brushes, 4
pastry cream (crème pâtissière), 301
   crème Saint Honorè, 301
   diplomat cream, 301
pâte fermentée (old dough), 81, 326
peach scones, 178
pearl sugar, 327
pectin, 292, 327
Penny's
   Ethiopian injera, 127
   Perthshire butteries, 158–9
peperonata, 33, 305
Perthshire butteries, 158–9
pesto and parmesan pizza, 33
pestos
   basil pesto, 312
   kale pesto, 312
   parsley pesto, 313
   watercress pesto, 313
   wild garlic pesto, 313
phosporus, 9
phytic acid, 80
phytoestrogens, 239
piadina romagnola, 116
pistou, 314
pitta, 124
pizza
   baked dough balls, 106
   barbecued, 102
   chargrilled pizza margherita, 109
   cheddar cheese and spring onion pizza, 33
   deep-fried dough balls, 106
   Garden Café pizza dough, 105
   garlic butter pizza, 112
   gnocco fritto, 117

goat's cheese and fresh herb calzone, 113
griddle pan, 247
ham and cheese sfinciuni, 115
'nduja and bocconcini pizza, 32
ovens, 101–2
pesto and parmesan pizza, 33
piadina romagnola, 116
pizza Bianca, 112
pizza paddles, 104
pizza Stromboli, 110–11
potato bread pizza, 45
rolling out pizza dough, 104
sfinciuni, 114
spiced aubergines pizza, 33
stretching pizza dough by hand, 103
tapenade and soft goat's cheese pizza, 33
tips for cooking in domestic ovens, 102
Turkish pizza with tahini, yogurt and sumac, 108
types of, 101–2
plain flour, 9, 185
plastic scrapers, 4
polar bread, 129
polenta, 9
poolish, 80–1, 327
poor knights of Windsor, 268
poor man's praline ice cream, 288–9
pooris, 156–7
poppy seed scones, 178
porotta, 136
potato and rosemary focaccia, 121
potato bread pizza, 45
potato flour, 239
potato starch, 239–40, 241
praline ice cream, 288–9
pretzels, 58–9
   baked pretzels with cinnamon sugar, 59
   baked pretzels with sea salt and caraway seeds, 59
Provençal flatbread (fougasse), 144
proving baskets, 3
psyllium husk, 236, 242, 258
Puck, Wolfgang, 101
pumpernickel bread, 160
pumpkin spice bread, 204
pupusas, 149
pure vanilla extract, 303

Q
....
queen of puddings, 283
quick white yeast bread (one rising), 60–1

R
....
Rachel Allen's
   bagels, 162–3
   banana muffins, 205
   zucchini and walnut bread, 211
railway cake, 38
raisin and rosemary scones, 177